A Thousand Tiny Cuts

ATELIER: ETHNOGRAPHIC INQUIRY IN
THE TWENTY-FIRST CENTURY

Kevin Lewis O'Neill, Series Editor

A Thousand Tiny Cuts

MOBILITY AND SECURITY ACROSS THE BANGLADESH-INDIA BORDERLANDS

Sahana Ghosh

UNIVERSITY OF CALIFORNIA PRESS

University of California Press
Oakland, California

Library of Congress Cataloging-in-Publication Data

Names: Ghosh, Sahana, 1984- author.
Title: A thousand tiny cuts : mobility and security across the Bangladesh-
    India borderlands / Sahana Ghosh.
Other titles: Atelier (Oakland, Calif.) ; 10.
Description: Oakland, California : University of California Press, [2023] |
    Series: Atelier : ethnographic inquiry in the twenty-first century ;
    vol. 10 | Includes bibliographical references and index.
Identifiers: LCCN 2023005935 (print) | LCCN 2023005936 (ebook) |
    ISBN 9780520395725 (cloth) | ISBN 9780520395732 (paperback) |
    ISBN 9780520395749 (ebook)
Subjects: LCSH: Borderlands—India—Bengal. | Borderlands—
    Bangladesh. | Border security—India—Bengal. | Border security—
    Bangladesh. | Boundaries—Anthropological aspects.
Classification: LCC DS450.B3 G473 2023 (print) | LCC DS450.B3 (ebook) |
    DDC 303.48/25405492—dc23/eng/20230302
LC record available at https://lccn.loc.gov/2023005935
LC ebook record available at https://lccn.loc.gov/2023005936

Manufactured in the United States of America

32 31 30 29 28 27 26 25 24 23
10 9 8 7 6 5 4 3 2 1

Contents

List of Figures

ILLUSTRATIONS

MAPS

TABLE

Introduction

On an auspicious day in 2013, as dusk flickered on the horizon, a wedding was about to start in a border village in northern West Bengal, India. The groom was a Rajbangsi man, just a bit past his youth and blind in one eye. The bride was a petite young woman of a lower caste. No sooner had the wedding begun when the state police and the Indian Border Security Force (BSF) appeared at the venue. The bride was Bangladeshi. She was arrested on suspicion of being an infiltrator, an illegal border-crosser, under the Foreigners Act. The groom, the BSF alleged, was her abettor. Beneath the arches of trees twinkling with fairy lights, the two were whisked away to the BSF outpost and then to the police station. The man who'd rented the loudspeakers for music to blare late into the night would later forego his payment from the anguished family. By all accounts, the police and the BSF had waited politely for the priest to speed through the ceremony, so the couple could be married first. The Indian Penal Code made accomplices of them faster than a Hindu marriage could.

This incident was fresh in everyone's minds in the summer of 2014 when I moved to Kathalbari *panchayat* in the same area.[1] I was told this story—with roughly these particulars—countless times. Sometimes there were barely any details; occasionally, it was narrated with great gusto and

1

more elaboration by someone who had been in attendance at the wedding. The story would come up as an example of either the BSF's violent intrusions into people's everyday lives (sparing not even a wedding) or the treachery of compatriots, fellow borderland residents, one of whom had "informed" on the Bangladeshi bride. The story was quintessential *simanta jibon*, borderland life: it captured the hardships that ordinary borderland citizens, Hindu and Muslim alike, suffer in the name of national security, and served as a cautionary tale to prepare me for the uncertainties of security practices. One time, when Iman Ali—a part-time shopkeeper and full-time carpenter in the Kathalbari bazaar—told me this story, his piercing eyes looking straight at me, I had the distinct feeling that the storytelling had a subtler message, too. "Don't believe anyone; *ekhane kothar kono daam nei* [words have no value here]," he added darkly. No one could be trusted with confidences, least of all me: I was a stranger, a young unaccompanied woman in their midst, professing to carry out "research" that no one really understood. No one ever remarked on whether or not the bride was actually Bangladeshi. Was that so obvious that no one cared to mention it? Had the families or the community protested the arrest? Border security turned everything upside down: whom you could trust, which marriages were attractive, and what was an injustice.

As I started spending time in the adjacent Bangladeshi borderlands, I casually asked after the young woman's family in Madhupur, the border village that she was allegedly from in the adjoining Lalmonirhat district. My inquiries shed little light: most families have cross-border marriages and kinship ties and searching for "a young Hindu woman who married into a neighboring Indian family" was like looking for a ripe jackfruit in the month of July. Almost a year later, in 2015, I was buying vegetables in the Madhupur bazaar one morning when the shopkeeper, with whom I was friendly, took the liberty of introducing me to a man standing next to me, buying a coconut. "His daughter is married in India too! Have you met her?" Before I could assure this man that he should feel no pressure to discuss his daughter with me, the man was pulling me by my arm, his face all lit up. "I've heard about you! What luck, my daughter is still at home, just about to leave. You must come and meet her!"

Imagine my surprise when I learned that the man's daughter is the "Bangladeshi bride" of the much-told marriage-arrest story. "Haven't you heard about me? I am the girl whose marriage was interrupted by the police," Rani asked, as she scrubbed her feet at the tube well in the court-yard of her parents' home. Rani Barman, née Das, was getting ready to set off on her journey back to her husband's house, but she insisted that I stay to talk for a few minutes. There was a ritual quality to the series of actions by which Rani put on a particular version of her self: she wound around her "Indian" sari,[2] stuffed the coconut into a black duffel bag, and while I tugged the zipper to urge it shut, she closed her eyes in a *pronam* (rever-ential bowing) at a shrine in a dark corner of the single room that was her parents' home. She then took Bangladeshi notes out of a frayed purse, replaced them with a handful of Indian notes, and carefully slid in what I guessed to be her Indian voter identity card before she zipped up the purse and tucked it into her blouse. Rani was flustered. Her infant, Borsha (named after the fulsome monsoon in which she had been born), was howling; her parents were in tears, reluctant to bid adieu to their daughter and their granddaughter.

"*Mamoni'r basha ekdom shamoney, mui je jamu, tahar upay nai. Apni jaiben* (Mamoni's house is right there in front, even still, there's no way I can go there. You must visit)." Rani's father sobbed, dancing all the while to comfort the baby, the *mamoni*, a common Bengali term of endearment, potentially referring to both his daughter and granddaughter. Rani retorted with some impatience in her voice. "What can I do, I have to go. Borsha's father's calling every hour. He needs to harvest the jute now, he needs me to cook at the right times. If I'm not at home these days, it's very difficult for him."

This little exchange between husband and wife encapsulates a perfectly familiar and historically enduring dynamic of agrarian production: wom-en's domestic labor is essential for the peasant household's productive and reproductive work. Yet there was much more going on here in this pair of border villages, Kathalbari and Madhupur, than a petulant husband want-ing his wife back from her parents' house. For countless people, living in the borderlands means being vulnerable to surveillance and carceral security practices, but also being able to continue being mobile and maintain multi-ple transnational connections. They related to unequal places unequally.

What do we make of these unequal relations and the profoundly gen-dered risks of clandestine mobility, ubiquitous across the borderlands of

1. The colonial rail bridge that hangs suspended over a changing river, between land and water, India and Bangladesh.

northern Bengal? Rani was indeed a Bangladeshi bride, a most-wanted *anuprabeshkari* (infiltrator), a much-maligned figure against whose mobility India's eastern border has been gradually militarized. Rani's acquisition of Indian citizenship via marriage was imagined together with, not in opposition to, a foreseeable future of clandestine crossings. As a religious minority in Bangladesh, her family risked this marriage to take a step toward acquiring Indian citizenship. Kamalesh, unmarriageable in the Indian borderlands, needed her to reproduce his family. With the militarization of this border, they counted on Rani being the right kind of body—Hindu, female— to remain mobile amid the border's closures. Rani's marriage was predicated on this interdependence and unequal relations, not despite it.

"I'll come again soon," Rani reassured her father, "*border thik thakle* [if/when the border is alright]"; the qualifying clause dangling, like the damaged colonial rail bridge, suspended between land and water, India and Bangladesh (fig. 1).

A THOUSAND TINY CUTS

This book explores how borderland mobilities shape the relational value of the national, such that the injustices of bordering are braided with the possibilities and gains of transnational living. While the India-Bangladesh border owes its political existence to Partition, the force of the border in shaping the lives, lands, and relations of those who live adjacent to it, and formations of the national that depend on it, are anything but inevitable, settled, or fully known. I have learned over a decade of ethnographic research in northern Bengal that *bordering* continues to unfold everyday through the transnational connections across different domains of borderland life: not a watershed event, a singular structure or policy, but a thousand tiny cuts across time, space, and imaginaries. The border is a risk and a resource. On days when the price of crops was high and the price of meat was low, and when both countries were winning cricket matches,[3] I even heard farmers describe it as the best of both worlds. But most of the time, neither the national domain of India nor Bangladesh offers much in isolation. Rather, the border generates a series of devaluations that hold "India" and "Bangladesh" together interdependently through a hierarchy of value. I take the border to be not a fixed thing in time and space; instead, I take bordering to mean an ongoing and historically layered process of cutting, through which physical, social, political, and mental landscapes are remade. I focus on how the transnational lives of borderland communities are generative of and deeply shaped by hierarchical relations of value through gendered mobilities and immobilities. At stake is the worldmaking violence of bordering, at once intimate and geopolitical. Through a thousand tiny cuts, borderlands come to be not only the privileged sites of clandestine mobility but essential to the subjectivities and forms of value that constitute and shore up postcolonial state power through transnational relations and separations.[4]

Although I have long been committed to understanding how borderland communities on both sides experience the militarization of this border, I did not begin by seeing bordering as worldmaking in this way. I came to this project having worked at a human rights organization, documenting the extrajudicial instances of violence inflicted by Indian and Bangladeshi security forces on borderland residents. I began by looking for explicit kinds of violence (torture, killings), framed in terms of legality and rights (extrajudicial, justice claims, protests), with a presumed idea of villains (the BSF, the Border Guards Bangladesh [BGB]), and valiant political actors (borderland residents on both sides). As I lived in the border villages of Cooch Behar (India) and Lalmonirhat and Kurigram (Bangladesh) districts for two years between 2013 and 2015 and visited for shorter periods between 2011 and 2019, this was not the kind of story I found. Bordering was devaluing *and* productive in all kinds of ways. The BSF and the BGB were only some of the actors who surveilled clandestine mobilities; I began to see how borderland residents were identifying themselves and remaking their lives and relations according to several distinctions that the border afforded.

A Thousand Tiny Cuts follows fragmented borderland mobilities into an expansive world of transnational connections. The divisions of the private and the public—kinship and familial matters from political economy, state institutions, and borderland publics—do not hold. While the India-Bangladesh border has been written about as a site of violence and an artifice of division,[5] this book highlights relationships brought about by the border that largely go unseen. In the analysis I offer, bordering—an ongoing and accumulative cutting of time, space, and imaginaries—produces and calibrates relationships of value, that we see across different scales connecting the intimate and the geopolitical. My use of the term *value* follows anthropologists who view the concept as dynamic and emerging, rooted in action rather than things or people themselves.[6] Following David Graeber and Elizabeth Ferry, the book posits bordering as productive of and rooted in a relational hierarchy of values that depends on the idea that valuation—and its corollary, devaluation—is a series of interconnected relationships within which "difference is made meaningful."[7] Borders everywhere signify difference at multiple scales: of currency, law, identity, and belonging. By being anthropological about relations, as Marilyn Strathern says, I deploy "*the relation* as an expository device."[8] I use it to describe and analyze shifting hierarchies—between people, places, and goods on one side of the border as well as across, and between borderland residents and distinct state actors. These are the grounds of bordering: an expansive archive of cuts.

In what follows, you will read about bordering and its shifting hierarchies of value as the disconnection of roads and rail lines when a region is cut up into national borderlands; as ordinary borderland sites, journeys, and networks become objects of national security surveillance; and as a surprising range of actors are complicit in assessing gendered threats. Agrarian commodity flows of tobacco and ganja flourish across the border because of the distinctions of national markets and currencies, for farmers devise strategies when their cultivable land is devalued by militarized border security. As we have already seen, intimate kin relations recalibrate identities as "Indian" and "Bangladeshi" as people marry and contemplate the past and future reproduction of their families. Young men coming of age navigate livelihood options amid stringent policing of male bodies and the pressures of productive masculinity. Finally, there is the impossible task of sorting citizens out from migrants and refugees, an enduring and fractious policing of migrant pasts that has exceeded the borderlands and come to direct terms of exclusionary political belonging across South Asia. Each of these chapters will trace an aspect of relational value that emerges through a distinctive kind of borderland mobility, paying attention to how people try to lead meaningful transnational lives as the grounds of those connections are devalued, criminalized, and actively reconfigured. I propose that an ethnography of bordering could be viewed as an anthropology of value-making, which "as a generative force of difference"[9] shows how profoundly unjust, naturalized, and consequential differences such as that of the national are unstable relations, still becoming.

Over time, I have found the metaphor of a thousand tiny cuts, which I use to describe bordering as a relationship of value, to be compelling for several reasons. First, the idiom of cutting was often invoked by people in relation to bordering as polysemic: a sharp structure of barbed wire (*taar-kaanta*), an architecture of dispersed security practices (*border*, the English word incorporated into Bengali speech), a variably controlled physical borderline (*zero point*), clandestine crossings as "cutting across,", and, finally, the borderlands as a cutoff place.

Taar-kaanta, kaanta-taar, try saying it out loud. It trips you up, inside your mouth.

In Bengali, the language in use on both sides in this region, India's border fence is referred to as *taar-kaanta* (literally, barbed wire). Yet the term and object have come loose from the steel fence and are distributed in a way that exceeds the visual repertoire and vocabulary we have for the

2. Banana gardens, Bangladesh, damaged by insects attracted by the Indian border floodlights in the background.

enclosures and intrusions that militarization brings to the agrarian ordinary. On walks in Indian border villages, my companions pointed out concertina wire by the side of the road where goats used to graze; in Bangladeshi border villages, farmers complain that the glare of the halogen lights illuminating India's fence all night attract insects that damage their banana gardens (fig. 2). The direction of the lights is fixed in one way, leaving little room for imagining common cause or solidarity.[10] Borderland residents on both the Indian and Bangladeshi sides used the Bengali phrase *taar-kaanta* to refer to the physical border fence. However, they use the English word *border* to refer to the larger visible and invisible structure, including the unfenced parts, security practices, and historical conditions. *Ei border ta khola chhilo* (this border was open); *ekhon border ta khub gorom cholchhe* (the border is very heated these days). It is through a combination of these temporal, spatial, and textural openings that build on social stratifications of caste, class, and gender that Rani and

Kamalesh were able to marry and carry on cutting across their part of the border.

A Thousand Tiny Cuts tries to capture this interrelated sense of bordering: as a tense in the present continuous, a profoundly gendered relationship of power, and an embodied experience of mobility produced historically across multiple domains of life. The descriptions I offer ethnographically theorize a complicated matrix of militarized bordering—the material infrastructures, a gendered geography, the social relations, the political-economic categories—that exceeds the visuality of the fence or the acts of physical violence that have come to dominate our understandings of border architectures and clandestine migrant trails, predominantly from Euro-American cases. To narrate how people navigate and live with the violence and injustices of bordering is to reach beyond a victimhood/resistance binary for agrarian residents of northern Bengal, predominantly Bengali Muslim and Rajbangsi.[11] As Sharika Thiranagama notes, writing about the complexity of violence in the context of the Sri Lankan civil war, "social life is thicker than survival tactics."[12]

My second reason for thinking about this metaphor is its ability to capture the braiding of bordering with people's crossings in working out the hierarchies of value which make the injustices of the border so tangible. In the anthropology of borders and borderlands, statist categories of identity, law, and economy have been studied in opposition to those of borderland society.[13] While this body of work has richly documented social and economic life and histories of mobility to question the stable geography and politics of borders, it implies the solidity of a separation, the prior existence and cohesion of a social realm in which people have faith or retreat for protection with the onslaught of statist imposition of policing.[14] This presumes a relation of separation and antagonism between the two in binary terms of state/society and private/public. For years I puzzled over the fact that across agrarian northern Bengal, borderland residents were not "evading" the state, per James Scott, nor fashioning transborder ties "beyond" it, per Willem van Schendel.[15] In arguing for a less settled or predictable cause-and-effect relationship between state institutions and borderland publics, this book invites you to consider how they are differently but equally invested in gendered policing and leveraging of forms of difference, mainly *the national*.

The national as an epistemic category and imaginary is not the domain of the state alone; it is laid claim to, manipulated, and interpellated by a range of actors for a variety of distinct ends. Bordering is this interplay of crossings, real, desired, remembered, with the relational hierarchies of value that make the "national" attach to things. This interplay, where the difference of *the national* is made meaningful, resides in marriages, the arrangement of homes, encounters with security forces along paths, the buying and selling of crops in markets, and offers of work refused. The national has a powerful hold on people's imaginations, desires, and senses of self; indeed, ambivalent structures of feeling combining love, fear, and loyalty bind borderland peoples to national projects.[16] If the state has been theorized as magical and alluring by anthropologists,[17] the national, too, heterogeneously imagined and located, is desired, embraced, deployed and also made concrete through borderland mobilities and transnational connection.

Against invocations in which "the national" appears as a self-explanatory qualifier or an innocent description, this book takes the elementary aspects of the national and its production through calculations of value as a subject of inquiry. I explore borderlands as a particular kind of transnational site at which the national is constructed, policed, and continuously exceeded. Each chapter of the book considers how in living with and through gendered mobility in borderlands, formations of the national appear and entrench in distinct domains of everyday life. These mobilities demand a transnational view to grasp the ways in which their distinctions emerge in relation to one another: a hierarchy of value across the borderlands that devalues some mobilities and makes some others viable, or even profitable. While I begin the book by showing how northern Bengal is cut up and produced as remote and underdeveloped national borderlands in relation to the centers of Delhi and Dhaka, I end it by elaborating how borderland residents render their own—and the region's—demographic change as they attempt to align dwelling and mobility practices with senses of belonging and bureaucratic citizenship. Acutely sensitive to the politics of national histories, borderland stories about migration illuminate the constitutive instabilities of the categories of citizen, refugee, and foreigner that bind India and Bangladesh.

This introduction outlines the book's three main ethnographic enterprises. First, the book weaves together accounts of the violence and injustice wrought by the border and its militarization with those concerns endemic to agrarian northern Bengal through half a century of decolonization and postcolonial citizenship. I do not focus on spectacular instances of violence and death as the primary feature of life in a militarized borderland. Rather, following other scholars of life in conditions of protracted violence and surveillance, I query the forms of violence-by-other-names that militarization takes in places that are expressly designated as peaceful, such as this "friendly" border. Second, the book shows the political economy of bordering to be a space- and world-making project. The borderlands of northern Bengal do not feature in this story as the self-evident sites of action; they are analyzed as new kinds of spaces that are continuously being manufactured, even as residents learn to (re)inhabit them at different scales—rural paths newly surveilled, neighborhoods changed with migrations, remembered villages in the neighboring country, markets frequented in clandestine trading trips—through reoriented social selves and relations. Third, in seeking to make sense of the mobilities of people and goods, I jettison facts and figures of volume, rife in our newspapers and parliamentary debates, to examine instead the gendered and embodied logics and experiences with which (im)mobilities are crafted, lived, and evaluated as threats in relation to one another. Gendered bodies and their sensations—such as of fear, hope, pleasure, and fatigue—guide us in this story of bordering and its hierarchies of value.

NORTHERN BENGAL AND THE MILITARIZATION OF A FRIENDLY BORDER

The Bengal borderlands constitute about half of the 4,056-kilometer India-Bangladesh border. Officially, this eastern border is "friendly", in contradistinction to the India-Pakistan border which from its inception in 1947 has been closed, hostile, and a site of ongoing conflict. The India-Bangladesh border is typically not viewed in exigent frames: it is not a place of territorial disputes (India-China), refugee crises (Bangladesh-Myanmar), or occupation and counterinsurgency (as in Kashmir, Mizoram, or the Chittagong Hill Tracts). The "friendliness" of this border is ceremoniously marked by shows of fraternal camaraderie

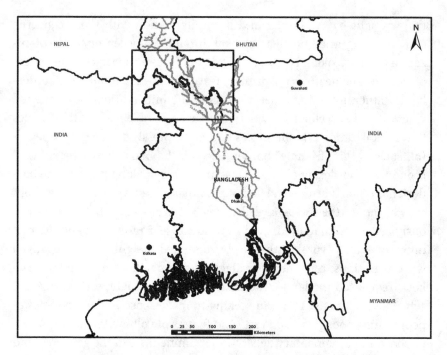

Map 1. The Bangladesh-India border. Map by Radhika Bhargava.

between the primarily male Indian and Bangladeshi border security forces, from the exchange of sweets on national holidays to volleyball matches. Unlike in places of protracted war and violence such as Kashmir or the Chittagong Hill Tracts, the qualification of the Bengal borderlands as peaceful *in contradistinction to* places and times of conflict conceals a recognition of the kind of militarization that is becoming normalized. Alongside the discourse of friendliness, a globally circulating lexicon around "terror" and "infiltration" post-9/11 has dovetailed with regional histories of religious and caste majoritarian politics to shape a partisan political consensus in India around militarizing its side of the border with Bangladesh. What, then, does militarization look and feel like in everyday lives of predominantly Rajbangsi and Muslim agrarian peoples of northern Bengal, a region that has been transformed into national borderlands? To what kinds of violence does "the friendly border" give cover?

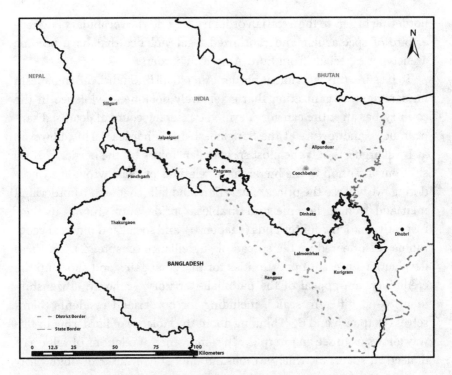

Map 2. Northern Bengal, a region of multiple borders. Map by Radhika Bhargava.

My analysis adds to a growing body of work on South Asian border-lands that demonstrates how militarization from both sides has escalated risky migrations and contestations over land, protected extractive ecosystems, made the politics of exclusion profitable, and rendered life and live-lihood more uncertain for borderland communities.[18] As residents of bor-der villages in Cooch Behar district attest through embodied memories and surveillance encountered on walks, the presence of the Indian secu-rity state has transformed from a rusty single-wire fence in the mid-1980s, with BSF outposts several kilometers apart, to a density of co-habitation (chapter 2). As the security gaze defines and translates its targets—clandestine mobilities—on the ground, sociality across these agrarian borderlands carries the weight and tear of this everyday evalua-tion under the security state's rubric of friendly cooperation. It is impera-tive that we grasp the visuality, texture, and forms of militarization that bordering brings to the agrarian ordinary, beyond the vocabulary and repertoire of spectacular and routinized legal violence that have become archetypes especially from Euro-American borders.

To be sure, this is a violent border. Ain o Salish Kendra, a Bangladeshi human rights organization that extensively documents violence in the country, has an entire category devoted to keeping count of deaths, disappearances, and torture at the Bangladesh-India border.[19] This, however, as I will argue, is only the most spectacular "injury" of the border.[20] If we shift our attention to the hierarchical relations of value wrought by bordering, we will see the prices of agrarian land fall (chapter 4), borderland men and women become undesirable as brides and grooms in their respective national hinterlands (chapter 3), and social and physical geographies disoriented by the spread of surveillance (chapter 2). Yet these devaluations present opportunities for marginal gains and shore up the credibility and appeal of the national—territory, economy, citizenship, identity—at different scales, including for borderland residents themselves (chapter 5 and 6). Thinking about the violence of bordering in this way allows us to see an interplay: the emergence of relations of value as a dialectical space, in which a thousand cuts are surfaced through hasty marriages, crops not grown, hidden migration histories, risks worn on the body, and interceptions narrowly escaped.

If the India-Bangladesh border has been upheld as the region's model of friendly bilateral management, contemporary northern Bengal is a region of multiple and differentially friendly borders between India, Bangladesh, Nepal, and Bhutan. In northern Bengal, the border runs through the foothills of the eastern Himalayas and a densely inhabited agrarian region, floodplains between the Teesta and Brahmaputra rivers. Considering the space of northern Bengal as a "meeting-up of histories,"[21] the region provides an especially fruitful starting point from which to trace the longue durée of postcolonial bordering. In precolonial times, this was what has been described by historian Richard Eaton as an exemplary "frontier zone" within the larger entity of Bengal.[22] Covered by swampy marshes and jungles, it was an ecological frontier between the deltaic plains in the south and the mountains to the north. It was the political frontier to territories ruled by the sultans of Bengal and the governors of the Mughal Empire before the settlement of the region under the East India Company. It was a cultural frontier, in religious terms, to Brahmanical structures moving northeast from the Gangetic Plains before the gradual expansion of the Islamic frontier with the incorporation of indigenous communities into what Eaton calls a "Muslim-oriented devotional life.[23]

There is another aspect to the regional particularity of northern Bengal in contrast with deltaic southern Bengal. While Partition brought a sudden division to many parts of the Bengal and Assam province, in northern Bengal it followed a deep history of successive jurisdictional boundaries of kingdoms, princely states, and colonial provinces, in a way that was simply absent for many other parts. In the wide circulation of origin stories of the Koch Rajbangsi peoples and their cultural and political history, I found the articulation of a lively historical sensibility among older generations about Rajbangsi identity. This identity is rooted in the regional specificity of a *distinctive* cultural and political geography that exceeds people's contemporary realities as citizens of national borderlands across India, Bangladesh, and Nepal. Whether it is the oral histories of material connections between places such as Rangpur and the princely capital of Cooch Behar, now in Bangladesh and India, respectively (chapter 1), or through the histories of trading families mapping the commercial sinews of the region (chapter 4), these inherited memories shape and direct contemporary borderland mobilities, whether of kinship or agrarian commerce. They query the picture of borderlands as backward and remote places in the spatial grid of the postcolonial nation, revealing the devaluation *as a borderland* to be central to a militarized national order.

The story of borders in South Asia is told through the Partition of the subcontinent in 1947. An important body of literary and historical work has established that "Partition in the east" was distinctive from that in the west.[24] Unlike the state-managed catastrophic population transfers in the west, people continued to migrate and seek refuge in both directions across the eastern border, "sometimes in trickles and sometimes in big waves," until the lead-up to the India-Pakistan War of 1965.[25] In the political history of the subcontinent that follows, the eastern border has been consistently declared to be porous. First drawn as the India-East Pakistan border (1947–71), this border was reestablished with Bangladesh's liberation from Pakistan in 1971. During the 1971 War, India had opened its side of the border to host millions of Bengalis fleeing the genocidal Pakistani army.[26] Immediately after, to consolidate the geo-political relationship of friendship, the two states inaugurated a special Indo-Bangladesh passport, with visas issued at the local level to facilitate easy travel across this border.

This standard political biography of the India-Bangladesh border and bilateral relations is made to do a lot of work, whether for domestic audiences in the two countries or in negotiating regional imperialisms as India and China compete for Bangladesh's affections and markets. Yet it sits somewhat uneasily with the contemporary realities of militarization, as well as the temporality, of bordering across northern Bengal. Despite frequent declaration of a special relationship of friendship by the Indian and Bangladeshi states, ongoing disagreements around migration, trade, river-water sharing, and a violent border security regime punctuate the volatile and unequal relationship between India and Bangladesh.[27] This book does not take the political history of the India-Bangladesh border as settled or for granted. Rather, it explores *how* borderland residents experience the border regime and mobilize different versions of the border's biography to make their own (im)mobilities and attachments to place meaningful amid militarization. Bordering, from this vantage point, is not a series of big historical events causing ruptures and crises, but an *ordinary eventfulness*—tiny cuts—that require falling apart and coming together in shifting relationships of power each time at the level of individual, family, and social networks. Through these stories, from continued cross-border marriages (chapter 3) to security encounters embedded in social life (chapter 2), we see how regional geopolitical claims of friendliness rely on and are constituted by everyday social and political life in the borderlands. The textures of transnational relations in the borderlands matter for the kinds of geopolitical stories that can be told about Bangladesh-India relations to different audiences.

Religious and caste identities articulate through the difference of the national. Over decades of bordering, from being cohabitants of a consolidated Cooch Behar state and a shared Rajbangsi cultural identity, Rajbangsis and Bengali Muslims have come to be related to one another through majoritarian-minoritarian relations within postcolonial polities. This social engineering is deep, often insidious, and widespread in India, and Bangladesh, formerly East Pakistan. In an explicit instance, Narendra

Modi, in a campaign speech delivered in West Bengal as a prime ministerial candidate in 2014, declared: "Those [from Bangladesh] who observe
Durgashtami, they are a part of our Hindustan, and they will stay here.
But we will deport those who are infiltrators." The weight of such hegemonic sentiments in the Indian political mainstream has a layered history
in the Bengal borderlands. Partition dramatically "changed the position
and status of the Muslims of West Bengal," reducing them to a minority in
the state. Over decades of post-Partition migration and resettlement, they
have clustered in border-lying blocks.[28] The idea that Hindu migrants
from Bangladesh are refugees and Muslim migrants are infiltrators goes
back to the post-1971 years, after the first flush of humanitarianism
toward Bangladeshi refugees ebbed, combined with a politics of resentment around welfare for refugees in the post-Partition decades.[29] Paranoia
around the figure of the "Muslim infiltrator," made synonymous with "the
Bangladeshi illegal migrant," has come to be an integral part of Indian
public discourse since the 1980s.[30] The discourse of the demographic
reconstitution of the eastern borderlands with the settlement of
Bangladeshi migrants underpin movements such as the antiforeigner
Assam Movement (1979–85), which have entrenched a deep suspicion
towards the eastern borderlands in mainstream Indian imaginary and left
traces on the citizenship laws of the country.[31] With the Bharatiya Janata
Party (BJP) coming to govern at the center on a platform of muscular
Hindu nationalism in 2014, the sanctity of Hindu demography, territory,
and economy have been stitched together with precision, consolidating
the India-Bangladesh border as a religious borderline, symbolic of the
unfinished business of Partition.[32]

Hindu nationalist anxieties sanction militarization of the border with
an implicit criminalization of the borderland's minority residents—
Muslims, historically marginalized castes, *adivasis* (indigenous groups)—
as untrustworthy citizens.[33] Borderland residents are portrayed as publics
with natural sympathies with the neighboring nation, sharing linguistic
and cultural identities as Bengali Muslims or Bengali Rajbangsis; with
these transnational ties, they are pathologized as criminal rather than
understood on their own historical and highly heterogenous social terms.[34]
Successive political frames such as these nationalize and separate communities along religious majoritarian-minoritarian lines, undermining

common cause across caste and class lines, within and across the national border. As I describe in the book's final chapter, Muslim migrations eastward to East Pakistan between 1947 and 1964 and Hindu migration westward to India post-1971 are perhaps the least known and most poorly understood strands of this kind of simultaneous incorporation and separation of mobility and settlement across the Bengal borderlands. While in northern Bengal, Hindus from both sides of the national border count on recognition as Indian citizens by supporting this overarching Hindutva imaginary of a Hindu homeland, a transnational yearning I describe in chapter 6, the policing of *all* borderland residents as potentially suspect render the grounds of their inclusion, documentary and otherwise, continuously shaky. These migration histories are central to the lived categorical instabilities of "citizen" and "refugee" that have emerged through relational nation-state formation.

WHERE ARE THE BORDERLANDS, AND HOW DO YOU KNOW YOU'RE THERE?

If this is a study *of* the borderlands, holding up a messy view of the national, it is equally a study *from* the borderlands. Borderlands are not spaces that simply house the force of a border; they are spaces that exemplify multiple, unequal relations of value. But how do such unequal relations come to be, and how do they so reliably endure?

To go from identifying and describing the inequality of borders to digging deeper into the conditions that produce and sustain them demands a move away from a dual analytical focus that has come to preoccupy activists, artists, ethnographers, and political commentators: the fence and the migrant. The border line is the synecdoche of separation and violence in postcolonial histories. Haunted by the iconicity of Partition, this fetish of the line is inescapable. This dominant visuality of the border-as-line in South Asia converges with the visual spectacle of European and American securitized borders: the drama of the border fence. Together these assume that borderlands accompany these spectacular borders, a settled and fixed common noun, a known and knowable place. Against this scholarship on security regimes and militarized borders, *A Thousand Tiny Cuts* reveals instead that producing and settling borderlands is an ongoing project of space- and world-making. Regimes of national security do not appear fully formed to be imposed on always-already borderlands; they are co-constituted through grounded and perceived relations between gendered and classed bodies, spaces, and imaginaries. So, to ask "Where are the borderlands? How do you know you are there?" as empirical questions is to begin an inquiry that upends the idea that borderlands are self-evident and neutral spaces where the stuff of borders happens. In asking a prior question of constitution, this book steps back to focus on the very modes and forms of spatial and social stratification that make borderlands a principle for the relational hierarchy of value. Such a relational hierarchy of value is both specific to the physical borderlands *and* a principle of world-making in a nationalized order. This could be the criminalization of young men as they consider livelihood options in a shared regional context of agrarian distress or the intergenerational dilemmas of intimate kin as they learn to live as national neighbors. Even though I tell this story through northern Bengal, I hope this pair of empirical and analytical questions will travel.

When I lived in the Indian and Bangladeshi borderlands in 2014 and 2015, I constantly found myself sent in different directions and to different sites as appropriate for my subject of study—*simantey jibon* (life in the borderlands)—by different actors. For instance, keenly interested in my research on everyday borderland life and struggles, I had numerous conversations with the middle-class family I roomed with in Dinhata (India) over the years, as they tried to match the "what" of my project with its "where." Over and over again, Reba-kaki, the mother in that family, would kindly offer help, convinced that I was lost and somewhat directionless by being in Dinhata. "I will take you there, right into the borderlands (*simanta elaka*), we will go right by the barbed wire fence, then you will understand. You can see roads and autos that are in Bangladesh and we can talk to the people there." For her it was thrilling to see the new additions to the border fence, the watchtowers of concrete, the spots from where the outposts of the BGB or autorickshaws on roads in Bangladesh were visible. She was not allowed to alight from her car—the BSF strictly controlled civilian use of the road by the border fence—but that momentary encounter with the BSF soldier who gruffly turned her away was part of the experience she enjoyed and considered definitive of being in the borderlands. Shielded by her visibly worn middle-class and Hindu identity—one she assumed I shared—Reba-kaki regarded the strangeness of the soldier with curiosity, not fear. They were part of the borderlands that she believed she could ride in and out of.

There were contradictory opinions on where the borderlands were on the Bangladeshi side, too. I was told in no uncertain terms by the area's commanding officer of the BGB that I could not live within twelve kilometers from the border, as that was their designated jurisdiction and deemed sensitive to national security. However, the town of Lalmonirhat, headquarters of the eponymous district, where I was instructed to stay instead of in a border village, was itself within that twelve-kilometer range. So, while there seems to be little doubt about the location of the border between India and Bangladesh, marked on the Indian side by a serpentine fence of concrete and barbed wire, a visible and immoveable entity, I found little agreement on where the borderlands are. The borderlands seem to be nebulous, their contours and limits fixed and moved by different actors in a variety of ways for distinct purposes. I explore this historically in chapter 1: marginality is not simply a spatial and social outcome or inherent spatial feature. It is an outcome of material relations of value, constituted across multiple scales.[35] A transnational view brings this political production of space into sharp relief *as a set of relations.*

Borderlands, then, do not simply exist where there are borders. They are spatial entities produced through historical and political processes and contestations, and it is not invariable that they feel the way they do for the those who live there. Indeed, as I write this introduction, the political stakes of this question become ever more urgent: in October 2021, India used existing executive powers to designate a wider swathe of territory extending from its borders under the jurisdiction of the BSF.[36] Yet, borderlands themselves are *lived* spaces, with a "liveliness"[37] that is vital to grasping the gendered arrangements of power that connect people to land and ecologies, communities and economies. Borders certainly "turn space into territory,"[38] but they do much more, spatially speaking. Such space-making is not the domain of the state alone, but a site of intense politics and competing desires for the national. These spatial orientations are not merely practical and methodological decisions to be resolved for an outsider-anthropologist.

They index descriptions of space in material, moral, and affective ways, as chapter 2 details, through gendered and embodied experiences of the borderlands transformed into geographies of national security.

The men and women portrayed in this ethnography are acutely aware of the regional geopolitics and histories through which their transnational worlds are viewed. I am attuned, throughout this book, to the analysis of geopolitical hierarchies that borderland actors themselves advance, often as structural critique but equally as heteropatriarchal and nativist national visions, such as Reba-kaki's, that she shared with other middle class residents. Upon learning that I was Indian, the typical fieldwork conversation on the Bangladesh side would begin with complaints about the many ways in which India, the regional hegemon, terrorizes Bangladesh (e.g., "*India boro utpat korey* [India harasses us too much]"). Cartographic images or references to the barbed wire border fence as a national imprisonment are scalar ways for borderland residents to talk about bilateral and regional geopolitical matters, such as Teesta water sharing, inequities of trade agreements, especially food crops, and violent border security. The everyday production of spatial distinctions comes alive in relation to borderland agrarian commodity flows, such as those of tobacco and ganja that I discuss in chapter 4, fixing the spaces of "India" and "Bangladesh" as national in political-economic terms. As the crops travel from the field through various transformations of value along the commodity chain, they sort people and spaces out as relationally separable and comparable. Such daily evaluations and geopolitical imaginaries foreground the incisive analyses of hierarchical spatial relations that are available in and from borderlands.

Images in this book tell stories about the gendered geographies of mobility that emerge and shift through bordering, disrupting the fetish of the spectacular borderline. At the same time they also draw attention to the multisensorial experience of its cuts. Over the course of a decade of ethnographic research, my photographic practice developed as a method of archiving, diagnostic of the ever-expanding presence of national security, the *feeling* of being in a militarized borderland. At first photography seemed impossible, for I could not point a big, fancy camera at the fence from either side, let alone carry it through frisking at checkpoints. As a young, lone woman, living with and accompanying Muslim and Rajbangsi borderland residents on daily itineraries made me suspicious in the male gaze of the security state like the "locals," an English term used in Bengali and Hindi speech by the BGB and BSF respectively, who are routinely criminalized and harassed. Although my privileged positionality afforded me protections that meant we were unequally vulnerable in the risks we could take.

Many of the images in this book were taken with a mobile phone camera, much the same way that residents do, pausing to frame and steal sights of security eruptions. Residents and security forces alike practice a visuality of partial, "situated knowledge" as necessity, not inadequacy. Embracing this partiality is to reckon with "the untaken, the inaccessible, the unshowable" in the visuality of bordering.[39] My use of images in this book furthers the argument that "vision is always a question of the power to see—and perhaps the violence implicit in our visualizing practices,"[40] brought to bear on the spaces, times, and scales of militarized bordering. The more Euro-American borders become archetypal, the more repetitive is the visual repertoire of borders; *A Thousand Tiny Cuts* calls that into question. Over the chapters of the book, especially the first three, images narrate a spatial history of borderlands at the scales of region, neighborhoods, paths, and bodies. Along the side of the road where goats graze (fig. 9), under the harsh glare of floodlights in cultivated fields (fig. 2), and in the ruined infrastructures of connection (figs. 1, 3, 5), the scatter of barbed wire across these agrarian borderlands challenges the selective visual economy through which only particular images have come to represent the violence and devaluation of bordering.

GENDERED MOBILITIES, GENDERED THREATS

Mobility is gendered and gendering. A final aim of this book is to examine the power relations that constitute what feminist geographer Doreen Massey has called "differentiated mobility"—that is, the uneven and unequal positioning of different groups and persons in relation to structures and processes of bordering.[41] In the chapters that follow, I explore *how* this differentiation of mobile bodies is gendered and worked out in relation to concerns of national security, categories of citizenship, and belonging. In particular, gendered mobilities that fall outside the bounds of or frustrate "heterosexual forms of political control, which are fundamental to national narratives of harmonious domesticity" risk being seen as security threats and excised.[42]

My own mobility was considered a threat by the border security forces of both India and Bangladesh. In India, my mobility as an unaccompanied young woman across numerous border villages, spending nights in "dangerous places" where "antinational elements" abound, was deemed suspicious by the BSF; in Bangladesh it was my cross-border mobility that was most suspicious and that scaled the threat from my body to national interest through gender and citizenship.[43] These readings were a function of location intersecting with gendered identity within a heteropatriarchal framework of the national. As the tensions of cross-border marriages that continue to be brokered across the borderlands show in chapter 3, mothers and daughters can mobilize the heteropatriarchal moral force of "the family ideology"[44] to legitimize their clandestine mobilities even in the eyes of state agents, at the cost of distinguishing themselves from men's mobilities "for business." On the other hand, the contours of kinship geographies surfaced through women's familial associations queer the straitjackets of the national community; their stubborn kinwork gestures to a future in which disobedient intimacies might be recuperated. Sitting beneath the turbulence of contemporary citizenship disputes, they become unruly oral archives of mobile pasts, as we see in chapters 3 and 6, and can host powerful critiques of present political structures that attempt to fix categorical boundaries of identity and belonging.

Yet, these are not innocent relations nor redemptive narratives.[45] As Farhana Ibrahim cautions in her work on the Kutch borderlands, "the idea of mobility cannot be presumed to be axiomatically a source of resistance and critique."[46] Taking mobility to be the primary political question of the twenty-first century, the "new mobilities paradigm" in the social sciences, with social justice at its core, focuses on "the organization of power around systems of governing mobility, immobility, timing and speed, channels and barriers at various scales."[47] While the politics of the Anglophone academy have resulted in this being framed in terms of mobilities between the Global North and the Global South, the vast majority of migrations are *within* regions of the Global South, making analytical groundings from such a vantage point essential. Gendered mobilities across the India-Bangladesh borderlands reveal this relational hierarchy of value at the heart of bordering *within* a region that in the global schema can only appear as "the south." State actors and borderland residents marshal multiple attachments to place, social and political claims, *and* heteropatriarchal figurations of threat to make certain mobilities possible in relation to constrained others. As I show in chapter 5, for instance, young men, and especially Muslim men coming of age in these borderlands, confront criminalization by the state as well as intense social surveillance on their clandestine activities.

In paying close attention to dress, bodily comportment, and sensations, I extend a feminist ear and eye to show how the tiny cuts on the body scale gender hierarchies in bordering from individuals to nations. The nexus of the "body-territorial"[48] is vital to understand how bordering assigns value to spaces, people, and mobility and arranges them in hierarchical relations. South Asia has an especially violent history of imagining the nation as a gendered body.[49] Bodies acquire identities, threats, and vulnerabilities through social and economic relations. Partition was enacted around demographic alignments on religious lines, fault lines that continue well into the present. Within the borderlands, the same physical border "does not interpellate all subjects equally" and as border residents move, they feel the intensity of this scrutiny on their bodies.[50] Gendered evaluations of danger and threat to the somewhat abstract mandate of national security become evident. Class, religion, gender come together in marking the terrain of permissible mobilities. In this, state actors and borderland residents share in gendering mobilities and threats with a common grammar, though not always to the same ends. The chapters of this book ethnographically track the processes through which such threats are embodied and gender scales mobilities, building on and bringing together discussions in feminist scholarship and political anthropology on unequal mobilities.

However, Partition and the end of the British Empire was hardly the start of fragmented mobility in the Bengal borderlands. Postcolonial borders, such as this one, are the culmination of centuries of what Anne Stoler calls the "principle of managed mobilities" in which colonial rule across the colonies of Asia and Africa named, tamed, sequestered, and settled as necessary the poor, vagrants, criminals, and laborers.[51] Contemporary iterations of citizenship, regional political economy, and mobility in the crossroads of northern Bengal can be considered in this longer history. While I begin this exploration in the first chapter with the spatial history of borderlands, chapters 4, 5, and 6 trace how the mobility of brides, agrarian crops, young men, and putative refugees, respectively, pivot on relational hierarchies such as that of currency, markets, labor, and religious majoritarianism. Their mobilities are not linear progressions in space or time, towards less mobile or more settled relations. They cut recursively over generations, appearing in unpredictable relations whether of masculine longing, commodity value, or political claims making.

MOBILE ETHNOGRAPHY AS A TRANSNATIONAL FEMINIST METHOD

Residents on both sides of the borderlands face similar structural disadvantages, though they experience them quite differently—for example, the halogen lights on India's border face that only shine in one direction, drawing insects to the banana fields owned by Bangladeshi farmers (fig. 2). As one young man in Madhupur village (BD) pointed out wryly—referring to the rifles of the Indian BSF trained towards Bangladesh and, in his emphasis, Bangladeshis—the mouth of the gun faces in only direction. Even when they share experiences, residents separated by distinctions and hierarchies of national identity seldom make common cause. National frames come in between, fracturing possible transnational solidarities.[52] That is perhaps the deepest cut of bordering. I observed this as a human rights worker in South Asia before I began my doctoral research, and I was determined to undertake fieldwork on both sides of the border. That is but one step to avoid the pitfalls of methodological nationalism. Conceptualizing borderland mobilities as fundamentally transnational can show how they are shaped through a relational hierarchy of value, the "scattered hegemonies" of caste, heteropatriarchy, class, and religion.[53]

   A Thousand Tiny Cuts puts into practice what Lisa Lowe calls an analytic of relationality.[54] In tracing the mobilities of people and goods across the borderlands, my research made connections between adjacent but always directly related or intersecting networks. It is this following in multiple senses, a process of khunje berano (searching around) for traces of people, things, connections (real and conceptual), without neat endings necessarily, through which my practice of mobile ethnography emerged. Each chapter demonstrates a different method in the service of a mobile ethnography—spatial history, walking, commodity chain analysis, kinship charts, and family histories of migration. Taken together, these operationalize a transnational feminist praxis that makes visible "the national" as it emerges in multiple domains of *transnational* borderland life. To put into practice this ethnographic analytic of relationality is "to contribute a manner of reading and interpretation."[55] I have tried neither to explain away the patchiness or unevenness of this knowledge nor to ethnographically balance out, as one early critical reader of my dissertation asked for, the "India part" with the "Bangladesh part." The unevenness—mediated by my relationships and positionality—has a particular story to tell about the intersection of mobility, security, and the hierarchical regimes of value that we see so acutely from borderlands.

Mobile ethnography as a feminist epistemology and praxis is a particularly powerful vantage point for a study of normative claims about social and economic life that attach to national borderlands but are predicated on less evident *transnational* making of those spaces in South Asia.[56] Inspired by feminist scholarship that foregrounds the body as political instrument and diagnostic,[57] this book traces the spatial politics and histories of the India-Bangladesh borderlands as theoretical questions to be known, felt, and navigated in and through gendered bodies. Bodies know through excitement and fear, they sense without seeing, they are pressed and gazed upon by others just as they turn toward or away from something, individually or collectively.[58] Countering the cartographic dogmas of the state means not only to map in other forms (though that is possible too, as the kinship counter-maps in chapter 5 suggest) but to recast how space is known, inhabited, and narrated. By ethnographically studying the ostensibly small scales of the body, the home, the household, the rural neighborhood, I hope that *A Thousand Tiny Cuts* will offer a way to think about spatial formations—such as agrarian borderlands—that are vital to the relational hierarchies of multi-sited connections. An *ethnography of relation*, then, can show what sites mean to each other.[59]

Between 2011 and 2019, I accompanied border residents on their daily itineraries and followed networks of people and goods, as well as everyday spatial practices. These daily itineraries were to villages, markets, homes, schools, and offices in neighboring border villages and towns across the districts of Cooch Behar (India) and Lalmonirhat and Kurigram (Bangladesh). In the Indian borderlands, I also spent considerable time at BSF outposts, interviewing officers, shadowing their daily work when allowed, and with soldiers on duty at checkpoints or patrols. This was in addition to encountering them with other borderland residents as we traversed village routes that were patrolled. In Bangladesh, while I was denied permission to officially conduct research with the BGB, I encountered them frequently, especially as I came to be surveilled by them. I followed the work of the district police as they carried out many tasks shared with the BGB—often in competition with them—such as seizing contraband goods, particularly narcotics, and intercepting crimes related to the border.

What networks, sites, and routes I came to know well over the long course of my research were radically marked by who I was perceived to be in gendered, religious, kinship, and national terms. I retain Bengali kin terms—kaki (paternal aunt), di (short for *didi*, elder sister), mama (maternal uncle), da (short for *dada*, older brother)—as suffixes to some names throughout this book to acknowledge the kinds of relations that mediated my presence. As an upper-caste Bengali woman from Calcutta, my presence in the Indian borderlands was often associated with NGOs and journalists. In Bangladesh, my identity as an "Indian" brought out as many complaints as histories of intimate connections. There were times when my identity as a Bengali trumped that of being Indian and when violations of my perceived caste identity offended Bangladeshi Rajbangsis; the chapters bear these shadows. Besides, my own mobility changed over a decade's acquaintance; the deeper I became entrenched in particular family networks, the more I came to be treated as kin. This structured my mobility in surprising ways: social expectations of kin-work from me expanded as my previous mobility (which came from being marked as an outside-stranger doing research, walking and talking with strangers, often male) shrank. Gendered identity was of tremendous material consequence, as I parse in chapters 2, 3, and 5, for both my mobility and "the field" as physical referent and socio-political location changed shape over time, with varying distances and intimacies.

Feminist scholars have long emphasized the intellectual acuity and honesty of partial epistemologies, arguing that "'subjugated' standpoints are preferred because they promise more adequate, sustained, empathetic and transformative accounts of the world."[60] Conducting fieldwork about that which is itself a subject of pervasive surveillance and security—borderland mobilities—requires further ethical and political engagement with the conventions of ethnographic research and writing. I eschew the role of the omniscient narrator in this book and espouse instead "the analytical importance of staying with, rather than trying to resolve, ambiguity."[61] In the western Indian borderlands of Kutch, Ibrahim writes, "to know what not to know" is scripted into interpersonal relationships.[62] Negotiating public secrets then, such as about clandestine cross-border marriages like Rani's, become tensions in social relations, and not for interloping ethnographers alone. The politics of transparency, visibility, and knowledge production certainly cannot be bracketed within the now-standard acknowledgment of the researcher's identity and positionality in the introduction to ethnographic monographs.[63] I offer these remarks on methodological and ethical questions of ambiguity and epistemology as an opening of a thread that runs through the book.

Toward the beginning of my fieldwork, the rumor that I was a *agent* (spy) or a *goenda* (detective) raged on both sides. Sometimes it was my fast strides, sometimes my use of Indian and Bangladeshi SIM cards in my phone, even how little rice I ate: all read as evidence that some greater powers were behind my small frame. At first, I was devastated and fearful. One night, Malati Barman in Kathalbari (India), my landlady and dear friend, explained how entirely reasonable this speculation was.

> How can you blame people? Like the police you are following people around everywhere, asking them questions, people can see how easily you are learning everything about their lives. On top of that you are not making any distinctions between good people and the *blackdar* [smuggler]—one day everyone sees you with me, and then the next day they see you with Shobuj [a young Muslim man known to be a smuggler; see chapter 5] hanging out in the bazaar. You are mixing with everyone equally, eating with them. How are people to understand what you actually want, no matter what you say to them [about your research]?

I was breaking down social distinctions, for instance by not observing religious and caste rules of commensality (in other words, eating in Muslim and lower caste Hindu households with an upper caste *"title,"* as I was frequently told). In Malati-di's analysis, this confounded a clear conclusion about who I was and what my objectives were. My own daily itineraries from one home to another, one site to another, one social domain to another, linked typically unconnected people and places. Eventually it was a scary interrogation by the BSF—witnessed by dozens of Balatari (India) residents and regarding caste betrayals, indiscriminate socializing, and most emphatically the absence of a husband that I claimed to have— that demonstrated to borderland residents my vulnerability to state security institutions. Stories like this about me and others circulated transnationally, incorporated into existing anxieties and shaping new ones about the value of connection. These anxieties are not only about information, intentions, or visibility. Connection was not indiscriminately desired; there was no before-times of the border that everyone universally longed for. The cuts of bordering show people always already learning to be apart and live together in renewed ways.

1 On and Off Rangpur Road

That the word simanta means the end is not entirely true.
There is much that begins here. . . . Wherever there is an
end, there are beginnings.

—Anarja Anwar, *Simantey Par-Abar*

A border is a dividing line, a narrow strip along a steep
edge. A borderland is a vague and undetermined place
created by emotional residue of an unnatural boundary.
It is in a constant state of transition.

—Gloria Anzaldua, *Borderlands/La Frontera*

THE RUMORED RETURN OF THE ROAD

Simanta is the Bengali word for border. In the summer of 2012, I was
traveling along the border in northern Bangladesh, east to west across the
districts of Kurigram, Lalmonirhat, and Nilphamari. It was already mid-
day by the time I arrived in Madhupur village in Lalmonirhat district,
using multiple modes of public transportation to cover about fifty kilometers from Rangpur city. Mr. Rahman, who met me at the auto stand in
Madhupur, took one look at my sweaty face and said, "Just see how long it
takes to get from Rangpur today. If only the rail line was working, we
would reach Rangpur in no time! Why Rangpur, we could get to Kolkata
directly." He pointed to something in the ground beside the road that I
hadn't noticed until then (see fig. 3), and when I asked about the defunct
rail line he was referring to, he admonished me for not knowing that
Madhupur had been an important colonial railway junction (*Shudhu*

3. Remains of rail tracks in disrepair next to Rangpur Road that runs through what is a Bangladeshi border village today.

station noy, junction chhilo!)[1] I duly noted that Madhupur had been no blink-and-you-miss-it rail stop but a junction where more than one rail line crossed. The memory and imaginary of connection clearly mattered for this resident of what is today one of Bangladesh's most underdeveloped and distant (from the capital, Dhaka) border districts. *Pratyanta, durabarti, bichhino, prantik* (remote, distant, isolated, marginal): these are the adjectives that routinely accompany any reference to these northern borderland districts in Bangladeshi media. And these are the same adjectives that sneakily accompany the arrival of anthropologists to the scene of borderlands on too many occasions. I thought I was journeying to the "distant" and "remote" borderland too, but in Mr. Rahman's rapid-fire Rangupuriya, it soon turned into a lesson on the antiquity and historical connectedness of that place. That was also the first time I heard about the rumored return of Rangpur Road.

Mr. Rahman, who would soon become Rafiq-mama to me as I came to live with his family over the next few years, introduced me to the history of Madhupur and the Cooch Behar-Rangpur region. He referred to ongoing efforts to revive the rail and road connections with India, gesturing emphatically to "India" right across the rice fields and the river by the village. "You should meet these people in Lalmonirhat, they have all the records," he said, rattling off names and referring to saved petitions and newspaper clippings. It seemed the return of Rangpur Road was imminent. For a new visitor to Madhupur like myself, Madhupur's Mughal existence, its historically famed bazaar, and its thriving life as a rail junction seemed a bit dubious. All I could see, on this first guided tour, were bits of iron beneath a heap of hay or outside makeshift mud houses built by landless families on what Mr. Rahman urged me to see as the elevated land on which railway tracks once ran. Pointing to the jagged mud edges of an eroded riverbank, he said that the international border had "fallen" into the river at that spot, the very same land that had been the site of a precolonial bazaar. His words tugged me between this distant past, literally hard to see, and a future that he seemed sure of: all of these houses built on the rail track have received a notice of eviction from the government, he reported. Their removal was a sure sign of a revival to come.

As I traveled on and off Rangpur Road myself conducting ethnographic research, I repeatedly found the rumored return of the Road to be a conversational catalyst on *both* sides of the border. *"Ei rasta abar chaloo hobey?* [I hear the road will start up again?]" was a frequent refrain, and one I also learned to ask as a conversational prompt.

How far, literally and metaphorically, the glorious history of road and rail connections went depended on who you spoke to. Rangpur Road can be traced to Mughal times, when it connected the kingdom of Cooch Behar with the Mughal-allied region to its immediate south. Like many other precolonial roads across the subcontinent, this became a major thoroughfare under British colonial rule,[2] serving as the political and commercial conduit between the princely state capital of Cooch Behar and the British administrative headquarter in Rangpur at the very north of the Bengal presidency. The extraction of resources like timber, coal, and tea and the agrarian settlement of this frontier region occupied the British in Bengal for two centuries.[3] In the late nineteenth and early twentieth centuries, eastern India was incorporated into the British Empire's dense commercial networks, with Bengal at its center, through the creation of a transport grid designed to connect particular labor and commodity markets.[4] Rangpur Road and its adjacent road and rail networks became an integral part of this transport grid, stratifying regions and peoples according to mobility. After Partition, the rail connection was first stopped in the India-Pakistan War of 1965; elderly residents animatedly recall attempts to bomb the rail bridge across the river. As the rail lines and roads slowly eroded over the decades, with no maintenance from India, Pakistan, or newly independent Bangladesh, passenger traffic on this route across the international border dwindled, and eventually ceased in the early 1990s. Over the decades, business owners and town associations in Dinhata, Lalmonirhat, and other prominent market centers of the region have periodically organized petitions to political leaders and bureaucrats to revive Rangpur Road. But these transnational collaborations in the borderlands have not been legitimized by either state. There have, however, been occasional signs of state actions that are read as heralds of large-scale projects of infrastructural repair and revival.

The latest of these rumors arrived In these borderlands of northern Bengal in 2015 as Narendra Modi and Sheikh Hasina, the prime ministers of India and Bangladesh, respectively, signed a slew of bilateral agreements to improve regional transit and connectivity by road, rail, and waterways.[5] The rumor that I had first heard in 2012 was revived: the buzz was in the markings to widen the road on the Indian side and the roadwork contracts allegedly circulating in block offices on the Bangladeshi side. Mr. Rahman's discourse on the antiquity of Madhupur and the rumored return of Rangpur Road's broken connections across the border are present as signs on Rangpur Road itself, to be seen and reinscribed by the discerning resident of the region. Beside and beneath its stretches, Rangpur Road holds a history of a sense of a connected place.[6]

This chapter is about that sense of a connected place and its history as it becomes a *simanta elaka* (borderland). Bordering is neither severing of mobilities nor connection alone; it is an interplay between the two. The making of a borderland, as a particular kind of spatial entity, sets in motion new ways of being held apart and coming together, which unfold variously over decades—Anzaldua's "constant state of transition." This chapter follows imaginaries, infrastructures, histories, and experiences of connection and remoteness as they come to intersect on Rangpur Road. Picking up on the provocation posed in the introduction—Where are the borderlands?—I demonstrate that a borderland does not appear where a border is drawn. It is laboriously produced in its geographic, political, economic, and experiential aspects. These labors are undertaken by heterogeneous actors in ways that are contingent, incomplete, and ongoing. This heterogeneity is important also for the spatial qualities that attach to the borderlands. In other words, *how* borderlands feel is a question of relational value with tremendous consequences for life in and governance of that space, and *where* these qualities are manifest is a matter of contention. Anarja Anwar, a young writer from a border village in Kurigram, vividly depicts this range in a collection of short stories: the borderlands can feel terrifying or be a place of possibility; this is a place of ends and of beginnings.

In using Rangpur Road to tell such a story of the borderlands, I draw on scholarship on landscapes that considers the social and political importance of place-making and the experiences and memories of inhabiting physical spaces.[7] The rumor of Rangpur Road's return brings together diverse habitations of this landscape, including those that invoke sovereign pasts. Scholars of borderlands have drawn our attention to the dynamism of sovereignty and state-making and denaturalized the stability of national territory to highlight, instead, its historicity, productions, anxieties, and instabilities.[8] I share the critical impetus "to see beyond framings of space as simultaneously self-explanatory and illegible" but push beyond this singular relationship between land and territory.[9] This chapter slows the rush to explain state territorialism as manifest *in* borderlands and achieved *through* borders and instead questions the assumed spatial facticity of borderlands themselves.

THE UNBEARABLE REMOTENESS OF RANGPUR ROAD

> Stories congeal around imperial debris, as do critiques.
> —Ann Stoler, *Imperial Debris: On Ruins and Ruination*

So here we are, off and on an approximately twenty-three-mile-long stretch of Rangpur Road between Dinhata and Lalmonirhat, two important border towns now in India and Bangladesh, respectively. Google Maps is confounded by a river, the firmly etched international boundary, and the visibly interrupted road that runs between the two towns. On the Indian side, Rangpur Road remains a busy thoroughfare, the main road in Cooch Behar district going eastward from the city, eventually becoming a village road until it ends abruptly. A narrow village road picks up on the Bangladesh side, runs its course beside the bare remnants of the adjacent rail tracks toward Lalmonirhat (see fig. 3), and then becomes a highway heading to Rangpur across the Teesta River. While this road—and all those leading to and from it—continues to be in heavy use in the borderlands, it is disconnected at and by the border itself. Its historical capacity to connect and facilitate the mobility of people and goods thus ruined, parts of the material infrastructure of this road and its ancillary structures—such as the dilapidated remains of rail tracks, warehouses, a bridge—are considered by borderland residents as ruins. They are Ann Stoler's "debris," they are debated and debatable archives.

I use the term "ruination" to refer to the deliberate work of severing connections— whether infrastructural, commercial, and imaginational— that constitute the making of borderlands as particularly devalued spaces within the national. In distinguishing ruins from ruination, Stoler theorizes "ruination as an active, ongoing process that allocates imperial debris differently and ruin as a violent verb that unites apparently disparate moments, places, and objects."[10] The rubrics of "colonial legacy" serve us poorly; as explanatory frameworks, they presume we know everything we need to about the postcolonial present. Not only do such frameworks prevent an understanding of the "connective tissue" at work, they are unable to constitute as a subject of inquiry "the perceptions and practices through which people are forced to reckon with features of those formations in which they remain vividly and imperceptibly bound."[11] Rafiq-mama's devotion to Madhupur's glorious past and its prosperous future-to-come, amid its dismally poor present, compels us to view the borderlands of India and Bangladesh as spaces-in-making. Refusing the label of a settled historical formation in this way questions what seems obvious or readily known about postcolonial borderlands: in a most basic sense, where they are, what their features are, and how they came to be. To travel on and off Rangpur Road is to home in on signs of an ongoing process of becoming on the landscape—of roads ruined, of connection severed, what the river sutures, and what it washes away.

In his thesis about the production of space as a commodity in a capitalist world, Henri Lefebvre draws attention to the dialectical character of this production process: the "coming-into-being" with the "disappearance of codings/decodings."[12] To appreciate the rising rumor of the return of Rangpur Road, then, is to acknowledge that there is a long history of the road's importance that is alive in the present, and that the equally long history of the production of remoteness bears the imprint of a dialectic. Remoteness and connection, in these oral histories, feature not as a static, spatial locations but a sociological set of relations or historical forms of state control.[13] Moreover, the interplay of remoteness and connection is experienced as a mood. Along Rangpur Road, the colonial railroad, the customs office in the new postcolony, and the border area road of the developmentalist security state all reek of new *de*formations, of the spatial and political productions of these spaces as borderlands, connected, disconnected, reconnected. In exploring this production of space, I retain some of the disorienting tugging between an invisible past and difficult-to-imagine future that sedimented histories invoke.

The four structures through which this chapter is routed—a customs office, a warehouse, a link road, and a shop—are unremarkable sites in many ways, easily missed for either their ubiquity or their present insignificance. They are mossy, dusty, rusty. In narrating them as nodal points of historical connection and potent debris in the present lives of the region, I am less interested in reading these buildings as receptacles or embodiments of history than as cues for opening up the sedimented layers that make these borderlands. Traveling on and off Rangpur Road—in space and time—seeks to understand how ruination and remoteness come to be braided together so that borderlands appear, naturally, as distant wastelands, the place where the road ends.

THE CUSTOMS HOUSE

Bordering as well as mobility are old, familiar phenomena in northern Bengal, a region frequently described as the Duars. Samir Das notes that the term, literally meaning "doors" to Bhutan, Assam, and Bengal, is widely used in Assamese, Bodo, Bengali, Nepali, and Rajbangsi languages spoken across this region.[14] The customs offices of postcolonial India and Pakistan came onto a map thick with borders and routes of connection. For example, the political and jurisdictional border between the princely state of Cooch Behar and the British Indian division of Rangpur in northern Bengal was widely known: I found that elderly residents of borderland villages referred to this spatial distinction frequently in the oral histories I recorded of the region. By the early twentieth century, Cooch Behar, Lalmonirhat, and "Rungpore" were well-known place names on road and rail maps. Dinhata, an old market town in the Cooch Behar state (India), is about forty kilometers to the north of Lalmonirhat (Bangladesh). As I learned from a Bangladeshi bureaucrat serving as the district magistrate of Lalmonirhat, who pointed out a Union Jack designed into the porch of his official bungalow, the urban foundations of the town were due to its rail station in the early twentieth century. That prominent bungalow was built to house the colonial rail official for whom Lalmonirhat would have been the most distant northern outpost in British Bengal. Colonial extraction paid for the building of an Officer's Club, with chandeliers, fancy tapestry, and even a ballroom, just so that the few white men who were posted to Lalmonirhat—to oversee the railway line and the

4. The customs complex for the Dinhata area, Cooch Behar, established next to what became one of India's last/first train stations after Partition. Children, cows, and goats are the only visitors today.

smooth passage of extracted commodities—could suffer its unbearable remoteness.

The infrastructures of bordering—for example, the customs office (fig. 4)—point us to where the adoption of the border was *not* so seamless and where respatialization of the region was indeed necessary, more emphatically and forcibly within national imaginaries. A parallel political reorganization was going on: after Partition, when princely states were being merged with either India or Pakistan, there was a clear demand for a separate, independent state of Cooch Behar. This would protect the Rajbangsi language and cultural identity and span a territory that would disobey the newly announced Radcliffe border.[15] Rafiq-mama's elderly neighbors, and friends in their generation across the Bangladeshi border villages in today's Lalmonirhat and Kurigram districts, emphasized that they were originally subjects of the Cooch Behar state. In talking about the history of the region, they would unfailingly remark that the princely state wanted to join Pakistan but the treachery of Indian National Congress political leaders ensured the signature of the king to the accession agreement. That the India-Bangladesh border could have run its course in an altogether different way is a spatial and political imaginary that gently weeps through the borderlands of northern Bengal even today. How would this region, its political economy, and its relations to security, migration, and citizenship in South Asia have been affected if the Cooch Behar princely state had become a district of East Pakistan? What entrenched and naturalized truths do these imaginary detours allow us to question?

The year 1946 was vital in the *re*spatialization of Cooch Behar: from a princely state to being incorporated as a borderland district in an imminently independent nation-state. Cooch Behar's political turmoil began in earnest with the 1946 elections to the Council of State, the precursor to India's Constituent Assembly. The newly founded organization Hitasadhani Sabha came into prominence in this influential governing body. Consisting of both Hindu and Muslim Rajbangsis, the Sabha voiced popular resentment against non-Rajbangsi Bengalis, referred to (even today) as "*bhatias*," Bengalis who were from southern Bengal.[16] At the time of the elections, Cooch Behar was demographically made up of 40 percent Muslims and 46 percent Rajbangsi Hindus; the remaining citizens were *savarna* Hindus, including Marwaris and *bhatias*.[17] Muslims occupied 50 percent of the higher services of the Cooch Behar state and owned 50 percent of the state's total land,[18] a distribution that was to change dramatically over the next two decades in the aftermath of Partition (see chapters 4 and 6).

The leadership of the Hitasadhani Sabha reflected this distribution, consisting of Hindu and Muslim *jotedars,* with its main positions occupied by prominent Muslims.[19] Across Cooch Behar, these leaders spoke publicly about supporting a merger with Pakistan and obstructed the hoisting of the Indian flag, a ceremonial signal organized in many border districts and parts of various princely states across the subcontinent.[20] A branch of the Indian National Congress was established in Cooch Behar as late as 1947, as political activists who saw themselves as "secular" and sought to align with India hastily organized meetings in Kolkata to draw wider attention to the activities of the pro-Pakistan Hitasadhani Sabha.[21] This *savarna* Hindu minority of Cooch Behar used political channels to petition Sardar Patel directly to act against what they bluntly described as a Muslim League conspiracy to "divide the Hindus of the state into two factions ... two nation theory ... to Muslimize the whole State, effacing the Hindus."[22] Politics was all about rearranging communities and spaces, identified along religious lines. The border was a tightrope stretched across the chasm of these widening ideological fractures.

Between the formation of the independent governments of India and Pakistan and the merger treaty ultimately signed on August 28, 1949, multiple sovereignties and territorial visions at the scales of the region, province, and nation were in the fray.[23] It is against this political volatility in northern Bengal and the overall contingencies of nation-state formation that the spatial reorganization of the region was undertaken through border delineation. National bureaucracies were established to manage the enormous traffic of people and goods flowing across this new border on a daily basis. The customs office, pictured here in a derelict condition (fig. 4), was at the center of this new postcolonial infrastructure of regulating movement that simultaneously stood for the border and was tasked with the labor of mapping "identities, geographies, and histories into bounded nations."[24] It was built next to a railway station that in 1947 became one of many "last" stations in eastern India. The station—and subsequently this customs office and checkpoint—were located along Rangpur Road. With two lines, one ferrying coal and tea between Assam and Kolkata, the metropolitan center of Bengal province and later the capital of the Indian state of West Bengal, and the other connecting northern Bengal to Kolkata, the establishment of border control in the form of immigration and customs checkpoints severely interrupted mobility across this region.

These days it is no longer a local landmark. You could easily miss the entrance to the customs office complex for the row of food stalls that first came up to supply customers there. The complex is a ghostly world now; plants come out of the walls, and only bats and the occasional grazing animal look for company. The place is best known among village children for the mango trees heavy with fruit. Imagine six blocks of two-storied buildings that served as office, storage for seized goods and files, paperwork stacked to the ceilings, and residential quarters for customs officers. The material infrastructure and spatial expanse of this complex attests to its bureaucratic prominence in the first few postcolonial decades.

With the partition of the Bengal province into the Indian states of West Bengal and Assam and East Pakistan, migration became the lynchpin of politics and political identity for the postcolonial states.[25] Scholars of Partition and historians of the postcolonial state have argued that citizenship and refugee regimes in South Asia are co-constituted in postcolonial sovereignty and in its structural violence toward minority populations.[26] I want to extend our analysis, beyond political identities, to the *spatial* work accomplished by the bureaucracies of bordering at sites such as this customs office. This spatial work occurred at two levels: one, the borderlands of India and then–East Pakistan were viewed and administered as a transit zone due to the management of mobility at this border; two, the border was spatialized at the scale of the body, with all the markings of gender, class, and religion. Regional geopolitics were embodied in the management of mobility at these sites.

Take, for instance, the tale of the twisted testicles. In 1950, a note from the government of West Bengal to the government of East Bengal complained of improper and intrusive body searches, even inside train compartments, as passengers traveled from Dacca to Calcutta.[27] It narrated the plight of one passenger who had felt compelled to complain urgently to the Indian Liaison Officer at the border that his testicles were twisted by one of the East Bengali peons when searching his body at the border crossing. Taking a solemn view of this complaint, the secretary in question wrote that "this Government is of the opinion that body search of passengers should be done only by Customs Officers and that also only in cases of suspicion."[28] This was the scale at which bodies were joined to new states as citizens; bilateral ties hung in the balance of intimate intrusions deemed to be significant.[29]

In the middle of 1948, first India and then Pakistan announced a permit system for travel across the border. Historian Vazira Zamindar documents the plight of families divided, individuals stuck on one side or the other, and also the bureaucratic and political debates over East Bengal's opposition to the extension of the permit system to the eastern border.[30] This uncertainty remained in the years that followed; ordinary people as well as lower-level government functionaries at these customs and immigration checkposts speculated about the imposition of the permit system. This speculation—should an "Indian" passenger's testicle-twisting by a lowly Pakistani functionary matter?—encouraged geopolitics to play out on bodies in borderlands in these everyday encounters.

This tale of the twisted testicles is anything but unusual. From 1950, many of these diplomatic, official notes complained about the harassment of border-crossers. The making of this eastern border in the Indian subcontinent was from its very inception the making of a classed border. The indignation of the man whose testicles had been twisted was not only that he had been so affronted, but specifically that the search had been conducted by the peon, a lowly state employee. This basis for indignation was heard, recognized, and addressed as such in the letter from the government, which deemed searches "only by Customs Officers" as fit for bona fide (read: respectable and elite) passengers. Furthermore, it unequivocally calls for the exercise of discretionary power and judgment on a case-by-case basis—that is, "only in cases of suspicion." As customs and immigration authorities sought to carry out the mandated task of classification and management, the religious and class dimensions to sorting people and their mobilities were as decisive then as they are now.

In December 1950 a set of letters had been forwarded from the government of East Bengal to that of West Bengal about the harassment of Muslim passengers while traveling through West Bengal.[31] For instance, one Muslim tea merchant from Jalpaiguri—the part of the district in undivided Bengal that now fell in Rangpur district, East Pakistan—and another passenger traveling with his family had their possessions seized with no receipts given. When they asked for receipts, they were summarily dismissed, with the threat of slaps by the Land Customs staff at the border railway station in Haldibari (West Bengal). The formal governmental complaint forwards the report from the East Bengal Border Inspector stationed at Patgram (East Bengal), while also noting that this instance was one in a line of persecution that "has reached a boiling point that no Muslim dare to dress themselves in their national costume for fear of harassment and insult."[32]

Communal violence linked to bodily religious markers has been widely documented in the year immediately preceding and following Partition and its mass displacements across the western border.[33] Trains that smelled of burning bodies and women jumping into wells to avoid being raped by men of the antagonistic religion have become emblematic of the intense and concentrated violence that characterized the "madness" of Partition. These historical records of the eastern border, on the other hand, archive a starkly different mood, embodiment, and pace of Partition's bor-

dering: the routine yet relentless bureaucratic ordering of mobility, mediated through hierarchies of caste and race that were manifest in the colonial railways project.[34] Bodies on the move were being joined to
nation-state territories via identifying markers of dress and comportment.
Public and state spaces like the customs house at the postcolonial border
came to be associated with sympathies for one religious community or the
vilification of another. As with colonial railway stations, these postcolonial
state spaces were foundationally spaces of policing and segregation, staging relational hierarchies of caste, class, religion, and now nationality.

The recourse to visible markers of class and religion was a vital axis of
border enforcement, despite the heightened concern around the public
appearance of secular liberalism that guided both India and Pakistan in
their interactions with each other, especially pertaining to the welfare of
religious minorities.[35] The larger discursive and legislative frame in both
countries focused overwhelmingly on the bureaucratic definition and
management of "refugees" and "citizens," in particular Muslim refugees in
Pakistan, Hindu refugee rehabilitation in India, and the category of "the
returning citizen."[36] Border inspectors, customs officials, and a whole reti-
nue of workers in each of these departments were the foot soldiers of governments, entrusted with the task of interpreting and implementing "the
spirit" of customs laws. It is their attention to and imagination of the
match between individual bodies on the move, governmental categories of
border-crossers, and emplacement in nationalist terms that classed the
border through material and bodily signifiers.

A peek into the political correspondence between the governments of
West Bengal and East Pakistan in the first decade of independence attests
to the controversial issue of counting migrant traffic and classifying moving
people and goods. Disputed numbers were central to diplomatic ties
between India and Pakistan as each sought to define, defend, and better
their own record of minority protection on the backs of displaced peoples.[37]
The mandated work of this border bureaucracy was to manage the postcolonial borderlands as transit zones. Yet, beyond the points of entry and exit
on the linear border, these were spaces teeming with their own concerns
over continued mobility and connections. The regulatory infrastructures
on the ground—such as this customs and immigration complex—made
visible to the two governments that there were many more categories of

border-crossers than the two that they were most fixated on from the vantage point of transit: refugees and citizens. The new border was crossed not only in the form of an "exodus"—that is, religious and political violence-instigated displacements—but through forms of mobility that greatly varied in frequency, distance, and duration.[38] If the only people the state "saw" were passengers, not residents of these borderlands who were also border-crossers, passengers and local residents came to see the state in these spaces as marked with religious sympathies. Consequently, in these vital years of postcolonial transition, the region came to be spatialized *as* borderlands— that is, as spaces of crossings in which states codify border-crossers but render invisible those that live there with sedimented attachments and orientations to places and mobility, both now transnational.

A *GODAM*/WAREHOUSE

Rangpur Road, particularly this stretch between Dinhata and Lalmonirhat, is dotted with warehouses, concentrated near the *haats* and train stations of colonial trade, thinning out in between. Unlike the ornate one pictured here (fig. 5), most *godams* are unembellished structures of wood, cement, and tin sheets, their walls caked with the dust of the road. Jute, tobacco, and potatoes, the prized cash crops of the region, are stored here. Each of these structures was a nodal point along the commercial sinews of Rangpur Road. The warehouse pictured here stands on the Indian side of Rangpur Road. It once belonged to a Bengali Muslim family that exchanged its properties—home, agricultural land, and warehouses—with a Bengali Hindu family in the mid-1950s. (I discuss in much greater detail the commodity history of tobacco and its entanglements with the history of displacement and dwelling across this border in chapters 4 and 6, respectively.)

Multigenerational Bengali Muslim, Rajbangsi, and Marwari trading families, many of which still own such warehouses, are repositories of the commercial and connected history of the region. For them, Cooch Behar and Rangpur is a patchwork of *haats* and warehouses, categorized as active or in disuse. While some of these warehouses remain in use for tobacco and jute—the two main crops of the region that can be stocked, unlike perishable vegetables—traders emphasized that the *godams* were

5. A warehouse on Rangpur Road just outside Dinhata, built to store jute and tobacco.

shadows of their former glorious life. In her magisterial account of
Lemuria, a land that once existed but that is no more, historian Sumathi
Ramaswamy theorizes "labors of loss" as a form of place-making, insisting
that this multiply configures a place that "reappears as lost."[39] I follow
Ramaswamy in exploring spatial history that accommodates "apprehen-
sions of loss as a source of pleasure and hope, and not just poignancy and
pain." For those like Mr. Rahman and numerous merchants who nurture
accounts of proximity to state power—both past and in the hoped-for
future—warehouses such as these materialized the glory days of trade and
capital on Rangpur Road, belying its current conditions of disconnection
and the flight of commerce. In their optimism, traders refuse to forget the
imposition of disconnection, disrupting the national narrative of development imposed on borderlands by dreaming of an altogether different spatial history toward vibrant transnational life.

The economic implications of bordering are monumental. Bordering is
not merely a process of economic implementation, it is also a process in
which national economic interests come to be constituted as such. In other

words, at the time of Partition there was no a priori clarity on national economic interests. The cross-border movement of commodities that were deemed to be national economic assets was thus tied to mainland economic interests and treated with great sensitivity. These reflected anxieties dating back to anticolonial and nationalist movements in the decades preceding 1947—that is, the control of agrarian wealth from land revenue to agrarian production. Better-known instances of economic nationalism revolve around cash crops, such as jute, and subsistence crops, such as rice.[40] Historian Tariq Omar Ali writes about the foundational place of jute in the fulfillment of Pakistan as economic idea. He details the draconian control that the Pakistani state attempted to exercise over jute, bringing suffering and harassment to the Muslim peasantry, even as the state had been supportive of the future of Pakistan as a "peasant utopia" at Partition. As India covertly sought to remove all barriers to the smuggling of jute—or so the Pakistani government alleged—in 1954, Pakistan issued orders banning the movement of jute within five miles of the eastern border. The East Pakistan Rifles had been reconstituted just prior in 1951, and stationed in these borderlands to seize jute that was found to be moving suspiciously toward India.[41] When this level of policing was found to be inadequate, the Pakistani government called the army to the borderlands in February 1952, with a shoot-to-kill policy, to deter jute smuggling.[42] For the government of East Pakistan, jute smuggling was no simple border crossing; it was economic warfare.[43] For a brief period, Pakistan escalated efforts to militarize its eastern border with India by bringing its army, navy, and air force together in the short-lived Operation Closed Door, an unsuccessful attempt to stop the flow of goods.[44] The attempt to establish sovereign *economic* control over resources not only unfolded through militarized bordering but also relied on the delineation of areas of transit that were to be governed in special ways, whose residents' agrarian rights and concerns were to be made subservient to a greater economic sovereignty that was territorialized unevenly.

Scholars of borders and borderlands frequently account for the deleterious effects of national and regional trade policies on agrarian economies and argue that smuggling in borderlands should be viewed in the light of this larger picture of economic disenfranchisement.[45] However, the kind of economic policing through bordering that we see in the Bengal borderlands—to deliberately rupture and ruin the connections that preceded the production of the space as a borderland—is a distinctive form of spatial violence. This spatial violence is not a thing of the past, justified as necessary for postcolonial state formation. Entrepreneurs and traders in Bangladeshi border villages critiqued the existing governmental prohibitions on industrial activity and structures in a twelve-kilometer radius from the border. Drawing attention to the continued state view of the borderlands as a space of war-preparedness, despite the avowedly friendly border between India and Bangladesh, residents' geopolitical critiques point to the production of economic devaluation.

Pointing to the two-room red-brick building that served as the ticket counter and station office, visible through a window in his house in Madhupur village, Kamal Miah took me back to the 1950s when this was a bustling port. Bent over with back pain in his old age, Kamal-chacha recalled the years of his childhood and boyhood spent polishing and repairing shoes at his father's stall at the Madhupur rail station. In what is now Bangladesh, this station was the last stop in the Cooch Behar state. Hindu Marwari and Bengali Muslim traders stocked bales of jute and bundles of tobacco in warehouses that lined the two sides of Rangpur Road. Several laborers worked at the station daily, loading jute and tobacco on and off the trains depending on where they were headed—northward to Assam or Cooch Behar, or southward to Kolkata. Frequent visits by government officials and security forces of the newly formed East Pakistan meant that tea stalls around the customs offices were always busy. Kamal Miah recalled the times that young boys like him would get a treat from local traders after inspecting officials departed, listing the variety of non-Bengali savory snacks that were prepared to please the imposing Urdu-speaking visitors.

Other elderly residents in what is now considered to be among Bangladesh's most remote and socio-economically backward districts, Lalmonirhat, recalled the splendor of *naami-daami lokera* (high-class passengers) traveling Rangpur Road across the postcolonial land port and immigration checkpoint established there by India and Pakistan. One man remembered a "Hindu *babu*" who traveled frequently between Cooch Behar and Rangpur, always clad in a spotless, starched white *dhoti* with a group of attendants. He recalled that that if that *babu* was in a generous mood, he sometimes gave boys like him "*ek anna.*"[46] "You know, I never spent that money. For many years I kept these coins in a special tin box. That box, too, I found on this Rangpur Road," he admitted with a smile. "*Ei border-er aitijho chhilo*" (this border was of socio-cultural importance) was a frequent refrain in many of these recollections. The mood the memory invokes in the storyteller and the historical claim it makes come into sharp relief with Rangpur Road's marked national and transnational marginality. Pausing on these rare items of luxury that came from Rangpur Road and its "*naami-daami*" passengers that gave residents in these new borderlands a continued feeling of importance by association, then, illuminate the processes by which remoteness and marginality are made and can potentially be unmade or changed.

Shankar Das, a resident of Kathalbari village, across the border from Madhupur village, used to work as a porter at the customs office, the first stop in India before Dinhata town. He described the primarily Hindu passengers who would come across from Bangladesh by boat, given the dysfunctional condition of the rail bridge since the 1965 war (fig. 1). "Some of them were so happy to come to India that they would start crying. I carried their bags for free. How can I take money when they have come with such difficulty? Rangpur Road was so broken and you had to walk a long way before you could get the bus to Dinhata or Cooch Behar. Those days you could see the misery and hardship on Rangpur Road."

Piecing together the memories of elderly residents of Madhupur and Kathalbari villages of the infrastructures that connected on this route, a shift emerges from the mid-1970s to mid-1990s, when the immigration checkpoint at Kathalbari (India) / Madhupur (Bangladesh) was finally closed. The transition in these narratives marks two decades of border enforcement and majoritarian state formation processes underway in tandem in India, Pakistan, and subsequently Bangladesh. Unlike the iconic Jessore Road, the route that millions of Bengalis took to India to flee the Pakistani army in the 1971 war, and that has been memorialized in popular culture writings, Rangpur Road swings between intense remembering locally and obscurity in national and subcontinental frames. The very immigration and customs infrastructures that were established to regulate—and rupture—extant mobilities and flows in the region after 1947 lie ruined today.

The regional talks and agreements between India, Bangladesh, Nepal, and Bhutan in 2015, which allow speedy passage of motor vehicles and transit of goods, have been presented and hailed as new achievements under the leadership of the Narendra Modi government in India to bring "unprecedented" connectivity to the region. In this narrative of transnational connectivity and borderless flows, borderlands figure as rough and remote logistical terrain to be overcome by the entrepreneurial and friendly states. Unlike China's grand Silk Road project, this is not a narrative of the deliberate revival of old colonial and precolonial routes and infrastructures. For the Indian and Bangladeshi postcolonial states, these neoliberal projects of connectivity are profoundly ahistorical, erasing pasts that sit oddly within nationalist frames while producing empty spaces for capitalist extraction. Such erasures rely on the construction of remoteness and the corollary need for modernity. Madeline Reeves, writing about the experiences of the people in the Ferghana Valley with new borders across formerly Soviet space, puts it poignantly: "becoming disconnected is quite different from the fact or feeling of never having been connected."[47] Remembering these border villages and towns as railway junctions and bustling places of colonial commerce—subsidizing the rail infrastructures that carried tea, coal, tobacco, and a host of other commodities across this region and beyond—is a cartographic imaginary layered across today's borderlands that some residents actively maintain and inhabit. To debate and archive this spatial history counters the erasures wrought upon the landscape of northern Bengal.

A LINK ROAD

No other infrastructure signals state-led development efforts to modernize more than roads, with all their attendant economic and cultural valences of progress and prosperity. At the Okhrabari bazaar (India), a narrow road takes us off Rangpur Road, and south toward the border. According to the blue signboard posted where the road forks, it is built under the Border Area Development Programme (BADP). The fine print details the cost, the year it was completed, and that it connects Okhrabari bazaar to an Indian Border Security Force (BSF) outpost, in local parlance a *camp*. Where there is remoteness there will be the need for a road.

Colonial surveys in the late nineteenth century noted the presence of precolonial market hubs and paths that connected between and across the princely state of Cooch Behar and the neighboring districts; this included the Mughal infrastructure of defense and taxation, reflected in place names duly noted.[48] By 1911, such references establishing a link to commercial and governmental life were gone. Instead, the same precolonial roads and Mughal place names were archived under "religion" and "culture," and the "economy" and "people" sections of the Rangpur district survey reported that this was a remote region and its predominantly Muslim and lower-caste Rajbangsi inhabitants were lacking civilization for the want of good road and rail connections.[49]

Fast forward to the late twentieth century, and in these rural and riverine areas of northern Bengal, the focus of the developmentalist state has been on visible infrastructures, such as roads and small bridges. Reproducing the colonial material and discursive understanding of north Bengal as remote and backward and its racialized inhabitants as inherently less intelligent, district administrators from centralized bureaucracies in India and Bangladesh recite verbatim from the colonial reports, confirming the lack of "basic" civilizational needs in the area. In the borderlands, nationalist infrastructure building is invariably a transnational project since it requires the approval of (or risks conflict with) the neighboring state.[50] Besides, performing sovereign power to its own and neighboring citizenry is always part of the calculus of roadmaking for states. A history of national security and the ideology of preventive development work in uneasy tandem beneath these specifically *borderland* roads.

It was the Sino-India War of 1962 that jolted the Indian government out of its blinkered focus on border-crossers in the aftermath of Partition. It was forced to confront the strategic importance of its borderland residents. The genesis of the contemporary BADP was in the immediate months after the Sino-India War. Welfare programs targeting residents of areas bordering China and Tibet were rolled out right after the war and only much later expanded to districts along the border with Pakistan.[51] They were intended to compensate for the exclusion that borderland residents evidently expressed through their lack of loyalty to the nation in its hour of need; a deeply concerned Prime Minister Nehru urgently ordered the nurturing of "sentinel citizens."[52] It is exemplary of the relationship between welfare and warfare, which Mona Bhan describes in her ethnographic study of counterinsurgency by humanitarian means in Ladakh. "Development," she writes, is "a ubiquitous term, deployed unsparingly by officials from the government as well as the military to assert their moral and humanitarian role in Kargil's postwar polity and to bring strategic border spaces and communities under the state's territorial and sovereign control."[53] Regional geopolitics exposed the fragility of focusing too narrowly on the border as a line; the spatial figuration of the borderland as a peopled place, where loyalties could not be taken for granted, was the lesson of the 1960s. Welfare programs were identified as the quick fix to nurture patriotism, a legacy that continues to date across the Bengal borderlands, hung out in the BSF's banners and dressed up in occasional medical camps.

The BADP was initiated in the Seventh Plan (1985–90) and initially existed only for the "hostile" India-Pakistan border, deemed no longer necessary for the border areas with China/Tibet. Under the BADP, provisions were to be made for "the distribution and installation of community TV sets so as to counteract the hostile propaganda from across the border and suitably enthuse the local population."[54] Studying the decades of directives, it is clear that the operative terms "border area" and "development programme" shifted according to the perceived political and strategic national security needs of the time. As welfare programs for border areas shifted geographical orientation from China to Pakistan, the emphasis too shifted unapologetically to the development of infrastructure that would facilitate the long-term presence of the newly established Border Security Forces. Main roads and link roads dominated the spatial engagement with borderlands.

The eastern border, reborn as the friendly India-Bangladesh border after the Liberation War of 1971, in which the Indian army and BSF played an important supporting role, entered discussions of national security in India only with the eruption of the Assam Agitation (1979–85) and the political desperation of the Congress government at the center to conduct elections and retain power in the eastern state.[55] The shelter of United Liberation Front of Asom (ULFA) leaders across the border in Bangladeshi territory, out of reach of Indian armed forces, underlined the

inevitability and dangers of transnational connections in the eastern borderlands and the urgent need for states to keep up good relations both
with their borderland citizens and neighboring states. Accordingly, the
Eight Plan (1990–95) of India's centralized five-year plans extended the
BADP to cover the states bordering Bangladesh and revised its guiding
directives to focus not only on the development of remote border areas,
and their effective administration, but also to "involve people in strengthening their resistance."[56]

As documents that present the vision of the state, the archive of the
BADP showcases this arc from the crisis of war to war-preparedness in the
borderlands. The stated objective of the BADP is to meet "the special
developmental needs" of people living in "remote and inaccessible areas
situated near the international border" and to saturate the border areas
with essential infrastructure through the convergence of BADP with other
central/state government schemes.[57] In successive revisions to the guiding
principles of the BADP, spatial delineation does definitional and discursive work: borderlands are underdeveloped and therefore pose national
security concerns because they are remote and inaccessible. The "satura-
tion" of these spaces with infrastructural governance will not alter their
spatial location but can fundamentally transform their spatial qualities. In
the imagined future, strategic importance will be a positive marker of borderlands, not one of anxiety for the nation-state. West Bengal, though
lately inducted to the BADP, soon became its largest beneficiary, receiving
INR 31.36 crores in comparison to the older "problem" states of Punjab,
which received INR 26.52 crores, and Jammu and Kashmir, which
received INR 21.38 crores in 1998–99.[58] (A crore is ten million INR.)

These figures attest to how developmental visions respatialize these
discrete borderland spaces of national security in relations of equivalence.
West Bengal has the longest stretch of India's borders and the most
numerous border-lying districts, each of which is promised a certain
development budget. Thus, even as a "friendly border," when it lacks the
strategic urgency and counterinsurgency needs of other theaters of
national security, a developmental border governmentality can operationalize such spatial claims to resources, as interested bureaucrats routinely
do. Money secured must be money spent on developmental national security, thereby producing its object of intervention.

Table 1   Cooch Behar district's annual breakdown of BADP projects

Year	Roads/ Infrastructure	Education	Social Work	Total Budget	Total Projects
2012–13	47	5	2	Rs. 13,47,00,000	54
2013–14	41	1	4	Rs. 13,72,57,000	46
2014–15	5	0	1	Rs. 1,91,48,000	6

SOURCE: Author, based on information from the Department of Border Management, MHA, India, 2015.

Table 1 merits a moment's pause. I constructed this table from data I received from the central government. At first glance, this investment in the capital-intensive infrastructural development of border areas seems entirely laudatory, but a closer understanding of the materiality of the projects and their spatial politics tells a different story. For example, the only project in 2014–15 under the Social Work category was the construction of two toilet blocks for the newly deployed female constables at a Border Outpost (BOP) under Sitai block. The list of roads is telling. An overwhelming number of them—like this link road and numerous others we will encounter in the chapters of the book—connect existing roads, markets, or BOPs to other BOPs. The frequent construction of small bridges was for vehicular traffic—necessary for the passage of BSF vehicles, not for wider public use. As Bhan has shown in her analysis of the Indian army's developmental initiatives in Ladakh, in these "friendly" eastern borderlands, human security is mobilized by the security state and the perspective, needs, and interest of the BSF "to legitimize their expanded role in public life."[59]

This tension between welfare and security is neither unique to borderland contexts in South Asia nor is it a recent development in the twenty-first century.[60] Roads, the quintessential public good, were deployed as a tool to spatially and materially transform these "remote border areas" to be suitable for navigation by and for the Border Security Force and its particular vehicular demands, soon after the initial decolonizing decades. A link road fulfills ostensibly local developmental needs and meets national security objectives of reforming the borderlands into a physically more hospitable space for enduring military presence. Does this mean that these are of no use or benefit to borderland residents? Certainly, they are, but they *re*direct existing routes and traffic in ways that have their own socio-spatial lives. As I visited the famed *haats* of the Cooch Behar princely state across the borderlands, residents and shopkeepers spoke of vibrant markets rendered remote because of such rerouting of roads. Many such *haats* had "died," said residents, as they had come under the scrutiny of the BSF and Border Guard Bangladesh (BGB) as especially sensitive sites of national security.

Infrastructures such as link roads also introduce new temporalities. On the one hand, they make travel speedy by facilitating a transformation from movement by foot to vehicular journeys; on the other hand, they function as the visible emblem of the possibility of speedy travel denied to borderland residents. Nightly curfews and other prohibitions slow down and instill immobility along what is emphatically marked as infrastructure of national security, not for ordinary civilian use. Journeys between old sites are made novel and unfamiliar because of new link roads, requiring often circuitous routes. These developmental projects saturate the spaces through which they run with borderness. These border security infrastructures—the paved road next to the border fence, the new watchtower along the way—themselves became sights to behold, to be traversed, to be guarded. In addition to transit and remoteness, the landscape of northern Bengal comes to be decisively associated with national security.

KHOKON'S SHOP

According to the zoning of the Indian and Bangladeshi governments, during the period of my research the borderlands extended fifteen and twelve kilometers, respectively, from the border.[61] This question of jurisdiction has a contested history in relation to the enforcement of laws, or as some would argue, exceptional rules of law, such as the nightly prevalence of the curfews through Section 144 of the Indian Penal Code (as a preemptive national security measure) or the prohibition on building factories and other economic assets in the Bangladeshi borderlands. *Where* the borderlands are depends on *what* the borderlands mean. While legal jurisdiction and how they structure conditions of social and economic life are vital lines of inquiry, a phenomenological approach allows for a subtler way to grasp the politics of value and space-making. Over the years, I found that people would describe sites such as markets or shops, checkposts, or administrative offices as imbued with concentrated qualities of *borderness* quite apart from their physical proximity to the international border. The process by which people join the *what* of the border to its *where* is deeply illuminating. Such ways of knowing and feeling the borderness of a place do not follow the statist zoning as a flat and even delineation.

The spatial layers and qualities of borderness—*simanta elakar parichay* (the identity of a place as a borderland), as one faithful customer eloquently put it—manifest materially through gendered affects. This was made clear to me by the joys of shopping in Khokon's shop of cosmetics in Lalmonirhat. In the central lane of the town's main bazaar Khokon's shop of glitter and delight stood between a bookstore and a utensils shop. I must confess I had originally been interested in the utensils shop, which I had been told by a friend belonged to an itinerant caste-Hindu family that until the 1950s had lived between Assam and Rangpur. But that shopkeeper was dour and refused to talk, so I went over next door to buy shampoo and soaps for the NGO residential home where I lived in Lalmonirhat. I peered across necklaces, handbags, and shampoo sachets that hung like a glittering curtain over the shop's counter. "*'Indian' na 'Bangladeshi'*?" came the young shopkeeper's unblinking question when I asked for Sunsilk shampoo. "What's the difference?," I asked, puzzled. Khokon the shopkeeper—and two young women in crisp dupattas selecting nail polish and face creams—turned to look at me, exchanged knowing looks between themselves, and broke out in a laugh. The shopkeeper, who looked young but spoke slowly with an air of maturity, explained that most of these products—gesturing to the neat rows making up the walls of his shop—are of two types: made in India or made in Bangladesh. With these words he placed two different bottles of Sunsilk shampoo on the counter for me to examine. I persisted in questioning what the difference was if they were the same brand manufactured by the same global company, Unilever. I picked up the two bottles, examining them closely: one had Rs 60 marked as the maximum retail price, while the other was marked as 60 Tk, signaling the Indian and Bangladeshi currencies, respectively.

"Ohhh, there's a massive difference, where it's made," one of the young women chimed in. "Never trust the Bangladeshi ones, they are always *bhejal* [fake or adulterated]. At least the Indian ones are real Sunsilk."

Pointing to the Indian bottle and gently persuading me to choose that one over the other, the shopkeeper said it would cost 130 Tk.

"More than double?!" I exclaimed.

"Yes," said Khokon, firmly, as he continued to explain the economics to me in a matter-of-fact way. "It comes directly from India by a *chorai poth* [forbidden route] across the border, changing hands many times, each person making a bit of money, driving the end cost up."

When I asked (incredulously) if there are takers for these products, despite the big price difference and well-known markup, he nodded affirmatively with a big smile. One of the women cut in, rather impatient about my naivete. "Of course. This is one of the advantages at least of living in the borderlands—you know you are getting the real stuff from India. And at least here it is as cheap as it can be." She went on to say that there were many buyers, not just in Lalmonirhat. Her sisters and aunts who lived in Rangpur would ask her to stock up on these items for them, too. The very fact that they know these are Indian bottles bought from Indian suppliers and transported across the border is, in fact, what assures customers that it is a genuine Indian product.

During longer periods of stay in Lalmonirhat, I became better acquainted with Khokon, his shop, and the cosmetics trade, even working alongside him as an attendant at the shop during the busy weeks of Ramzan. He let me in on one of the secrets of the trade that he had learned in his first year in this relatively new and dynamic business. There were some products from brands like Dove, Fair and Lovely, and Clean and Clear that Bangladesh does not manufacture, but officially imports from India. These can be identified by a sticker of import. Khokon revealed that he would peel those "Imported by Bangladesh" stickers off to fully expose the Indian cost and manufacturing details. This helped to drive up the price and convince discerning borderland buyers that this was indeed a smuggled jar or tube from markets in nearby Indian towns like Dinhata. They had come, reliably, on or off Rangpur Road.

We laughed together at the irony on so many levels. Shops in Bangladeshi border villages did not stock these sorts of Indian consumer goods—chocolates, creams, and so on—because they are frequently raided by law enforcement agents expecting them to have smuggled Indian goods that undermine Bangladeshi products of the same kind. At the same time, there was a significant demand for such products, particularly among families of salaried members of the government administration. While a jurisdictional enforcement of the borderland, zoned and policed by the state, makes a shop like Khokon's into a hub of border-crossing flows because it lies outside that, for residents these sites exuded borderness, and frequenting such shops was the definitive experience of being in a borderland. The encounters at Khokon's shop reflect the tremendous unevenness of borderlands: where they are and how they are felt. Bordering in the form of border security practices rupture and ruins existing flows and connection, as with the agrarian trade and commerce of colonial and precolonial pasts. But bordering also drives enterprise underground, a move in which Khokon participates and from which he benefits. For some, the lived realities of the borderlands are measured in terms of these transnational flows—bits of there here, bits of here there. People feel the borderness across the borderlands variably, and they always feel it in and through their gendered bodies.

This sentiment of finding joy in transnational consumption was not limited to consumer goods transported clandestinely for customers at a distance from the border crossing. It was echoed more broadly across border villages. Everyday transnational connections through material consumption practices characterize the thousand tiny cuts that mobility makes across national segmentation. Framed neither in terms of legality nor resistance (to the state), these ubiquitous tiny cuts across the border are predicated on clear conceptions of national distinctions. They reflect how borderland residents understand and inhabit transnational connection through these national distinctions, not despite them. Farmers buying food for their households in the borderland bazars of Madhupur and Kathalbari declare matter of factly: "We get our fish in Bangladesh and our spinach from India."

If Khokon and his customers appear to be a far cry from the "smugglers" who populate the political imaginary of this border, it is because these labels mislead more than they illuminate. Tidy conceptual, and normatively moral, categories of "smuggler" and "trader" may come loose in transactions that are embedded in the ordinariness of social life and the desires of transnational connection made possible by the borderlands. Not only is it impossible to view entrepreneurs, "smugglers," and borderlanders as distinct categories, here we see how women's desire for beauty products creates space for a gendered participation in networks of clandestine mobility. For Khokon and the young men who transported his supplies, the risks of being caught and violently punished by the police and the BGB were real, and it animated their pragmatic calculations of what was likely to be safest. But the pleasures of transnational living and connection were real, too, and with each strand of connection the contours of the borderlands were imagined, perceived, and narrated a little bit differently. These different strands entwine in a heap on the shop counter and matter for how the spatial qualities of the borderlands are described: in moral, social, and material terms, the borderlands can be remote, underdeveloped, connected, thrilling, criminal, or all at of these at once.

.   .   .   .

What do the ruins of the customs office, emblematic of an enthusiastic postcolonial state, have to do with Khokon's shop, a corner of the bazaar that thrives on skirting that state security infrastructure? To understand the many ways in which mobility and security intersect in everyday lives across the Indian and Bangladeshi borderlands, we must see the borderlands themselves as particular kinds of spaces produced through ongoing processes of postcolonial state-making and inhabited with multiple imaginaries and memories. Stories about the unruly and underdeveloped borderlands serve a distinct national and neoliberal capitalist imaginary, most often one in which residents of these spaces are absent. Stories from the borderlands that foreground alternative historical accounts of the region most emphatically expose this historical fabrication of the borderlands. These stories compel us to think critically not just about *how* the borderlands came to be but also about *where* they are most acutely felt—inscribed on particular bodies, concentrated in some sites more than others. The construction of "remoteness" of the borderlands of India and

Bangladesh has proceeded by severing existing connections, including material infrastructures, driving new flows and connections outside the monopoly of the state underground, and building roads and other infra-structures selectively to alleviate—and therefore prove—the remoteness of these spaces.

For various groups of borderland residents, the histories and futures of Rangpur Road mean very different things. For instance, for Mr. Rahman and the relatively influential residents of the border villages, the road tes-tified to the importance of the place, an importance in which they had historically enjoyed an advantageous position. But for those who lived in homes built on the old rail tracks, whether on the Indian or the Bangladeshi side, the possibility of return meant an eviction notice in the face of which the accompanying talk about reinvigorated commerce and new jobs seemed quite chimerical. "Rangpur Road" comes to mean the actual road, and also the other modes of connection that accompanied it, as well as a mood of connectedness.

2 Walking through the Borderlandscape

Kathalbari theke Balatari hata lagey bala
Tar upore achhe BSFer jala.

From Kathalbari to Balatari you must walk on sand.
On top of that is the BSF's heavy hand.

WAITING

Aminul Hossain chanted this rhyme in his most nasal voice. All of us burst out laughing, a change from the complaints that were getting louder and louder as we waited in the afternoon sun. On this day, when Aminul made up this little song, I was waiting with him, his wife, Najma, and about a dozen other men, women, and children on a sandy riverbank for a boat to take us across from Balatari to Kathalbari[1]—that is, from an Indian border village adjacent to Bangladesh to further inland in India. Standing or squatting, we were all looking across the river, our squinting eyes on the passenger boat on the other bank, taking too long to leave the Nazirghat jetty—and a Border Security Force (BSF) checkpoint. The comic relief passed as quickly as a breeze on a muggy day, and my fellow passengers resumed their various complaints, hot, cross, and it seemed to me, rather anxious. Not everyone was well known to each other, but the collective wait had brought us together as a group as, one by one, we shared our concerns about the delay. It was a weekday and several people wanted to combine business at the village council office in Kathalbari with visits to the bazaar. This was Aminul's and Najma's plan, too. I had just spent the

6. Walking with Malati Barman on a village path in Kathalbari, India, now lined with concertina wire where the goats used to graze.

night at their house, and I was to accompany them on their day's itinerary. Whatever each person's plan, everyone who lived in Balatari had to be back to cross the checkpoint and the river before the jetty closed at sunset. The BSF's strict patrols on this and all other village paths going toward the border structured people's schedules. "*Ei boshe thaka* [this sitting and waiting], this is our daily condition," Aminul said to me. He was both resigned to and sarcastic about being incorporated thus in matters of national import. Waiting was no empty time: it crackled with commentary. An annotation to borderland mobilities and my initiation, too.

I joined Najma on a log and took in the scene. There were a few fishermen out in a boat on the river, throwing their nets out in strong, deft moves, cutting through the sparkling surface of the water. On the raised embankment on the Kathalbari side, I could see the outlines of a man leading his calf to graze and two women arranging jute sticks to dry in the sun. The Balatari side, where we were waiting, had no embankment, and recent floods had left several meters of sand deposits exposed (the *bala* in Aminul's rhyme). India's border fence, which cuts the visual field in these flat plains of Bengal no matter which side you were on, is notably absent here. Riverine, and thus unfenced, this part of the borderlands is deemed especially "sensitive" to—or promising for, depending on your point of view—border crossings.[2] Residents of the Indian border villages of Balatari and Mansai spoke of being marooned between the river and Bangladesh, as they had to cross the river and a checkpoint each time they made their way north to the rest of the Kathalbari *panchayat* (district) country. I was always tickled by the call of "*India jachhi!* [Going to India!]," sometimes cheery, sometimes wary, with which residents of Indian border villages hailed each other on these paths as they signaled the direction in which they were going. It was as if other directions and destinations—*opar*, Bangladesh—were perfectly normal and possible too. Orientations, feminist theorist Sara Ahmed writes, "are about the direction we take that puts some things and not others in our reach."[3] Bodies, their movements, their gestures, their relations to/in space, are shaped by histories to be oriented one way or another, so that what they "tend to do" express such sedimentation rather than being "originary."[4]

As we waited in the scorching heat, an older man from our group went over to the makeshift bamboo hut under which the BSF soldiers stood to inquire about the delay. They had already checked our identity documents and bags, and like us were looking toward the other bank; I could hear the whirring and muffled voices over their radio sets. Although we couldn't hear their conversation, Najma and I noted that this man and the BSF soldiers seemed to be having a pretty friendly conversation. He soon came back with a triumphant smile and some news. "*Dhorse, Mishti-boudir jeera dhorse. Informer chhilo. Ekhon deri hobe, saheb ashchhe.* [Mishti-boudi's cumin has been seized. There was an informer who gave them the lead. Now it will take some time, the officer is coming]."[5]

This news, that the BSF had found ten kilos of cumin being transported on the boat by a woman well known to conduct cross-border trade, provoked all kinds of reactions, to my surprise. It appeared to be "an identity-fixing event."[6] The police found a smuggler and the audience found an informer, too.[7] The BSF officer-in-charge—referred to as *saheb* in a colonial remainder—was on his way to this location, which was now no longer a village thoroughfare but a site of national security. The officer's arrival in a jeep with a cloud of dust behind, having traveled a short distance of a couple of kilometers that residents typically walk or cycle, would be a spectacle. As this man quite rightly concluded, his speedy arrival meant interminable delays for residents.

The arrival of national security on the scene was a slowing down of time over an increasing expanse of space. A small wait was about to turn into a big long wait, and no matter how harmless or respectable you were, you just had to sit down and give in to waiting.

The checkpoint at Nazirghat where the boat was stuck on this day is one of hundreds that have proliferated along this border in the last decade in the eastern state of West Bengal. The English term *checkpoint* is used by the BSF to refer to a site along the border at which a semi-permanent point has been established to routinely check, identify, and search all those (and their goods) moving along that route. There are no Bengali equivalents of *checkpoint* or *patrol;* even in Bengali media, the English words are written in the Bengali script in both countries.[8] Cooch Behar district in the north of the state shares 549 kilometers of the border with northern Bangladesh along its Nilphamari, Lalmonirhat, and Kurigram districts. Despite India's persistent efforts to seal this border with the construction and defense of a fence, only about 300 kilometers of this district's border is fenced. The remaining parts are unfenced due to land acquisition problems, riverine landscape, or both. At checkpoints such as at Nazirghat (unfenced border) or at gates along the border fence, BSF soldiers check identity documents and search bags, frisk, and interrogate individuals. This makes such sites a nerve center of negotiation between the security forces and various groups of borderland residents. As permissions are withheld, transacted, and contested, under the scrutiny of the BSF as well as other borderland residents, all passages are subject to surveillance and evaluation.

Mishti-boudi's smuggling of cumin—hardly a threat to national security by any measure—did not meet with a unified defense. Some people even condemned her harshly. A Hindu woman, whose fresh streak of vermilion was melting down her forehead, spoke in my general direction. She seemed certain of my sympathies. "Look at these *du-nombori bou* [illicit

7. A BSF checkpoint at Nazirghat, the passenger ferry between two Indian border villages along a riverine and unfenced part of the border, closely surveils and filters all mobility. Boats on the river are required to fly their national flag.

women], can they have any value [*daam*]? Even quarreling with the BSF! They've sent their *man-shonman* [dignity and honor] down the river. But all of us women suffer because of them—the BSF may behave badly with any of us. We have to all suffer for them."

If our protracted wait while the BSF policed mobilities generated some measure of sociality among borderland residents, it also exposed multiple fractures among them, including tense speculations about who the informer was. Alerted to Mishti-boudi's tactics, the BSF made *all* women renewed targets of suspicion, upsetting carefully established social differences of class, religion, and respectability, where women in general and respectable Hindu women in particular were deemed to be beyond suspicion. Security instills fear of becoming the target of surveillance while inviting residents to blame their compatriots for their experiences of violence, especially through gendered norms of respectable masculinity and femininity. Indeed, Najma had warned me against hanging out at checkpoints such as this to talk to the BSF; she urged me to display friendliness instead of docility, as a young woman who presumably wished to be considered respectable. Interactions between borderland women and male soldiers affirm "the masculinist logic of protection" for the security state, whereby femininities are either transgressive or docile.[9]

As in this instance, the rationale of "national security" is neither rejected on political principle nor simply submitted to as opaque and incomprehensible. Waiting, while walking, opened up the time-spaces of national security: where, who, and what was a threat to national security in borderland mobilities was worked out through a variety of negotiations and calibrated through an existing rubric of heteropatriarchal social relations. Whether or not someone's mobility would be considered a threat depended on how it was related to this thing called *secoority*, regional Bengali accenting the English word. From scenes of everyday waiting in courtrooms to petitioning for governmental care, scholars of the state and bureaucracy have written evocatively about waiting as a mode of power that the law and governmental institutions exert, especially on women and other vulnerable bodies.[10] I am interested in how waiting is experienced as a mode of power, but more specifically, we see here how it produces "fragmented solidarities" through differences of gender, class, and religion when the organizing principle is national security.[11]

Border security practices exploit differences and fractures among border-land communities even while homogenizing "borderland people" as a population.

Yet, despite this intense social commentary and incessant reflection on how not to be perceived as a threat (or to know it when you see it) to security, nobody was ever sure. This uncertainty is vital, for as we will see through the rest of the chapter, it makes space for both egregious over-reach of authority by the security forces as well as claims, doubt, and humorous cheek by borderland residents. The work of security brought all these registers of sociality together, making residents and security forces (and me) bristle with discomfort at times, unmistakable thrill at others.

WALKING AS METHOD: TOWARD A COLLABORATIVE ETHNOGRAPHY OF NATIONAL SECURITY

In the Bangladeshi national media, the fence being built by India since the late 1980s has been the focal point of growing critique. In 2019, a group of students and activists staged a month-long protest in central Dhaka against India's killings at the officially "friendly" border, demanding their state to *man up* to the more powerful fence-building neighbor.[12] These critiques reinforce a globally circulating model and understanding of mili-tarized border security regimes, while engaging South Asian statist narra-tives for *more* border security as expressed in bipartisan political policies and bilateral talks.[13] When I began my research in the Bengal border-lands, I expected to find explicit resistance to the widespread infringe-ment of rights and liberties of citizens taking place in the name of national security.[14] But my "romance of resistance" yielded little understanding of the messy ways residents live with the dispersed violence of border secu-rity and in surprising ways reproduce and further entrench its logics in their everyday lives.[15]

This chapter explores how something called "national security"—*desh ka suraksha* in the BSF's Hindi phrasing and *secoority* in Bengali—becomes concrete and spreads, spatially and temporally, in the border-lands. A unified construct of the border—and the associated criminalization of borderland residents and their lives as suspicious—has justified India's expansion of a militarized security architecture along its friendly border with Bangladesh as a bipartisan project since the 1980s.[16] While the BSF are ostensibly working to protect *in cooperation with* borderland residents, they are simultaneously policing and surveilling this Bengali Muslim and Hindu Rajbangsi population as potential suspects. The preemptive and preventive practices to control the illegal movement of people and goods across the border are directed to routes, flows, and movements within the Indian borderland. The processual and incomplete nature of this security architecture's control is as visible on routes as is its violent presence and intrusions.

In northern Bengal, residents and security forces live and work with a riparian and agrarian borderland that is shifting. For instance, the physical nature of the route we were traversing that morning varied tremendously depending on whether it was winter or the monsoons. For most of these border villages—whether in India or Bangladesh—the closest bazaar, health center, or school was often in the neighboring country, the wrong side of the border in statist terms. Forced to travel in one direction and not the other to access the mundane stuff of life—groceries, education, materials for housing, and bureaucratic services—people were highly conscious of and joked about the ironies of statist belonging that took them on circuitous and troublesome routes. On the Indian side, people joked that you could tell a Balatari person from their dusty clothes. Power and inequality are spatialized and felt through the tired and tense body, dusty clothes, and aching feet. Walking with borderland residents, as ethnographic method, revealed that *all* residents (Hindu, and especially Muslim) and their ordinary, everyday mobilities are presumed to be suspicious and dangerous by the BSF, who seek to intercept border-crossing and smuggling. Yet, as I learned, the *BSFer jala* that Aminul sang of did not materialize in the same way for different people: gender, class, and religious identity intersect to produce the vulnerabilities that people worry about, experience, and seek to overcome as they walk these surveilled paths and try to keep moving.

The aims of this chapter are twofold. One is to track ethnographically the various ways in which "national security" comes to be inscribed across the borderlands, felt and located in people's bodies, and assigned proper times and places. The other aim is to show how such emplacement of self and other constantly works to differentially value mobility and time and produces the militarized borderlands as a gendered geography. As we will see, this work of surveilling and policing is not the business of the state or the BSF alone; rather, in seeking to legitimize itself, the BSF acts through social relations and institutions.[17] I use the term *security socialities* as an ethnographic frame to address the heteronormative social relations—among residents and between residents and security forces—as a key site where the effects of security are felt and that constitute the very scaffolding through which "national security" becomes intelligible, oppressive, normalized, and also unstable. These relations make space for security in the intimate reaches of borderland lives, well beyond the times and spaces of visible civil-military encounter. In particular, I hope to highlight how the phenomenal links to the political—such as *this sitting and waiting* and singing and discussing—in ways that define the particular political economy of militarization that emerges at friendly borders such as this.[18] I suggest that security logics attach to existing social hierarchies, relations, and forms of policing, and expand through them, rather than operating as a forcible imposition from above.

Feminist analyses of conflict and war have emphasized the need to push beyond a victimhood-agency binary that is intrinsically colonial, evermore important when discussing the experience of security regimes in the Global South.[19] Civil-military encounters are bookended by *socially familiar* rather than hostile relations.[20] In the sections that follow, we will see how neighbors, friends, and kin evaluate mobility—their own and that of others—through the gaze and logic of national security. Civil-military interactions occur as ordinary social conversations such as the banter, mutual requests, disagreements, and empathies that arise out of sharing space routinely, as much as through the structures of law and institutions.

The "walking through" of the chapter's title refers to a diagnostic method for security practices and their history: gendered and classed bodies as archives of uneven mobility. In 1999, the Kargil War between India and Pakistan had resulted in a complete overhaul of national security policy in India. The BSF emerged with substantially increased manpower, a bigger budget, and new agenda for "effective" national security at *all* borders under the motto One Border, One Force. Borderland residents turn to their immediate material environments as a record of the spatial transformations by which their villages, fields, and paths in between have been turned into a site of *national* security to which all *local* concerns must be subservient. For one woman, this shift came through longer and slower routes to go to her mother's home, still only two villages away. Aminul-da, for instance, invoked an embodied archive—"*Ei book pocketey card niye jawa asha shuru* [walking around with the card (the voter identity card) in the shirt pocket]" (quintessentially male, with the reference to the shirt)—to historicize the surveillance of mobility on borderland paths. Histories of documentary identification, recorded in terms of political personalities, such as the "Seshan effect,"[21] or governmental regimes, is viscerally recalled in the borderlands.

Walking as method is particularly helpful to grasp how "the military normal" expands and entrenches among borderland residents who suffer it, critique it, and participate in it.[22] Walking could not be the unreported part of ethnographic work, a functional task, for walking was *the* everyday target of security. It is in walking through the borderlands that the particular "texture" of militarization along the officially friendly Bengal border is felt.[23] "Walking" demands to shift our conceptual gaze away from incidents of spectacular violence. It was only when I began to document daily (often mundane) walks that comprise the variety of borderland mobilities that I could see the normalization of border security practices in heteropatriarchal terms of gendered behavior, the social tensions that people come to live with as suspicious subjects, and the profound devaluations of time and labor, simply because they are located in borderlands, a site where national security must be privileged.

DETOURING

Sumon Barman is the nephew of Malati Barman, in whose house I lived in Kathalbari. When I first met him, then nearly twenty years old, I had asked if he'd be interested in accompanying me on my walks in and between border villages. His mother told me right away that Sumon would be entirely useless: he didn't know any of the village paths and she was sure I would soon be more familiar with the local geography than he was. Not convinced, I persisted with my request and soon Sumon promised to take me around his part of the village on a day off from work. At that time, he worked at a store selling mobile phones in Dinhata, the nearest town, about thirty minutes away on his motorcycle. He enjoyed this job in spite of his parents' concerns about the low pay. They were eager for him to develop a more reliable career so that they could sell their homestead and tiny patch of land in the border village and move closer to Dinhata; they believed moving out of the borderland (*simanta elakar bairey*) was key to their future prosperity, especially Sumon's prospects of marriage (see chapter 3).

On the day we were to meet, in the thirty-minute walk between Malati-di's house and his, I had crossed two BSF checkpoints, each with a pair of armed male soldiers. The BSF referred to these structures as "*naka* points," their numbering and cartography delinked from local place names to deliberately prevent mutual comprehension between locals and soldiers. Along the path, coils of concertina wire occupied the side of the road, where goats used to graze not so long ago (fig. 6). Soldiers at both tempo-rary checkpoints had asked to see my ID card and asked me where I was going and why. Speaking in Hindi, their lingua franca and a language not spoken locally, showing my voter identity card with a Kolkata address had sufficed. I heard one whisper to the other that this was the journalist they had heard about. On days when I didn't have somewhere to be, I would have used this as a pretext to start a chat; however, on this day, I didn't correct them, and I continued walking. Sumon came out of his house but-toning his shirt over a pair of jeans. It was sweltering hot and I remember remarking on how overdressed he was.

We continued on the narrow footpath in front of his house. Sumon took my invitation to tell me about his rural neighborhood seriously and began to point out the houses of his friends and distant relatives. Within min-utes, he was not only pointing out what's what and who lives where but also offering commentaries on the shifting geography. "This entire row of houses belongs to *nadi-bhanga lok* [those broken by the river]. There was a whole village on the other side of the river that got destroyed when the river changed course. Over there, the river took a turn into Bangladesh.

All those people have come here. I have heard that most of those homes were in Bangladesh, I never saw it, it was before I was born."

We soon turned a corner, the brown of the fences broken by the brilliant red of flowering hibiscus shrubs. He pointed to a cluster of houses: "This was almost exclusively Hindus who came from Bangladesh." Braided into his descriptions of the changes in this riparian landscape were accounts of displacement and settlements induced by flooding, a changing borderline, and the shifting value of land in relation to emerging architectures of border security. "Even *I* haven't really thought about how much this area has changed," Sumon mused, as I hurriedly sketched our route and noted the changes he was pointing out. Much like Rafiq-mama's account of Madhupur's connected history (see chapter 1), I couldn't "see" these historical markers in today's material landscape.

As we walked back, our conversation turned to my experiences of walking in the border villages and navigating the BSF's "checks." Sumon had a lot of questions for me, but I was distracted by the slippery ground. I lifted up my salwar to gingerly navigate puddles along this narrow path, muddy and wet in the monsoons. Not wanting to land on my butt, I asked Sumon why we were taking this terrible path instead of walking back on the elevated gravel road, which would surely have been a better choice. "I'm sure there are snakes here, too," I muttered, still shook up from seeing snakes for the first time only a few days before. At this time of the year, they are frequently spotted on footpaths to which they retreat when their habitats get filled with water after rains.

He replied: "Better to get bitten by a snake than beaten by the BSF." That remark made me stop and look up. "What do you mean, Sumon?" We continued walking slowly as he spoke:

This is an incident from the past winter. I was walking back home from the auto stand [on Rangpur Road, where the main road terminates beside Kathalbari bazaar] having just come back from Dinhata. The days are short, right? So, it had already become dark and I had no light because my phone was out of charge. So, I thought, let me take the *boro rasta* [big road; here, the elevated gravel road]. Normally, I never take that road, ok? I always go *bhitorer rasta diye* [taking inside paths]. Now, the BSF patrol the big road much more during the dark hours than during the day.

Bhoyanok! [Frightening!] No sooner than I had turned on to the big road than they surrounded me and started beating me. *'Kahan ja rahe ho? Kya irada hain?'* [Where are you going? What's your plan?] They started shouting in Hindi. I tried to say that I lived right there—less than 300 meters from the road—but they wouldn't let me speak. *We have never seen you before,* they said. I tried to say that they hadn't seen me because I work in Dinhata, because I stay far away from this place [Sumon recounted his words in broken Hindi]. When they said, 'we are going to take you to the camp,' then I started shouting and some neighbors ran out hearing the noise. Only when they explained who my mother and father were and where our house was, the BSF let go of my collar and let me go home. Since this happened, *mairi bolchhi, BSF rastaye aar haatbo na* [I swear, I will not walk on BSF roads again].

Sumon added, bitterly, "This is a place for *du-nombori* people. Those who are loitering up and down these paths all day are known to the BSF and are never stopped, it's only the *bhalo manush* [the good people] who have no business with the BSF that are harassed."

His censure was only as strong as his hurt; he was a stranger to the social geography in which the BSF and allegedly *du-nombori* people were familiar. The importance—as well as the irony—of being well dressed and asserting himself in appearance as a *bhalo manush* (respectable person) through sartorial signals, shone through in this moment. Spatial control has long been a form of power for government and marginal communities, whether in the name of development or security,[24] but Sumon's experience questions whether embodied knowledge is *necessarily* a source of community for the marginalized or a tool against the state's spatial capture.[25] Rather, Sumon had at first refused to acquire the knowledge that was dependent on and signaled intimacy with the premises of border security. Sumon became a target of suspicion because he was unknown to the BSF and unaware that a young man walking on a border road in the dark would surely be read as a threat: a confluence of the spatial and temporal logics by which border security fixes its gendered object. While each year, the BSF argue that night-vision equipment will make their interception of clandestine mobilities of humans and animals more effective and precise, and even reduce erroneous shootings, instances such as this make clear that that "relations among persons are a crucial requirement and product of this work" of policing.[26] The very neighbors from whom Sumon maintained a distance and who he disdained as "*du-nombori* people" came to his rescue that night. The neighborhood is a unit of policing; the neighbor, called upon to mediate, is an accomplice to both sides.

Du-nombori literally translates as "second-order" in the sense of being counterfeit, illegal, suspicious.[27] This Bengali term, used on both sides of the border, is a capacious referent insofar as it is used to refer to practices, transactions, goods, and indeed individuals that straddle legal and socio-moral borders. *Du-nombori* is a vague and unstable term. What is *du-nombori* (clandestine, illicit) is a matter of policing for all and, in a way, by all. As Nosheen Ali argues, writing in the context of Gilgit-Baltistan in Pakistan, militarization creates not only "suspected subjects" but also "suspicious subjects."[28] Dramatically violent security measures may be reserved for policing mobilities at night, yet beneath the fractured socialities bubbled a violence that manifested in spatial and temporal ways. Sumon and his neighbors, daytime detours, and nighttime testimonies made this perfectly clear.

The incident had scarred more than Sumon's back. It had eaten into his personality; it guided the routes his feet took. Walking with Sumon dramatized this embodied nature and political ecology of security and surveillance, as we stopped, looked around, and went a different way. The contours of this securitized landscape were in Sumon's muscle memory; he knew when and where to take a detour onto the low, muddy path to avoid the one with the patrols. Sumon's detour showed that it was no longer adequate to have particular topological knowledge—as in, which path would be waterlogged in the rains. A socio-spatial knowledge of this gendered geography was key.

LOITERING

One morning I was making puffed rice with Radha-di, Sumon's mother, when through the mud walls of their kitchen located on the side of the road, we heard women's voices calling to each other "Come, come, there's about to be a fight." "Must be the Phensedyl women," said Radha-di with a chuckle, "go have a look."

I ran out in the direction of the gathering to see an elderly Muslim woman confronting two male soldiers patrolling the gravel road near their house.

"Does the road belong to your father? As the *sarkar* [government] has sent you to do duty on the roads, just so they have built it for us to loiter [*ghora-phera*] on it."

She looked around at her approving audience, which delivered applause on cue. Later, her friends teased her: "What filmy dialogue you gave!"

The BSF soldiers walked away to the side of the road; it looked like they did not want to prolong the confrontation. Like me, a couple of other young people had quickly snapped a picture of the face-off on their mobile phones, bad angles and jutting in shoulders be damned. I asked a woman I recognized as Radha-di's neighbor what had happened. "The BSF asked them to stop loitering and get off the road, so she got angry and started arguing with them."

The contemptuous tone and diminutive "*tui*" register in which the woman had spoken was a far cry from the usually deferential verbal and body language in which locals typically spoke to the BSF. The BSF expected the deference and took offense when it was absent.[29] Given that context, it was more than a mere verbal squabble. The question of who had a right to the road and how it could be used quivered beneath the surface. At first glance, it posed a moral challenge to the legitimacy of the BSF's presence by publicly questioning their authority. What made this moment so tense was the ostensibly deeper assertion of rights to space. Everyday negotiations such as this challenge the "logic of masculine protection"[30] and feminine docility for the abstract mandate of security, scaling from the body to the national geobody.

For the male soldiers of the BSF, their appearance in uniform with arms did not automatically translate into legitimacy. They were feared but not necessarily accepted as a legitimated authority among residents. They found that to build this legitimacy, which would allow them to be effective soldiers carrying out their duties of border security, they first had to establish themselves as empathetic moral beings. To attend to these encounters with those manning the border is to grapple with the "intensity of gendered sociality" in civil-military relations.[31] The friendly eastern border allows for a framework of sociality that few other border-fronts do, even as this sociality proceeds through heteropatriarchal norms of masculine and feminine propriety, fraternity, and kinship. Residents recognized with sympathy the long hours of hard duty that the soldiers put in, far from their families. This laid significant groundwork for times when disproportionate expressions of anger or harassment by male *jawans* on duty were officially explained away in terms of tiredness or misjudgment under stress.[32] Far from being rational security bureaucracies, security regimes everywhere are animated by affective and kinship relations. Residents and security forces enact, improvise, and coproduce gendered norms and economic subjects continuously.

Everyone knew that women on this path were transporting Phensedyl to be smuggled to Bangladesh. Phensedyl is an over-the-counter cough syrup that is commonly available in India but banned in Bangladesh since it became a substance rampantly abused in the country. In 2014, while I was living in these border villages, the BSF, enabled by the increased deployment of troops on the eastern border, had started to patrol village roads like these to preempt unauthorized border crossings and intercept smuggling. Previously, anyone could carry anything unhindered on this path. Ever since patrols were introduced on this path, women, who the male BSF soldiers are not allowed to physically search, had become the only ones who could smuggle goods hidden under their clothes. They were paid in cash for this labor of transportation, as smugglers were desperate to get the goods past the patrols. This brief history of patrols epitomizes the "paradoxical character of borderlands" writ large: the introduction of the patrol makes it a profitable opportunity to be crossed.[33] Risk means profit, and the patrol introduces risk—and profit—on this route, in particularly gendered combinations.

The claim of loitering, however reasonable, was a ruse, or so I was told by Radha-di. She made no secret of her disapproval of her neighbors' activities even when she enjoyed a saucy story and a good laugh with them. The neighborhood's women gathered to discuss the morning's showdown at Radha-di's doorstep, after lunch had been cooked and families had been fed. Over *paan-supari* that afternoon, I learned that there was a whole group of women who transported bottles of Phensedyl along this path, hidden in the folds of their saris. They deposited the bottles in a designated spot close to the border, where they would be collected by a handler on the Bangladeshi side. "They have to hold their pee for hours waiting for the right time to cross [the path] because they can't sit down when these bottles are arranged under their clothes," Radha-di said, pointing to these women's bodies, in a voice part sympathetic and part critical.

One of the ladies (I recognized her from the morning's showdown) objected: "It's not easy, ma go. You laugh, but it's a lot of trouble." She tucked a folded paan into the corner of her mouth and leaned into a big sigh.

"Don't do it," chided Radha-di promptly. "It's because of you that we have stopped walking on that road."

Women who barely earned the equivalent of the daily wage rate from petty smuggling were deemed to be *bechare* (pitiable) and not threatening to *desh ka suraksha* (national security); the BSF squarely placed all those who dealt with narcotic substances in a category for which there was *koi chhut nahi* (no leeway). The BSF *and* residents refer to women who transported goods like Phensedyl bottles as victims of drug lords and businessmen, who earn the real profits but remain concealed behind the use of these women's bodies. That is, a paternalist argument about protecting women from exploitation is routinely invoked to both condemn *and* make a case to overlook their *du-nombori* involvements. Illegal practices not only sit at the heart of state power;[34] here we can also see how state actors are drawn out of their logics of legality into empathetic considerations through patriarchal and paternalistic norms while evaluating clandestine mobilities. *Du-nombori*, then, is not inherent in persons or things but can be thought of as a classic question of value in action.

Du-nombori is a marker of difference: it produces mobility and immobility as conditions for each other. These differentiations in security socialities challenge the presumed purity and polarity of moral economies that underpin the study of illicit flows and borderlands. As Radha-di noted resentfully, the patrol on this road had ended her own bona fide loitering too. In their free time in the afternoon, women would go for a short walk in twos or threes, often with the additional task of bringing their grazing goat or cow back home. The concertina wire that now occupied the side of the road had marked it as a privileged site of suspicion and security; goats and loitering had been driven off. Like the female passenger who'd scorned Mishti-boudi, caught while smuggling cumin, Radha-di blamed these women for working a *du-nombori line* that had brought a BSF patrol out there, to that fork in the road, as it came to be associated with women smuggling. But she didn't do so by invoking religious differences; they lived side by side with neighborly intimacy. In this context, the surveillance of mobilities has unfolded along—and is expected to conform to—

the lines of existing social fractures of gender and class, more than caste and religion. But in any case, it is most disruptive of the social order when it rearranges power hierarchies anew.

The borderland society versus the (security) state opposition, around which much scholarship on borderlands and border identities is built, is inadequate to grasp the social drama of the security-induced wait, detours, loitering, and enclosures.[35] Indeed, as Allen Feldman writes, "the transgressive aura of certain branded spaces are complementary signs of social deformation."[36] All residents were subject to the same prohibitions on movement and the use of public spaces, but they were not targets or victims in the same way. The discussions and disagreements between "respectable" Radha-di and her "*du-nombori*" neighbors were folded into the intimacy and solidarities they shared every day. Their children played together between their houses and were equally vulnerable to the BSF's surveillance and rough handling; they shared the risks of militarization but, in the meantime, its differentiations cut the social fabric, too.

STOPPING

Manipulations of time are a key mode through which security's violence and devaluation impacts borderland lives, including the division of the day and the night to the slowing down and lengthening of routes. Residents have an acute understanding that the temporal is a mechanism of control.[37] As one resident put it, you don't really understand that the BSF exercises this power until you are stopped, your day's solid plans evaporate into the humid air, and you are made to feel that they are "the owners of time [*somoyer malik*]."

My introduction to Girish Das in Kathalbari was occasioned by his need for mediation with the BSF. Girish-da lived in a dilapidated tin-walled house in Kathalbari and hawked baked goods in Balatari and Mansai. He had a routine hitched to the local bakery's production rhythm: in the morning he cycled to the neighboring village where the bakery was, collected the goods that had been baked the night before, and then cycled on the same village paths every day to supply buns, biscuits, breadsticks, savory patties, and syrup-soaked sponge cakes to small home-run shops in

Balatari and Mansai, border villages that fell beyond the fence and/or the BSF line of control. Mondays were his day off. To preempt the smuggling of goods to Bangladesh, the BSF closely regulates all possessions (from domestic animals, such as goats and cattle, to agricultural implements) and consumer goods (from building materials to edible products).[38] To achieve this ostensibly impossible task, anyone traversing the patrolled rural paths is required to have written permission from the local BSF officer-in-charge for the goods they are transporting. However, each time the deployed officer changed, which it did frequently and irregularly, the signature had to be renewed for it have any value.

Since this hardening of controls on mobility within the borderland, a series of cheap notebooks recording these signatures—sometimes at monthly, sometimes fortnightly intervals—had been added to Girish-da's bag of baked goods (fig. 8). In the autumn of 2014, when a newly arrived BSF officer wanted to review all such permissions before renewing them, Girish-da needed a letter writer at short notice. He was illiterate, poor, and poorly connected to the lettered few at the *panchayat* office who typically helped locals with these bureaucratic processes. I was known to have helped others negotiate with the BSF by writing letters for them in English and I sought no favors in return, unlike local scribes who integrated this mediation into a wider economy of political patronage.[39] One evening I was summoned back to Malati-di's house to write for Girish-da. It was a note stating who he was, why he moved on the routes he did, and that he should be allowed passage. I gathered that it was meant to function as a message from one soldier to another, obviating the need for further social interaction and translation.

Some weeks later, Girish-da and I were returning together from Balatari. He was an affectionate and talkative man, beloved by all who knew him, and walking with him was a pleasure. Girish-da couldn't speak or understand any Hindi. On multiple occasions I heard him being teased by friends for his incompetence at communicating with the BSF. I thought his hearty smile always froze a little bit at these jokes. We had both stopped at a patrol by the road; we were on foot, he was rolling his rusty Hero cycle beside him, the empty bags hanging off the handlebars.

"*You!* Where are you coming from? Where did all the things in your bag go? Sent them all to Bangladesh? Show me your *permission!* No more trips from tomorrow!" a middle-aged soldier, sweating profusely in the

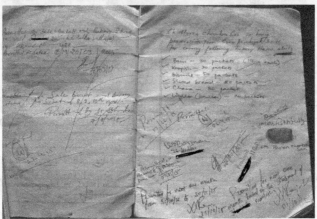

8. Girish-da's bag of baked goods (left) to which has been added this notebook of permissions, signatures, and units of time measured out by the BSF (right).

late afternoon sun, said curtly in Hindi. He addressed Girish-da in the uncomplimentary "tu" register. This manner of speaking was clearly disrespectful and its utterance was an assertion of power. Girish-da was at a loss, his weather-beaten face stricken with fear, as he turned to me. "*Bon,* what did he say? They keep saying *permission-permission,* what do they want? I've been to the camp and got a signature [*shoi*], why won't he just take that?" Terrified, Girish-da made multiple trips to "the camp" that day in a bid to meet the officer-in-charge and resolve the matter, but to no avail. He was told that it was not "the right time" and that he could not just show up at "any time" and expect an audience.

As a daily-wage worker, time was money, and being prevented from moving on his daily route was a direct assault on his labor hours. Interception for the BSF was not simply a routine measure of securing the border against potential breaches; it was a demonstration of power and supreme authority to its own citizens in the borderlands.[40] That evening in the Kathalbari bazaar, where Girish-da usually gathered for a cup of tea and exchange of day's news, he said to his friends, "I am really upset, feeling broken today. Look at my body—it has shriveled up, I won't be able to sleep at night, I won't survive this way." His bodily dread and experience of harm was not only the immediate intimidation and harassment he had suffered; it was also the anticipation of being stopped in future.

Over the next week, Girish-da's fears were confirmed. Despite a great deal of effort, he was unable to get the necessary signatures to resume his daily mobility. Stopped from hawking the goods which he had already bought from the bakery with a weekly advance, Girish-da's hand-to-mouth existence looked even more precarious. Time spent in any effort to overcome this imposed immobility was time spent out of work, out of money. His neighbors rallied around him sympathetically in the bazaar to comment on the multiple forms of stress: the use of an unfamiliar language in public humiliations, the prevention of his mobility, and most importantly, a disruption of his working days.

This harassment is neither unintentional, nor would it be correct to gloss this simply as the result of a malfunctioning security bureaucracy. Rather, as Yael Berda argues regarding Israel's permit regime, "effective inefficiency" is the hallmark of a system whose goal is to track, delay, and slow down movement. "The greatest and most persistent effect of the permit regime," she writes, is to generate "despair."[41] In addition to Girish-da's embodied experience of such despair, the force of the encounter with the soldier was not contained in the time and space of the checkpoint. He felt the physical effects of the encounter long after. It "extracted vitality"[42] from him, bit by bit, as he sought the advice of friends to prepare for the next passage on his daily route, considered alternative work, and prepared feverishly for the next potential encounter with the BSF. Like the patrol that turned the footpath in Radha-di's neighborhood into a suspected space, being forcibly stopped dissolved distinctions of work and leisure, public and private. The performances of being *un*suspicious that must appear at the moment of encounter in order to secure passage have a much longer life, backstage so to speak.

I want to home in on the political economy of time as everyday mobili-ties become the target of border security. Mohamad Junaid, writing about the claustrophobia of confinement in India-occupied Kashmir, urges us to consider the enclosure of time together with space. He writes that curfews imposed by the Indian state in Kashmir "freeze and unfreeze time at will, weaving it into the striated spatiality of occupation," and argues that it is in curfews and people's strategies to keep their bodies moving that the "spatio-temporal logics of occupation" are most purely expressed.[43] Curfews are imposed only at night along the border roads through the activation of Section 144, which prohibits residents from walking or cycling on these paths.[44] But if we deploy Junaid's method of viewing moving—and forcibly halted—bodies as barometers, then we can see that being stopped in these so-called friendly borderlands derives its force not only from the control of movement but by upsetting the most mundane divisions of time and space in daily life. Border security no longer remains confined to the time and space of encounter but streaks every aspect of existence and scales to the national. As matters of *national* security can erupt anywhere and anytime, superseding established distinctions of day-time free mobility and nighttime restrictions, the Indian security state can claim the Bengal borderlands are places of no-conflict while simultane-ously producing them as privileged sites in a differentiated national secu-rity geography. It is to this paradoxical simultaneity and the multiple gazes of surveillance that it enables that I now turn.

HIDING AND SEEKING

I regularly initiated conversations with BSF soldiers with the following question: What do you think of border duty here in Bengal? This was an implicit invitation to reflect on the specificity of the Bengal borderlands in comparison to wherever else the soldier had been posted before. I found that far from being merely diplomatic rhetoric, the discourse of friendliness regarding the India-Bangladesh borderlands structured how these soldiers narrated and made sense of the distinctive tensions of security practice in these agrarian borderlands.

Most of the BSF's six-hour shifts at "*naka* points" along village paths and at the gates of the border fence were uneventful, and once I had become a familiar face in the area, I generally found soldiers quite willing to chat. They were eager to convey how difficult their jobs were and to garner sympathy from me. "*Hamara bhi human rights hain. Likhiye aap.* [We have human rights too. You write that down.] Far away from our families, not being able to see our children grow up. . . ." I had to remind myself each time that telling me "the true reality" (so that I could write about it) was also a part of their job: this particular self-fashioning of the soldier as a family man, addressed to me, a female researcher, was part of the affective regime of rule at this friendly border to which the symbolic and relational power of gender and kinship was central.

In one such conversation, a soldier with twelve years of service underlined the demands of the friendly Bengal borderlands, locating the area's distinctiveness within the broader national security geography that his own itinerant career had traced.[45] "*Yahan duty bohot kharap hain, naukri ka khatra hain* [Duty is terrible here; our jobs are in danger here]." Such references to *khatra* (danger) in a time and place of *shanti* (peace) recurred. Descriptions of the hazards of security work—characterized as dangers to jobs in terms of disciplinary records and other punishments rather than threats to life—along the Bengal border was as pervasive a script for the BSF as was the one about harassments being a daily condition for borderland residents. The BSF found shape-shifting security socialities to be distinctive about the "friendly" Bengal borderlands but confusing. One day, at one of the gates along the serpentine border fence, I sat beside the soldiers on duty with no immediate company other than

9. A BSF checkpoint at a gate on the border fence; an example of a stolen frame on my mobile phone.

the occasional grasshopper and cattle grazing nearby. The gates are opened thrice a day for an hour each (see fig. 9), during which time there is a buzz of checking, frisking, questioning. As I remarked on the *shanti* of duty, the soldiers, who had been quite circumspect until then, burst out.

> *Bilkul nahi!* [Not at all!] Anything can happen in a minute! It's very unpredictable. One is always worried about keeping the job, you can get punishments. . . . *Larkibaazi* happens a lot. Women catch you and make accusations at you, try to trap you as a womanizer [his explanation of *larkibaazi*]. . . . I was in Bhuj before this and that was very good.[46] You see an enemy, you shoot straight away. Rest of the time you could be *easy*, relax. Here you really have to give duty properly. There is a lot of *smuggling* going on, we have to try and stop it. It is a very difficult task. There is so much pressure on us from the *civils*. You really have to be alert and give *duty* properly.

Militarization in these eastern borderlands is refracted through the insistent distinction made by the Indian state that this is *not* a place of conflict but rather a peaceful place of duty in cooperation with citizens and a friendly neighbor. Feminist scholars have directed attention to how safety (and danger) becomes embodied, gendered, and spatialized through these security practices.[47] Here we see how they are scaled from the body to an inter-referential national security geography. For the BSF, every hour of duty in these borderlands where they had to engage in social inter-action with local residents ("pressure from the civils," "*larkibaazi*") was fraught with gendered and sexualized forms of threat.

One morning, for instance, I was chatting to a pair of soldiers at the Nazirghat checkpoint—one young and one old. Mishti-boudi, whose cumin consignment had been the focal point of the delay with which this chapter opened, was standing nearby, probably waiting to arrange the transportation of her goods of the day safely across this checkpoint. Acknowledging her presence, the older of the two soldiers raised his eye-brows suggestively in her direction. One of the reasons they were sent out in such combinations of age, he noted somberly, was to manage the aggres-sive sexual humor from older women—the older man ostensibly to help the younger, inexperienced soldier. "*Yeh Bangali aurat bohot chaloo hain* [These Bengali women are very cunning]," he said with great feeling (pos-sibly having forgotten that I, too, was a Bengali woman). The fearful refer-ence to *larkibaazi*—roughly translated as "women-related fracas"—acknowledged the gendered and sexualized registers ever-present in civil-military relations. In pausing on this anxiety as indicative of broader social tensions, I follow in a well-trodden path in the feminist anthropol-ogy of South Asia, where scholars have written about the complex narra-tive valences of "forthright female voices."[48] The frame of fear that casts the male soldiers as victims and Bengali women as cunning reflects deep patriarchal anxieties.[49]

By this time, I had learned to read such comments as veiled references to sexual advances, all of which were referred to by the term *larkibaazi*. Wanting a concrete example, I turned to the newly minted *jawan*, barely twenty years old. A. Kumar, from rural Bihar, was hesitant. A few awk-ward minutes and silent steps away from the checkpoint and out of the other soldier's earshot later, A. Kumar confessed that he was terrified of being accused of sexual harassment. "Why? How can you just say that?,"

I asked impatiently and rather unsympathetically. After all, the BSF and other paramilitary forces in India have a notorious record of sexual violence in places such as Kashmir, Chhattisgarh, and Manipur.[50] "I'm in a bad way," he said, hesitating, embarrassment holding back a frank disclosure. Eventually, he started to talk about his predicament: he has been receiving calls on his mobile phone during *off-duty* hours (his emphasis) from an unknown woman. Soldiers are not permitted to carry mobile phones when they are on duty. While most use their phones to keep in touch with family members, there is also talk of monitoring phone usage to detect corruption. Inexperienced, A. Kumar was nervous that his colleagues might overhear the inappropriate sexual comments made to him on the phone—which he coyly referred to as "what-not" —and suspect him of being sexually embroiled with local women.

I was convinced about the sexual nature of the phone calls when Mishti-boudi walked up close to us, unnoticed by both of us. With her hands on her hips and a smile dancing on her lips, she said to A. Kumar in Bengali: "*Ki go*, you will also have to marry one day, why don't you practice some sweet talk here?"

I turned from her to him; he shifted uneasily, leaning his weight on his rifle and looking down at his mud-splattered black boots. He may not have understood her exact words but the flirtatious tone of her voice and her suggestive body language confirmed that the joking was not lost on him. Pleased with her assertion of power, Mishti-boudi delivered her punchline, complete with an exaggerated stage-wink at me. "*Ora meye-manushke khub bhoy paye* [They are very scared of women]."

A. Kumar's nervousness directs our attention to the anxieties of power within civil-military relations—in particular, the disruptive work of gender and sexuality. To attend to the ways in which the BSF watch, search, and categorize "civilian" bodies in the borderlands means that we must also recognize that there is an equally active domain in which the tall male bodies of the BSF are being watched, scrutinized, and discussed. In these onstage and offstage security encounters, borderland residents are not only victims of the security forces, as they actively strive to direct these interactions—which are certainly not of their own volition, structurally speaking—to desirable ends. The register of sexual playfulness in which many of these interactions take place serves several functions, especially as a subtle maneuvering of power. The transgressive sexuality that Mishti-boudi performed highlighted the vulnerabilities of border security regimes as embodied in a masculinist and heteronormative force.

A focus on these socialities also enables us to see the presence of *secoority* in spaces beyond highly determined sites, such as checkpoints to spaces of leisure, ostensibly beyond the pale of the civil-military encounters. As A. Kumar elaborated on his predicament, he confessed that receiving these "crank calls" in his barracks made him feel watched by his peers and borderland locals alike. The regimented on-duty and off-duty hours broke down and bled into each other. That was precisely the desired effect of the countergaze.

I had heard a different version of this same story from one of the women who had been calling him. Jahanara, a mother of two in her late thirties, is a government-employed health worker, in charge of three border villages in the Kathalbari area. She checked on pregnant mothers, newborns, and spread information about scheduled immunizations and other health camps on weekly neighborhood visits. Speaking of her experiences of sharing these paths with alleged smugglers and criminals and being subjected to the surveillance of the BSF, she had invited me to join her back in 2012: "Come with me, *moja hobe* [it'll be fun]." Jahanara's confession came up unexpectedly; we were talking about something unrelated as she and I were walking by a patrol one afternoon.

JAHANARA: He isn't here today. Last time I saw him was at this patrol. I want to see his face after the phone calls! Do you think I should give him a *hint?*

SAHANA: Who is the he? And *hint* about what? I don't know what you mean.

JAHANARA: Arre, you know we managed to get the phone number of that new BSF. He's boyish and *cute*. We called him [Jahanara burst out laughing at this point, bending over so we had to stop walking] and it was so much fun! [I looked over my shoulder furtively toward the patrol we had left behind, making sure they didn't hear us.]

SAHANA [SMILING AND VERY CURIOUS]:   What did you say? What did he say?

JAHANARA: First we began with "hi, hello" and asking what are you doing, what are you wearing right now, are you lying down? He said *'kaun hain?'*[51]

SAHANA: You're mad! What did he say?

JAHANARA: He kept saying who are you, who are you. And then he was just silent. I thought he will hang up so I said 'I love you!'—just like that for fun. Then Ruma snatched the phone and said 'Hey, I keep thinking of you and seeing you in my dreams. Will you sleep with me?' Then he cut the call.

Calling A. Kumar from the comfort of their homes, Jahanara and her friends asked probing and intimate questions. Anticipating that they would physically encounter him on duty along some route they would take, but not knowing when or where that would be, the thrill of causing stress and discomfort to a BSF soldier was lived and savored far from those spaces of encounter and built structures of the border fence, walled outposts, or checkpoints.

Among trusted friends, women joke about the sexual appetite of these lonely yet physically attractive men, expressing in turn their own sexual and romantic desires and the ways that BSF men find a place in those desires. Stories of fleeting flirtations and romantic encounters are told and retold, and speculations regarding who offers and takes sexual services in lieu of favors to facilitate border businesses is a recurring topic of gossip. This domain of desire and representation humanizes and sexualizes the force in the borderland, figures them as manageable, but also brings them into extremely private and intimate spaces of homes well before and after the time spent in encounters at classic militarized sites, such as the checkpoint. The narrative circulation of BSF stories is key to public perceptions, expectations, and scripts of sociality with the BSF and demonstrates that border security is shaped in homes and through everyday conversations where gendered modes of being are finely deconstructed and reconstructed, in public and in secret.

KNOWING TO LOOK, LOOKING TO KNOW

Let me return, then, to the questions of embodied knowledge, the time-spaces of national security in these borderlands, and the devaluation of borderland mobilities as threatening. Once I began to accompany Jahanara regularly on her field visits, it became clear what she meant when she alluded to "fun." "When they [the male BSF] are patrolling, they can tell by looking what type of a woman you are, are you *du-nombori* or are you straightforward." Jahanara, as we have seen, had been doing a fair bit of "looking" herself. But what she meant by the BSF "looking" is quite literal. Unable to frisk, male BSF guards must try to see if bottles and packets concealed in blouses and tied around stomachs are explicit through the folds of clothes. One afternoon, on the way to make some house visits, we exchanged greetings with a patrol. "That's why I wear my sari low and pinned up very neatly, so you can see my midriff and up to my cleavage if you want," said Jahanara, pushing out her bared midriff exaggeratedly right after we passed them. I giggled uncontrollably in my deliberately modest salwar-kurta.

Jahanara's playfulness made light of the idea that *du-nombori* mobility is simply there to spot or even unambiguously threatening as *du-nombori*. Some of the soldiers described the task of surveillance with embarrassment, but many more resorted to racializing and sexualizing Bengali Muslim and Rajbangsi peasant women as deserving of this gaze in order to justify their policing practices along what they nevertheless maintained was a "friendly" border. Walking is revealing because of the intensity of multisensorial communication. Words are but one of the ways in which secrets are kept, knowledge is shared, and bodies are schooled. While ethnographers of checkpoints and their modes of rule have focused on the biopolitical power and terror of the state to "turn the body inside out" at such intensely concentrated sites of scrutiny,[52] this chapter has explored the *dispersal* of surveillance, suspicion, knowing, and uncertainty. While walking with borderland residents allowed me to "fit in," it also produced and reproduced my status as an outsider to enable access, "on the verge of experiencing alterity," as Pratiksha Baxi notes about her experience of conducting research on rape trials in Indian courtrooms.[53] Female friends like Jahanara and Malati-di joked about how walking with Sahana-the-novelty meant getting stuck at patrols because the BSF "*phaydla parey*," a slang expression for flirtatious chit-chat. Male BSF officers felt entitled to draw different kinds of inferences based on my physical appearance: suspicion that I was a spy because I walked so fast or commiseration that "*weight loss ho gaya madam itna chalte chalte* [you've lost weight madam, with all this walking around]." Walking couldn't remain only a method and analytical approach for me; I was reminded constantly that my walking revealed a great deal about me to my companions and to the BSF.

Walking and looking with Jahanara made especially clear that the BSF were not the only ones in the business of looking or evaluating the threat of mobilities. Borderland residents were complicit in placing themselves and each other in this manner, drawing on existing social norms of class, gender, and religion. This chapter has moved our focus away from the spectacular performances of state security and panoptical regimes, manifest most dramatically in the border fence, to an embodied politics of security that is normalized through normative social hierarchies and "an even deeper regulation of local desires, affiliations, and aspirations."[54] Projects of state security are reliant on and constituted by social forms of knowledge, differences, and ethical horizons. The thousand tiny cuts of militarization are dispersed in space and time over what comes to be a gendered geography of the borderlands. Following the traces of these civil-military interactions takes us into the lives of borderland communities in ways that are contrary to the usual "civilians" who figure in discourses of border security. Such victims are typically framed in legalistic ways, such that only overt adversarial positions of violence are recognized *as* civil-military encounters: men killed while smuggling cattle at night, people injured while border-crossing clandestinely, individuals caught up in "lawfare" as targets of surveillance.[55]

However, as these security socialities unfold, dissonant discourses of danger and injustice are articulated. Embodied knowledge in the borderlands shows that knowing is necessary but also dangerous. It marks you, which is a dilemma with high stakes for many like Sumon, Jahanara, Mishti-boudi, and Girish-da. Who knows and who doesn't, then, becomes a process of social differentiation in relation to the targeting of borderland mobilities. Checkpoints, patrols, and choices of routes are not merely practical mechanisms in the infrastructure of mobility and border control. Neither are they inert sites at which security practices unfold and civil-military encounters find intense expression. They are both and more. The borderland is produced as a gendered security zone, taking spatial form and social, material, and affective texture. Clear demarcations of the times and spaces of security, of civilian and military, and the proper place of civil-military exchange are upended. Soldiers and residents alike grapple with these blurred boundaries in daily decisions through which the architecture of India's border security takes shape on the ground, etched on paths not taken and in flirtations carefully displayed.

"Security socialities"—as a broad frame for heterogeneous entanglements rather than the repression/resistance binary—offers a better understanding of how residents negotiate and live with militarization in the villages along this so-called friendly border. Collective scripts about the harassment and violence of state security are continually reworked by the wayside as gender, class, and religious identities intersect and punctuate everyday itineraries of mobility under surveillance. Songs, jokes, and the challenges of neighborly intimacy offer glimpses into security socialities, where acts of transgression are possible yet fleeting, where private spaces of safety are constantly under threat of being encroached, where friendships, vulnerabilities, and bearing witness are vital, fluid, and explosive. Intimate kin relations within the borderland family come to be altered over generations as distinctions of national identity take root. In the next chapter we turn to how security shapes senses of distance and intimacy across generations of the transnational family.

3 Relative Intimacies

During one of my earliest visits to Kathalbari, India, in 2012, I attended a *gram sabha*, a public meeting in the village, which is routinely held two or three times a year. Invited by the elected village leaders to introduce myself and my research project, I said I was interested in learning about the challenges that young people faced, especially as borderland residents. In this public gathering of about two hundred men and women, some children playing on the sides, a tall, lanky man stood up: "No one wants to marry us. It's a real problem. *Biyer bajarey amader kono daam nei. Ei dik tao dekha dorkar* [In the marriage market, we have no value. This is an aspect that needs to be looked at, too]."

Laughter rippled through the gathered Muslim and Rajbangsi crowd and a great chorus of voices rose to applaud the opinion expressed by Kader, a young Bengali Muslim and, at that time, unmarried man. My fieldnotes remind me that I was taken aback by the public articulation as well as the widely shared quality of this experience.

Kader's comment insists that we pay attention to the sedimented ways that transnational kinship geographies and a nationally circumscribed location are in tension in people's intimate lives in the borderlands of north Bengal. By "no one" he meant in India, a nationally delimited "marriage market." No family wanted to marry their daughter into border villages, which had poor infrastructure and economic conditions. Given the Border Security Force (BSF)'s increasing security measures in these villages, discussed in the previous chapter, the groom's house would likely be difficult to access for future visits by the bride's family. Altogether, this made prospective grooms in border villages undesirable, and a match with their families of little value.

If borderland men are worth nothing in the marriage market, unable to attract desirable marriage proposals or command gifts, borderland women suffered, too. Families of prospective brides in border villages were very keen to find matches *bhitore* or inside, away from the border, but these were elusive. Rajbangsi families, among whom dowries are widely demanded, found that to secure a groom away from a border village, they had to offer substantially larger dowries in cash and kind. Muslim families shared with Rajbangsis the taint of negative stereotypes regarding borderland residence. As Kader went on to explain and his own experiences illustrate, borderland youth either married in border villages among their compatriots, or clandestinely across the border in nearby villages of the neighboring country (as with the story of Rani's marriage that opened this book). The border's separation into "Indian" and "Bangladeshi" distinctions provided a measure of value with which to negotiate this shared devaluation of prospects in the borderland marriage economy.

KINSHIP GEOGRAPHIES AS COUNTER-MAPS

This chapter traces bordering by the distinctions, devaluations, and remaking of kinship and families. Although these processes of separation and reconfigured connection have been in play since 1947, they have intensified in key ways in the twenty-first century with the rapid militarization of the borderlands. As state border security practices and changing forms of transnational kinship and the borderland family attest, one articulates through another to the extent that an anthropology of bordering might very well be an anthropology of kinship.

In north Bengal, as in other Asian borderlands, marginalized men seek out cross-border marital alliances with less-well-off women to reproduce heteropatriarchal structures.[1] Indeed, in the story of the "Bangladeshi bride" with which this book began, Rani Barman's marriage hinged on such a calculus of gender, nationality, religion, caste. What Kader presents as a curse today was hardly new: for generations, the Muslim and Rajbangsi locals of northern Bengal, across the Cooch Behar and Rangpur region, have been marrying each other. A kinship geography overlays a social and political geography whose shared history and lively present disrupts the religion/nation isomorphism that Partition was founded on. The fractures of 1947 have found their ways into imaginaries of intimacy, reshaping families and reconstituting kinship over generations through a thousand tiny cuts: what appears today as a surprising transnational fix is actually a torturously slow embedding of the national as a criterion of value in kinship. "Territorialized and nationalized religious identity," writes Sara Smith in her powerful study of the geopolitics of interfaith marriage in the borderlands of Ladakh, "is enmeshed with the everyday violence of heteronormative and reprosexual expectations around desire, love, and reproduction."[2]

Disarmingly straightforward, Kader's commentary reminds us that marriages mean movement and, once formed, marital alliances and other kinship ties require movement for their upkeep. This chapter will explore what the promise of transnational kinship means in the borderlands over generations, with increasing militarization and a greater differentiation of gendered mobilities by the interplay of nationality, religion, and class. What these predicaments center are the gendered burdens of kinship: marriages often mean migration for women. And in the borderlands, if the marrying woman finds herself on the other side of the border from her natal family, it also creates a particularly gendered border-crosser. At the same time, heteropatriarchal sympathy toward kinship ties, shared by the security forces of both states, is critical for the innocence of a female border-crosser to be established, in clear contradistinction from the national security threat as figured in the male migrant that we glimpsed in chapter 2 and that I will discuss in detail in chapter 5. The gendered body of the border-crosser matters, as the structure of a friendly border conscripts people into reimagining themselves as national neighbors. Distance and intimacy are promises that don't hold still.

The rich ethnographic scholarship on transnational kinship has pushed against methodological nationalism, and feminist contributions have especially centered women's mobility and immobility as central to reimagining power in relation to the changing family form and investments in place, both material and affective.[3] Yet, what is considered transnational has itself been based on long-distance mobilities, typically from the Global South to the Global North, thus yielding understandings of space, time, distance, and intimacy that are particular to those material conditions.[4] Borderland mobilities in northern Bengal challenge us to revisit conceptions of the transnational and its elementary aspects of distance, temporality, and intimacy. The production of the national in the borderlands demands a separation and distance between neighboring villages and kin now in neighboring nations; borderland kin strive to live up to the potential intimacy held in the promise of transnational mobility and networks. Rather than view the family and kinship as a private domain of refuge from the state, this chapter shows how the two are thoroughly implicated in the unpredictable mirroring and occasional queering of heteropatriarchal norms and desires that constitute each other's modes of power.

Within South Asia, transnational kinship is bracketed as a thing of the past, whether in scholarly work or in statist visions. A past ruptured violently by Partition, the loss of a thriving life of kinship was inflicted by states invested in a national-territorial reordering of families.[5] This temporal framing of transnational kinship ties is reflected in the scholarly division of labor too: the study of Partition and its immediate effects is the domain of historians and literary scholars while the contemporary life and political economy of borderlands has come to be the province of anthropologists. Ruptured kinship is the past, today's transnational ties are part of the "illicit flows" defying border security.

Indeed, while the BSF and the Border Guard Bangladesh (BGB) are sympathetic to the plight of separated families—especially those from an older generation, newly separated by the border—I found them baffled by why people today risk clandestine crossings for the sake of reproducing transnational ties instead of simply reshaping their kinship geography and families to stay within national borders. The BSF, already inclined to consider borderland residents as suspect citizens, took this to be willful disregard of the obligations of the national; the BGB, enabled by linguistic ease, were more understanding, but nevertheless invested in teaching borderland residents to give up these "old" ways. Such a disposition toward the *continued* investment in cross-border kinship, including through new marriages, reflects the dominant idea that legitimate transnational kinship is history; borderland mobility of the present is necessarily illegitimate.

In this chapter, I use the multigenerational histories of kinship and cross-border marriages to trace the nonlinear timeline of postcolonial bordering. Kinship geographies are counter-maps to the oft-told biography of the border, and by extension, to the political history of the region, surfacing fissures, silences, and recursions. Doing so also shows how the particularly gendered and moralized mobilities of transnational kinship and the fiction of the "friendly border" produce one another. I parse this co-constitution by looking at how the value of neighborliness—what it means to live as national neighbors—impacts the life of kinship.

In my fieldwork, I repurposed "the visual imperative" of the classic family tree into diagrams of kinship geography in my notebooks.[6] These diagrams grew unevenly over the years, sometimes lopsided in one direction, sometimes crawling off the page as I "discovered" a generation.[7] For all the transnational families I was mapping, I moved up or down the generations, depending on whom I started with, making note of the place-name where each spouse was from. For the Partition generation, I recorded Cooch Behar, Alipurduar, Jalpaiguri, Moynaguri, Rangpur, Kaliganj, Phulbari, Nageswari, Bhurungamari, Dhubri, Gaibandha; these names plotted out the contours of a kinship geography that stretched across united northern Bengal and lower Assam, through the length and breadth of the Cooch Behar princely state and greater Rangpur region. As I traveled back and forth across the India-Bangladesh border through the northern land port of Changrabandha/Burimari, my movements facilitated the exchange of photographs, gifts, and messages between relatives. Family trees grew denser with details of little-known offshoots in between my own comings and goings, with eleven sets of transnational families whose histories and experiences I traced. My own research presence and methods were deeply mediated by kinship. I lived with Malati Barman, a nurse at the village health center in the Kathalbari *gram panchayat*, India. Although her parents and older siblings had migrated from Bibiganj village in East Pakistan, she grew up in a village in Kathalbari and married into a local Rajbangsi family. She thus had a vast network of kin relations on her natal and affinal sides across the region. As her "younger sister," I became adopted into this transnational family network, observed primarily through the use of kin terms of relatedness and claims of care and affection. I came to call on the hospitality and care of her extended family members, just as they made requests of me, which included carrying messages and gifts across the border. While this network introduced me to some Rajbangsi communities in the adjacent Bangladeshi border villages, my relationship with them was initially bumpy, given the fact that there I was living with the Rahmans, a Muslim family in Madhupur village,[8] and was known in the area as their "Indian niece." How could I be related to Malati but stationed with a Muslim family, calling them *mama* (maternal uncle) and *mami* (maternal uncle's wife)?

The feminist anthropological scholarship on kinship has established that there is nothing natural or universally biological about it, and the "private" domain of kinship is deeply imbricated with broader political economy and nation-state structures.[9] My own kinship-mediated ethnography bears out different aspects of this now common wisdom; at that level, this chapter is a study of the inequities and inexorable joys of relatedness, its gendered forms of power, and its imbrication with state structures and geopolitics. These kinship ties were not simply practical fieldwork arrangements. They established me as a transnationally active and mobile person on both sides of the border, and before long I was drawn into the calculus of transnational kinship-state-market relations, like most families I knew. Each time I crossed the border, I tried to hide the many jars of Dove beauty cream, Indian medicines, and chocolates that had been requested by Bangladeshi friends and kin; going the other way to India, my bags were heavy with *lungis*, vermicelli, dried fish, and savory snacks. This kind of embedded mobility established several things about my situation: I was not going to nip across in a *du-nombori* crossing, thereby bringing the state and *sarkari bhabe jawa-asha*, the official way of coming-going, into conversations. The frequency of my cross-border travels across the land ports of northern Bengal, and occasionally via air travel between Kolkata and Dhaka, all ensured that inequalities of nationality, class, and geopolitics were never far from the accounting of kin work, my own included.

IN BETWEEN COMINGS AND GOINGS /
JAWA ASHAR MAJHE

> You see, in our family we don't know whether we're coming
> or going—it's all my grandmother's fault. But, of course, the
> fault wasn't hers at all: it lay in language. Every language
> assumes a centrality, a fixed and settled point to go away
> from and come back to, and what my grandmother was
> looking for was a word for a journey which was not a coming
> or a going at all; a journey that was a search for precisely that
> fixed point which permits the proper use of verbs of
> movement.
>
> —Amitav Ghosh, *The Shadow Lines*

If Kader's words portray the experience of the border as a curse, growing
up, Shefali Barman experienced the same border as a promise. But promises, like the language of direction (as Amitav Ghosh's narrator discovers),
are treacherous paths. As a Hindu woman marrying into an Indian border
village close to her natal family in Bangladesh, her cross-border marriage
was forged with the promise of mobility but failed to live up to that promise. Close in age, we spoke frankly about family and feeling left out. One
hot afternoon we lay on her bed, fanning ourselves and chatting about my
upcoming travel to Bangladesh. Shefali wrung a promise out of me to visit
her brothers' families so that I could hear directly from them, her *boudis*
and nieces and nephews, how beloved she was to them. She sat up very
straight, beads of sweat around her mouth as she spoke. "*Hay re*, Sahana,
tor ki moja. Pakhir moto ghure berash. [What fun you have, Sahana! You
wander about like a bird.] I married into India out of greed for the *melas*
[fairs] and now I'm stuck . . . no *jawa-asha* [coming and going] for me."

In contrast to what appeared to be my unhindered travels, Shefali drew
attention to her own loss of mobility. Married at twenty, widowed at
twenty-three with an infant, Shefali continued to live with her in-laws in
Putimari, a border village neighboring Kathalbari. In 2014, she was particularly upset that she couldn't cross the border to attend a nephew's rice-
eating ceremony in the nearby Bangladeshi border village of Boraibari.
The circuitous path that Shefali usually took between Putimari and
Boraibari, across an unfenced portion of the border, was closed at that

time due to a newly stationed BSF patrol there. All her natal family would be gathered in her brother's house on this occasion, and the pain of being unable to attend was evident on Shefali's face. Shefali desired not simply to be on one side or the other—she wanted a transnational life of continued *jawa-asha*. She found, instead, that she had to navigate belonging to unequal places, unequally.

"Did you really marry for the *melas?*" I asked.

My question seemed to bring Shefali's usual good cheer back right away and she nodded with a chuckle.

> In my childhood, our father or older brothers would take my sisters and me to the Rash Mela in Cooch Behar and smaller *melas* during Durga Puja and Rathjatra in Dinhata.[10] You see, it was no fun being Hindu in Bangladesh— but each time we would come here [West Bengal, India], we would see that so many women, so many families, Hindu and Muslim, who would come to these *melas,* traveling to them from different places and enjoying them till late at night. . . . The *border* was open in those years [through the 1990s], and the distance between Boraibari and Dinhata was not very much. *Jawa-asha* was very easy, and when it was necessary we occasionally stayed a night or two at relatives' homes. Then we would return to Bangladesh with toys, new dresses, and sweets.

With two paternal aunts married in the same area of Cooch Behar district, Shefali had also grown up as a witness to the ease of their *jawa-asha* across this international border. One of her older sisters had also married into an Indian border village. Having traveled these cross-border routes herself, she was agreeable to the proposal of marriage she received, with the reassurance that it was close enough within the borderland for her to visit frequently. She recalled that the excitement of the wedding for everyone included feasts on both sides and journeys accomplished clandestinely. "Truly an international affair," she laughed, underlining the local importance of that event. Shefali's deep disappointment with her immobility is thus made sharper in contrast to the memories of these cross-border journeys of her childhood and her expectations based on those experiences.

Shefali experienced the border as open through the 1990s. India's construction of the border fence was underway along some parts, but not in this region. At the time of her marriage there was a fence, though it was not as formidable as the current version and border security practices were not so rigid. The variability of the border's closure at any given time became even more clear as Shefali bemoaned that her sister would likely be able to attend the rice-eating ceremony by crossing as she usually did: her husband's family had land in the area between the border fence and the border, so she typically deposited her identity document at a gate on the border fence and went through. On this pretext of going to her land, she would make a quick trip across the border to their brother's house, which was located right by the border, and return before the gates closed for the day.

Shefali sat up again, struck by a new idea. She wondered if she should try to join her sister. She had, of course, visited her sister numerous times, but never attempted to cross the border at the fence there. I accompanied her the next day on this journey to meet her sister at the BSF checkpoint by the fence gate. At the checkpoint, the BSF soldiers on duty inspected Shefali's and her sister's voter identity cards and informed them that holders with addresses not in that village required special permission to be allowed through. "She's my sister, she's come to visit me, we will go together and come back together," pleaded Shefali's sister. The soldiers refused, simply shaking their heads in silence. Shefali was trembling visibly, crestfallen and fearful of an argument with the guards. Hopes dashed, the two sisters consulted in whispers, and decided that Shefali's sister would go through and bring the gathered family right up to the fence at a point between the BSF patrols, and Shefali would see them and talk with them through the fence for as long as possible. Shefali swallowed back her tears as we marched down the border road (fig. 10). It felt like a defiant act because the BSF strictly control civilian use of this road, which is monopolized for guarding the fence and movement of security force personnel and their vehicles, even though it was built by the Public Works Department. After what felt like a long time, I could see an elderly woman in a white sari running toward the fence through the bare harvested fields. We stopped walking and waited, facing Bangladesh, breathing on the concertina wire that filled the space between the two rows of metal frames strung with barbed wire.

10. Shefali marches down the border road, prohibited for civilian use without permission from the BSF—a defiant act in itself.

I turned away, keeping a watchful eye out for BSF soldiers who might come along patrolling the road on their bicycles. Soon, the larger group of sisters-in-law, nieces, and nephews joined up with Shefali's mother, and a frantic and tearful exchange of news took place. "Please go for another round for five minutes," I requested the young BSF constable who had cycled up, clearly understanding what was going on. "You people hurry up, if my superior comes around by chance and sees this, I will be in trouble," he said nervously. I was surprised at how obliging he was. The voices, briefly paused, resumed as he cycled away slowly. I looked on from the side, as this group of women and children spoke excitedly. Shefali complimented the children on their nice outfits, new ones on the occasion of the rice-eating ceremony. Even through her tears she managed to squeeze out a wry joke: "*Amar sharee ta paona roilo* [a sari is still owed to me]."

The exchange was difficult to follow—bits of the lunch menu, news of Shefali's school friends, messages from guests at the family celebration pushed through the barbed wire, like pieces of a puzzle through a sieve. "Look after our girl," said one of Shefali's sisters-in-law to me. "We know there are a lot of rights and laws for women in India, but we don't want any of that. We just want her to be happy, to feel she has her rightful place. And she should be able to come to visit." Another barb, marking out the difference of jurisdictions, underlining the hierarchy of neighbors.

11. Shefali meets her Bangladeshi natal family across the border fence, while I am keeping a watch out for the patrolling BSF soldier.

The constable was spotted cycling back again, waving agitatedly. And so, the intense meeting ended abruptly. Both groups turned away from the barbed wire to walk back into India and Bangladesh.

THE FRICTIONS OF DISTANCE

Taking this whole sequence together—the condensed narration of Shefali's lifetime of *jawa-asha*, her cross-border marriage, being currently stuck on one side, and this day's experience of intimacy through the barbed wire fence—makes clear that the border does not mediate distance in any singular way. The "friction of distance" is defined as the time or cost incurred to traverse a particular distance, and in that sense the border is a friction.[11] But as Kader's diagnosis of the problems of value in the marriage market suggested, the isolation of borderland families emerges not from the mere presence of the border but from the "rhetoric of distance"[12] that produces the isolation and devaluation of borderland families in particular ways. This rhetoric is a social discourse of remoteness and alterity,[13] invoked through experiences of border security and surveillance and negative stereotypes of borderland peoples, and hinges on fixing *national* distinction in spatial and social terms. At the same time, Shefali's own experiences of successfully navigating the border through the 1980s and 1990s, in contrast to its rigidity in the 2010s, shows that the same border has posed different material frictions and required vastly different spatial practices to maintain the same degrees of intimacy. Fun in India felt proximate because border-crossing was easy; the cross-border marriage transformed over a decade from feeling desirable, a commonplace mobility, to an entrapment, a distance harder and harder to traverse, in more ways than one. The rooting of national distinctions within such borderland families and their transnational networks becomes like tectonic plates, pushing away from one another.

For countless borderland residents like Shefali, their comings and goings that span transnational kinship archive the life of the border: what emerges is not a watershed, a before/after of the border, but a multitude of cuttings of time and space through openings and closures. This biography indexes the frictions and affects of distance, experienced as material and emotional qualities. Women in cross-border marriages frequently shared their experiences of distance and the demands of "kinwork"[14] as related: the labor of caring for kin as managing these valences of distance. Using terms such as *kora* (heavy/strong), *gorom* (hot), and *thanda* (cold) conveyed the texture of the enforced border and its dispersed security architecture as well as how the frictions of distance felt in their fears, hopes, bodies, and dreams. Shefali's claim from her transnational kin—the gift of a sari on her nephew's rice-eating ceremony—remains suspended in time, a stubborn cut across distance.

Women's profound meditations on distance and the nature of *jogajog* (connection) linked the biography of the border to their own biographies and kin relations. In 2014, I spent Eid in the house of a Muslim family in Boraibari, not far from where Shefali lived. As I helped in the cooking, Tahmina-chachi, the elderly mother of the family, pointed out that the *lacchha semai* (vermicelli) had been sent by the sisters of her husband, Ibrahim; they lived in Lalmonirhat, Bangladesh, and this was their custom each year. But this year's meal, she noted, tasted a bit different because she had been unable to send any fruits to her in-laws as she usually did. "Right before Eid the border became *gorom*. Those people through whom I usually send fruits from Dinhata [India] refused to risk it this year. *Ei bochhor kachhe thakte parlam na* [I couldn't stay close this year]." In the short phone call between Tahmina-chachi and her sister-in-law, exchanging greetings and prayers on Eid, she repeats this last sentence to them, apologizing for the lack of her gifts.

In her discussion of postcolonial intimacies, Sara Ahmed urges us to move beyond theories of intimacy based on geographical proximity, and to engage with intimacies "as archives of cultural and historical complexity and of the messiness that histories of mobilities inject into spaces where bodies meet." Following this approach attunes us to the sharp critiques of the naturalization of spatial concepts of distance and scale used by nation-state projects of bordering. Gendered bodies and mobilities carry with them historical traces of being "oriented" in specific ways.[15] Shefali's Bangladeshi kin explicitly spoke of her inability to be present as indexing a structural hierarchy in reciprocity. While this structural hierarchy and difference in border regimes was plain to all, how to narrate it over time was a trickier matter. Relatives in India found they either had to grieve their growing distance and denounce the Indian state to their relatives in Bangladesh, or justify changing practices of Indian border security and embrace their national identity as exclusive of their kin identity.

The nature of communication profoundly shapes whether people feel close or far in their transnational relations. International calls between India and Bangladesh cost Rs11 per minute. Tahmina-chachi's house was not close enough to the border to be in the range of Bangladeshi mobile network towers, which would allow users in India to use a Bangladeshi SIM card to make local calls to Bangladeshi numbers. Conversely, their kin on the Bangladesh side living in Lalmonirhat, which was about twelve kilometers from the border, were out of range of the Indian mobile network towers. Using this overlapping coverage is how many borderland residents on both sides can afford to bypass the expensive international calling rates and talk with regularity to their relatives and friends at the cost of local calls. Night after night I stood by a *jamrool* tree at the edge of the Rahmans' back garden, to "catch" an Indian telephonic network so I could call my mother or friends across the border. In the Kathalbari area, the belated delivery of text messages on my Bangladesh SIM would delight and distract me as soon as I came into coverage area. Whether calls can be made as local or international matters a great deal, determining how frequently relatives talk and how extensively.

As the Indian state has attempted to police all manners of transnational connection over the decades, the possession of Bangladeshi SIM cards has also come under scrutiny. Although possession of such SIM cards is not a violation of any law per se, security forces allege that the process of acquiring this Bangladeshi commodity is evidence of border-crossing and cross-border engagements. Since the BSF cite the possession of Bangladeshi SIM cards as sufficient grounds to charge individuals with being "Bangladeshi" and to detain and arrest them under the Foreigners Act, possession of the "Bangla" SIM in India has come to be perceived as a risk. Tahmina-chachi observed that over the decades, remaining connected has not only become harder but also criminalized: visiting her in-laws in person is risky and even the act of keeping Bangladeshi SIM cards to call between families is a sensitive issue.

Meanwhile, national security has brought an older infrastructure of connection to a stop in November 2013: the India-Bangladesh passport.[16] India closed a passport system that had been launched in the flush of friendship of another political historical juncture, the independence of Bangladesh from Pakistan in 1971. While the eastern border had been opened to allow the flow of people fleeing the war, this special passport and visa were reciprocally launched as a symbolic continuation of the openness of the border when it officially "closed" again—that is, resuming border control regulations at the end of the war. It could be acquired locally in the districts through the District Magistrate's office. In Cooch Behar district alone this passport had been popular to the moment of its withdrawal—948 were issued in 2010, 1,074 were issued in 2011, and 1,290 were issued in 2012.[17] A great many of the applicants were transnational kin, using this somewhat affordable opportunity to visit family. While bilateral politics strive to build smooth highways and smoother connectivity that will transport goods and people that are desirable and profitable in the eyes of the state, the BSF patrol across Shefali's route and her inability to acquire a passport and visa led to a restless anxiety about kinship and well-being that grounded geopolitics in the frictions and affects of distance.

Shefali's encounter with border security brings out another aspect of gendered bordering: the value of kinship as a moral force. In numerous interviews, BSF soldiers asserted that they were certain that residents like Shefali's sister were, in fact, crossing into Bangladesh and not simply working in their fields. Yet they expressed their sympathies for the ordeals of women who were separated from their natal kin and declared that these kinds of mobilities, while illegal, were not only permissible but needed to be judged apart from the concerns of national security. Tending to the gendered burdens of kinship, soldiers recognized that enforcing the border would be enforcing distance in these intimate ties and they confessed that they tried to use their discretionary powers to accommodate these mobilities when possible. However, this distinction clearly relied on the naturalized image of the mother or daughter, fulfilling kin duties, with the implication that no male subject could be recognized with similar concerns. Such sympathy waxes and wanes in relation to the dominant political discourse on "infiltration." With the soldier on the cycle we see this sympathy at work, making possible the reproduction of the state-enforced border and the transnational, heteropatriarchal family at the same time.

GENDERED ASYMMETRIES OF KINSHIP AND BORDER CONTROL

Stories like Shefali's and Tahmina-chachi's—of divided families and arrested routes—have become recognizable to us in the context of the subcontinent's partitioned borders through film, literature, and scholarship.[18] However, what distinctly sets apart stories like theirs is that they are about the *continued* making and maintenance of heteronormative kinship ties across transnational family networks and over changing practices of border control, rather than about rupture. Partition is not a past historical event in the Bengal borderlands; the tiny cuts of bordering continue to be changing, lived realities. Villages such as Putimari and Boraibari across the region in northern Bengal were once all part of the Cooch Behar princely state, knit together by a dense web of kinship relations and a great deal of mobility. Practically every family in this agrarian region that has come to be reconstituted as borderlands in/of India and Bangladesh has kin relations who are now on the other side of the border. Instead of viewing the endurance of transnational kinship as evidence of cultural ties that subvert or supersede the artifice of statist borders, I argue that the asymmetries of kinship and border regimes of neighboring states intersect to produce new differences and hierarchies of value within the borderland family.

It was the morning after Shahida Bibi's youngest brother's wedding in Madhupur (Bangladesh). At the groom's house, an enormous vat of steaming *khichudi* (a dish made of rice and lentils) was at hand to feed all the relatives in the winter cold. "I never imagined that you would see me here, in my father's house," said Shahida-chachi to me, as we devoured the spicy *khichudi*, washed down with sweet milky tea. "I was sure I would not come," she says, listing all the work and responsibilities she had in Kathalbari (India) and referring to the physically arduous walk across the dry sand banks of the river that is a characteristic of the landscape in the winter months. "Then I came—*shudhumatro moner taaney* [pulled only by the strings of my heart]."

By this point I had known Shahida-chachi for a few years. In the border villages of Kathalbari, she was introduced to me as a local leader and organizer of the government-aided women's self-help groups. In her late fifties, she is an activist for women's and child rights, and had been a community worker for numerous NGO projects. She was clearly embarrassed that she had been "caught" in the position of being what the government of India would classify her: an "illegal" border-crosser. She immediately noted that she knew that I had not crossed in this way. This embarrassment tempered her delight at being able to share the joy and pride of her father's home with someone "from India." It was important to her that I understood what had driven her to take such a risk, and that it *was*, in fact, a substantial risk to her. "I am always worried before I come. You know people like us have nothing to do with the BSF. I start trembling just at the thought of being stopped and questioned by them." Ashadul, her elder son, who lives in Madhupur with his wife and children, interjected impatiently. He'd been sitting quietly in the room until then, playing a game on his phone. But he'd been listening.

> I am always telling her there is nothing to be scared of. She just has to be normal and cross the BSF checkpoint and the river. Once on this side, I go to pick her up from the [unfenced] border myself. Once when I was bringing her from the border on my bike, the BGB saw and stopped us. I told them the truth and they let us go. It was no problem! We are respected in society, people know us, there is nothing to worry about.

And with that Ashadul underlined that the Bangladeshi state knew and understood kinship ties in the borderlands, especially when it concerned socially respectable people.

A few days after the wedding, Shahida-chachi sent word for me and I went over to the part of the village in which her extended family lived. "How rarely I get to show an Indian person the comforts of my father's house," she said, ushering me into her mother's bedroom where she had been staying the nights. In the few quiet moments as we settled onto the double bed, the mosquito net folded up neatly, she stroked the well-worn *kantha* and mused that there could be no greater peace of mind than sleeping by your mother's bosom and bed. Unprompted, she explained why she had come, this time, and all the other times; *moner taan (attachments of the heart)*, she repeated over and over again.

> I have given up everything here—all my other sisters [all of whom are married in villages in the greater Rangpur region] have got their share of my father's land, our betel nut orchards. My brother even sends fish to them [the ones who live close by on the Bangladeshi side] when there is a big catch from the pond. I don't want any of these. But when I hear that my father is unwell or my niece or nephew will get married, I have to come. That is my duty! . . . Do you know what breaks my heart every day? Knowing that when I die my brothers and my elder son will not be there to lay me to rest. I live in fear—suppose I get news that something has happened to my aged father and mother. What if the BSF on duty are not good? What if I am not able to *manage* and come?

Such a call to duty, expressed as pure affective attachments to one's son, father, and brother, is the driving force of Shahida Bibi's decisions to undertake "illegal" travels across the border over the years. With women largely bearing the burden of these duties toward both natal and affinal families, it is significant that they frequently distinguished this commitment from claims to property and inheritance. *Despite* having forsaken her share of her father's property, knowing that she cannot consume the fruit of the orchards or the fish in their family ponds, Shahida Bibi continues to perform and nurture her duty and attachment to her natal kin. The anthropological literature on kinship has explored its inherent ambivalences, the politics of the normative demands of kinship, often serving as sources of anxiety in the face of inability to fulfill those demands.[19] For numerous borderland residents, like Shahida Bibi and Shefali Barman, kinship obligations were not moral compulsions or undesirable burdens. Their great desire to be a part of family rituals and occasions, to perform kin roles of a daughter, brother, sister, underscored an understanding of kinship as a form of relatedness that could not be taken for granted but had to be constantly performed in order for its reciprocity and profound pleasures to bear fruit.[20] They practiced and articulated a vision of kinship that involved "long-term bonds of intergenerational reciprocity."[21] They would simply *have to* cross the border and remain mobile to realize these long-term bonds. Shahida Bibi wanted to perform her roles as much as she wanted reciprocal kin roles to be performed toward her, imagined most poignantly at times of birth and death.

For the moral force of kinship to successfully push against border security, these stakes of long-term and intergenerational duty had to be made explicit. The BSF were "good" if they could recognize and assist in this work of kinship; they were "bad"—namely, unethical—if they purposely prevented it. But who could be recognized as this acceptable border-crosser was explicitly gendered: only women had a chance of being recognized as selfless, with no economic interest. The importance of this juxtaposition between pure familial duty and economic interest in inheritance became clear to me the longer I was privy to the tensions in Shahida Bibi's transnational family. During another visit from Shahida-chachi to her son's house in Bangladesh, Ashadul seemed embarrassed that he, the son, had made his mother cross the border rather than doing it himself. He related that "earlier" he used to go to his parents' house in Kathalbari two or three times a year. "Don't you understand, I am not a boy anymore? I am a responsible grown person, also." He looked down at his tucked in shirt and jeans. "I don't look like a village laborer anymore, it is hard to sneak past the BSF." Indicating that this is a contentious matter between them, his mother whispered out of his earshot, "His sense of pride and dignity is very important now, more than the *moner taan* for his parents. He has become obstinate against coming these days."

This time, Shahida-chachi was in Bibiganj to see her newborn granddaughter. "I have to do my duty, don't I?" she said, rocking the week-old baby in the cradle of her arms. It was a Friday. Her son, Ashadul, employed in the district government's agriculture department, was at home from work, busy with prayers and meetings at their neighborhood mosque. We chatted in the kitchen of his house as Shahida-chachi finished preparing the lunchtime meal we would eat together once he returned. In addition to lentils, greens, and spiced mashed potatoes, there was a fish preparation with vegetables, an egg curry, as well as a mutton curry made in my honor. When I remarked on this elaborate menu—meat and fish were clear signs of wealth and material abundance in rural north Bengal—she pointed out that it always surprised her to find her son's family here in "Bangladesh" eating very well, often better than she did in "India."[22] "Just imagine, as a mother I am not able to live out my elder son's salaried success and status," she said woefully, staring into the bubbling mutton gravy, shaking her head in regret.

Transnational separation had the potential to threaten the social reproduction of gender and kinship roles.[23] For Shahida-chachi, being denied the fruits of her son's success was particularly upsetting; after all, the ideal life-course of a mother's journey culminates in being taken care of by her son, her elder son in particular. To partake of that kin exchange testifies to the moral uprightness of his character and upbringing to his mother's credit. His relative success as a *Bangladeshi*, in contrast to the rest of the family's material conditions in India, stood out in Shahida-chachi's descriptions, even as this success grated against the structural inequalities of border control between the two nation-states. What makes it dangerous for Ashadul (as a young male Bangladeshi Muslim) to cross the BSF, compared to Shahida-chachi (as an elderly Indian Muslim woman) to cross the BSF and BGB, is elided. Instead, the matter is settled in terms of affective attachment that flattens the imbalances of risk and humiliations of being positioned as a "desperate" Bangladeshi, a threat to Indian border security. Far from the liberal publicity of state diplomacy, assumed to be the domain where geopolitical power is staged or claimed, the "fantasy of equivalence between national sovereignties"[24] crumbles in the compared menus of Friday lunch.

A mother visiting her son, a daughter visiting her mother: the moral power of these subject positions excluded them from the infamy of illegality in broader social eyes, even though Shefali, Shahida, and Ashadul each wrestled with concerns of social status being diminished through association with the "illegal" border economy and questioning by the Indian BSF. Their fears—as well as strategies employed—indicate that there is a hierarchy of exception for "people like us" (visibly marked through, for example, dress in terms of class status), whose compulsions to undertake such border crossings are sympathetically considered by the border security forces. The tremendous discursive power of the "familial ideology" is to naturalize it,[25] make roles such as the dutiful daughter and self-sacrificing mother inevitable. With Shefali Barman, the ubiquity of these structural expectations of gendered life-cycle exchanges and performances provide a counternarrative of value—albeit within the bounds of a normative patriarchal discourse—to the legal regime of India's unilateral border control architecture, subtly critiquing its validity from such a moral standpoint. This is remarkably different from the moral discourses within which women's mobility for work, unprotected by the shared ideology of the family, is prohibitively framed, as feminist scholars of sex work and trafficking have argued.[26] The Indian state's inability to provide a measure for these legitimate needs of its citizens—to the contrary, harassing and belittling them for these needs—is perceived as heartless, in contradistinction to the Bangladeshi state, which is characterized as more humane in the form of the compassionate BGB. Transnational kinship in the borderlands daily register the frictions and affects of distance between national and regional hierarchies.

The assertive reference of Shefali's "rightful place" in "India" as a widowed daughter-in-law (in the comment made by her sister-in-law) fuses heteronormative kinship obligations with a legal national jurisdiction. It does so by way of acknowledging the unequal structural relations between India and Bangladesh in gendered terms. What they are marking is a kind of a backhanded compliment—India as progressive enough to have rights and protections for women, yet not progressive enough to allow border crossings for the reproduction of families that exceed the geo-body of the nation. Changing regimes of border control have transformed networks of relatives into national jurisdictions.

LEARNING TO LIVE AS NATIONAL NEIGHBORS

What does it mean for intimate kin to learn to live as national neighbors? In seeking to answer this question, I am drawing on the anthropological interest in the question of cohabitation alongside conflict, especially with regard to caste and religious difference.[27] I build on recent scholarship that emphasizes neighborliness as a kind of fraught proximity, consisting of "the relationships between horizontal possibilities and vertical hierarchies."[28] However, I take a different tack to trace the historical emergence of a new form of difference and hierarchy among proximate kin: that of national identity as adopted and ascribed across the borderlands. Building on Doreen Massey's notion of "power geometry,"[29] Sarah Mahler and Patricia Pessar call attention to "social location" or people's positions "within power hierarchies created through historical, political, economic, geographic, kin-based and other socially stratifying factors."[30] Transnational kinship is neither a space of refuge from the state nor a site of socio-cultural transcendence; it is a gendered geography of power, a site of stratification, thoroughly interwoven with the long, slow cuts of bordering and relations of value, hesitantly articulating itself as such.

Neighborliness is an altogether distinct register of difference through which gendered family roles and asymmetric border regimes are articulated. The Indian state's investment in an increasingly militarized border security apparatus, including more boots on the ground, durable fencing, floodlights, night vision equipment and arms, and surveillance cameras, is in stark contrast to the Bangladeshi state's material presence on their side of border security (fewer troops, no surveillance equipment, no fence). If citizen-subjects imagine their polities in contradistinction to proximate others through objects, such as the map for example, we must consider the material and affective effects of unequal sovereign powers thus displayed at their shared border. To pose the question of difference a little differently, when there are numerous continuities across the borders of national maps, how is difference learned, imagined, and recognized?

The contrasting accounts of kinship hospitality within a single transnational family surfaced one set of tensions around neighborliness. Majidul Hoque, a pharmacist in Kathalbari, is of the same generation as Shahida Bibi, but his preferences for observing transnational kin obligations could not be more different. His wife, Fatima, is from what is today a Bangladeshi family; while she was married into a family across the border, her twin sister, Mamata, married in Bibiganj. Through the 1970s and 1980s, the sisters visited each other frequently. The border was not fenced and it was poorly enforced on both sides. When the drive to documentation picked up on the Indian side, border-crossing families such as theirs tried to acquire documents for all their members in the hope that that they would safely stay mobile with these Indian identity documents. Over the course of raising young children, the two sisters managed to maintain close contact. Fatima visited during Eid and Mamata and her daughters visited Fatima and Majidul's home at other times of the year. As the *dulha bhai* (brother-in-law), Majidul has received numerous invitations from Mamata to cross the border and the BSF checkpoint and visit them. In their perception, as an Indian citizen he may be able to do that more easily than them. In his little room in the Kathalbari bazaar, stacked with medicines, he confessed that he was uncomfortable with the lawbreaking that comes with such border crossings. "It is very difficult, they always put pressure on me to visit whenever we talk on the phone. As it is, they [his niece and his sister-in-law] come *abaidya bhabe* [illegally]. Bangladeshis have more courage than us Indians, they can be *desperate*. I am afraid to take them around on my *bike*, even though they have cards."

Mamata in Bibiganj (Bangladesh) has three children. When I got to know them in 2014, her eldest daughter, Jui, had started college. With her Indian voter identity card, Jui had crossed the border numerous times through the early 2000s. Over the years, she learned to navigate the BSF checkpoints as they came up, passing through as an Indian citizen to visit her *khala* (maternal aunt) several times in Kathalbari. She had not visited for three years, however, since such crossings had become riskier. Border security practices had become stricter and even Indian borderland residents had started to police those they knew or suspected to be Bangladeshi. Across the borderlands, cooperative neighbors were turning into active patriots. Like in other places with protracted policing and surveillance, the obligations of kinship sometimes felt like burdens, under the circumstance of increased policing of "illegal immigrants" by the Indian state.[31] Families like those of Fatima and Mamata were not sure how to navigate this changing face of the border and were not sure whom to trust. One evening I was visiting Mamata's house in Bibiganj at Jui's invitation. Seated in the courtyard of their modest tin-walled house, Jui plied me with steaming cups of spiced black tea, plates of expensive fruits and cookies, and homemade savory and sweet snacks. She wanted my advice on plans for her future and that of her younger brother, who was in the final years of high school. Did I think it was worth trying to look for jobs in India? As I thanked her for the elaborate spread of snacks, Jui responded, somewhat bitterly invoking her experience of the difference in hospitality between this side and that side.

> When someone comes to our house, whoever it may be, the very least we will do, however poor we might be is to put some tea on the hearth. Biskut, fruit, *chanachur,* if we have made some *nashta* [snacks] at home, at least two or three types of things. But I have seen what you are like on that side [referring to her visits to her aunt's home on the Indian side]—they will ask if you want tea, if you should say no then that's the end. You won't even get tea. Nobody bothers with anything else. People think too highly of themselves on that side. They think that you [Bangladeshis] should be happy just to be there.

While Majidul Hoque was quick to separate differences in attitudes toward border control by deploying stereotypes about national character as "Indian" and "Bangladeshi" among his own kin, his niece Jui too read the differences she noticed in the hospitality practices among her family in the light of larger national differences and inequalities in bilateral relations. Wielding a common joke contrasting the miserly West Bengalis with the generous East Bengalis, the placement of *us* and *them* along national lines was enabled by intimate knowledge circulating in a family and affirmation of cultural difference among proximate others. Ashadul's assertion of his self-respecting and proud national identity was jostling against such prevailing stereotypes of a "desperate," lawbreaking Bangladeshi, widely articulated by BSF personnel and residents in the Indian borderlands. At what point would one cease to be an *atmiya sajan* (familial relative), and instead appear as embodying these national types? This was an unresolved source of tension in cross-border family networks; in whispers, jokes, and declined invitations, it erupted in intimate relations.

While Indian kin in Bangladesh are rarely stopped by the BGB, Bangladeshi kin find it practically impossible to visit in the other direction.[32] As we saw with Shahida Bibi and Ashadul, neither mother nor son wished to relocate, devoted as they are to the national identities with which they characterize themselves and their worlds today. The resentment they share, deeply felt among transnational kin, struggles to find expression. The toll this takes within families is not negligible and puts a further strain on the inequalities of exchange and reciprocity that are integral to kinship. The family becomes a site on which the hierarchies of national identities stick. Transnational intimacy comes to be fraught with entrenched inequalities, as the moral discourse of kinship arranges a hierarchy of gendered mobility.

Master narratives of nation and national character are woven into the weft and warp of transnational family life that bear out the bitter reality of unequal neighborly relations. This is an "existential problem" with several parallels: the struggle of "coexistence with others in situations where the 'Other' is also one's 'neighbor.'"[33] If reckoning with norms of neighborly sociality test the ethics of dignity and respect in the context of the caste hierarchy, in these borderlands recasting intimate kin and existing neighbors in normative statist terms of nationalist identity can be a profoundly alienating experience. It wounds senses of self, identity, and cultural value. Considering this experience brings together the three distinct levels across which social reproduction operates: dispersed kinship networks, regional political economy in which hierarchical and unequal national identities emerge and entrench, and a borderland social and political geography within which the neighbor is not only kin but recast as a culturally differentiated "other." Distance is not a flat numerical figure or a meta-phorical measure of intimacy within relationships; it appears in terms of material, social, and affective textures and reflects the structural imbal-ances of power along gendered and national lines.[34]

"WE HAVE BEEN HERE, THE BORDER HAPPENED"; OR, ACCIDENTALLY TRANSNATIONAL

Close attention to these tensions in transnational kinship offers insights into the fraught relationship between subjectivity and national affinities in narratives of historical change. Nation-states have been central to con-trolling and rupturing processes of movement and settlement. They seek to effectively control the power of legitimacy of historical narratives itself. As Claire Alexander, Joya Chatterji, and Annu Jalais have argued, "The movement of brides thus calls to be placed in the context of national bor-ders and practices, not just in the regulation of who can enter and stay within a country's borders, but in the broader sense of who 'belongs' and who does not."[35] Cross-border marriages, a particular aspect of transna-tional kinship, are still being brokered "as a space for transfiguration" that takes the violent lessons of history and of territorial state-making seriously.[36]

Consider Shahida Bibi: her predicament is the product of a complicated life history in which the upheavals of war, its displacements and survivals, are explicit themes, although this is not an uncommon story in the border-lands. She was born in Kathalbari (India) and was a little girl when she moved to Madhupur, then in East Pakistan, with her family when her father (still remembered in Kathalbari bazaar) exchanged his house, shop, and four acres of land in Kathalbari with the Ray family of Madhupur in 1965 in the tense lead-up to the India-Pakistan War. Less than a decade later, they all moved back to Kathalbari for nine months to wait out the bloody war of 1971, putting up at the house of her father's old friend. That is where her fate was sealed, as she sees it. After the war, her father married her to the son of the family that had sheltered them during the war. It was a way of staying connected to his beloved Kathalbari, of infusing deeper meaning into the bonds that had kept them alive in that trying year of

1971. Such family histories were ubiquitous but recalling them were always tinged with the danger of disruption, for women's unruly associations in these borderlands gesture to a future in which disobedient intimacies might push against the straitjackets of the postcolonial nation-state.

Remarkable, too, are the silences about cross-border kin and keeping contact with them in the space of everyday life in India, whether through regular phone calls or irregular visits. I could know someone for months in the Indian borderlands before I would discover his or her family connections in Bangladesh. Unless you were known to be in the same position, people on the heavily surveilled Indian side—mostly Muslim—did not feel they could trust you with these confidences, which had transformed from being commonplace facts to sensitive information. Transnational kinship and kin practices are embodied archives; their memories and silences are both "the subject and the map," as Ruba Salih writes, of intergenerational work of "compassion, connection, and sometimes solidarity."[37] As the blanks in my kinship diagrams filled out, the arcs pointed to the regional geopolitics of migration, holding and embodying histories even when they couldn't be directly or widely spoken. In each instance of genealogical mapping, between rinsing, chopping, grinding, and stirring, the seams of the family, nation, and region would burst open.

In Bangladesh my Indian Bengali identity attracted unsolicited accounts of familial connections from Muslim residents; the Hindu minority was less forthcoming, in similar fashion to their minority counterpart in India. The state is, as Janet Carsten notes, "heavily implicated in the transmission of kinship memories,"[38] and my state-imputed identity of Indian nationality interplayed with my gender, religious, and ethnolinguistic identities. It was by chance that I came upon the now transnational details of Afzal Hossain's family network. A talkative septuagenarian, he would summon me at dawn after he read his first prayers of the day when he had no one else to talk to; I was to record his life history. The Bengali postcolonial trinity of Netaji, Gandhi, and Nehru hung on his wall alongside framed award certificates received for his contributions to education. He had been a village schoolmaster, spearheading educational missions across rural north Bengal, especially among its Muslim, lower-caste, and tribal inhabitants.

One morning, Afzal-master was giving an account of the high politics of the nationalist movement through which "Hindoostan-Pakistan happened." His kindly wife brought us tea and breakfast, a distraction I seized as a break from the school textbook history lecture. "Where is your *baper bari* [natal home]?" I asked her, a question with which I often began conversations with married women of different generations, alert for patterns among/across generations. A long silence fell as the elderly couple looked at each other uncomfortably. "It's not close by," said Afzal-master, his bushy gray brows furrowed.

You won't report this, will you? Her *baper bari* [natal home] is in Bangladesh; it is my *mamar bari* [maternal uncle's family]. When we got married it had just become Hindoostan-Pakistan, you wouldn't think there was a border for many years, everything continued as usual. Even trains used to run across the bridge here as before. Then it was only around the 6 September War that everything stopped.[39] The train that went from Kathalbari was stopped in Pakistan and war broke out. Our *jawa-asha* stopped completely, too. Pakistan kept *kora* [strict] vigil at the border; you could not get past the Khan-sena. I was in a government job, our children had grown up . . . what if they called us Pakistani? . . . Then came the *ekattorer juddho* [War of 1971], *border-torder* everything disappeared. *Pil-pil kore* [in huge crowds] people came here from Pakistan. My in-laws' family came and took shelter in this house—my brothers-in-law and their families. Indira Gandhi gave them all rations in the camps! They all went back after Bangladesh became independent, but the border was open for many years. We never went that way, of course, *abaidya bhabe* [illegally].

Clearly not trusting his "unworldly" wife to narrate their family history, Afzal-master presented one to me that was carefully constructed in reference to official national historical events. He wanted to me to read "domestic life *as* political history," not its deviance [emphasis mine].[40] His narrative emphasis on the righteous observance of law—embodied in his family's relinquishing the upkeep of kin relations by not crossing to East Pakistan/ Bangladesh—was integral to his public and self-image as a good citizen, and in these times, a good Muslim. Despite being a respected and well-known community elder, he feared being reported—for being married for over fifty years now to someone who may today be labeled as "Bangladeshi."[41]

Bengal's borders remained largely porous after Partition, and uneven attempts by the state to control them were unsuccessful.[42] From mainstream media to governmental reports and scholarly analyses, this porosity has been the defining characteristic in descriptions of the India-Bangladesh border. This affective narration of history—before the "what happened" has been entirely subsumed into the "that which is said to have happened," to follow Michel-Rolph Trouillot's important semantic distinction—bears strong resemblances to the responses of divided and displaced families in the long years after Partition.[43] As Shefali is faced with a new patrol stationed along the route she had been employing, as Shahida and her sons experience the permeability of the same border very differently in relation to their respective bodies, we realize that the openness/closedness of a border is neither fixed nor singular.

It was six months after the conversation I recounted above that Afzal-master announced to me that he had applied for a passport and had to travel to Kolkata for the appointment to deposit his biometric data. He revealed that one of their daughters was married across the border and lived in Hatibandha subdivision in Lalmonirhat district. Afzal-master's life history, highly organized and full of precise details, was dotted with ellipses. It was only with the passport application that he could proudly share his plans to visit his daughter in Bangladesh, indeed even acknowledge his daughter and her family across the border.

The silences and hesitations I recorded among Indian borderland residents regarding their kinship ties across the border "are thus active"[44] as historical data, as much as the emotional words and actions shared vocally by others. As several elderly residents put it, they have not started doing anything new or different by way of marriage practices or observance of kinship relations. It is the border that happened to them and turned their lives into transnational ones. Systems such as residence and giving birth in one's *baper bari* (natal home)—routinely practiced without much interference in the form of border control in the years between 1947 and 1965 and then again from 1971 up to the late 1980s—suddenly took on new significance. For those who had records of these births in the form of birth certificates in India, a documentary practice rarely seen before the 1980s, they formed the basis for the acquisition of other documents that marked residence and eventually citizenship, like ration cards and voter cards. For those born in Bangladesh, with childhoods spent in their *nana* (house of maternal grandfather) or *mamar bari* (house of maternal uncle)—that is, spaces that figured as places of generosity and care—these experiences provided a vantage point to speak of the neighboring nation, its people and places, with intimate affective attachments.

AN ALTERNATIVE BIOGRAPHY OF THE BORDER

> *"Jeta kachhe mone hoy, sheta myala dur* [What seems near,
> is very far]."
> —Shahida Bibi, at her home in Kathalbari village, India

As I drew kinship diagrams for the transnational borderland family over generations, they marked an alternative biography: that of the border itself. Starting with its birth in 1947, the biography unfolds in fits and starts and loops. Through closures and openings, porosity and impermeability, these cuttings of distance, time, and identity belie the modernist narrative of linear temporal progression from open to porous to increasing control, now approaching stability, that we are familiar with for this border as well as porous borders more generally. People explicitly related these cuts of openness and closure, permissibility and porosity to one another: it was the absolute openness at the time of the 1971 War, which came after the experience of strict enforcement and closure of the border on the Pakistani side in the years leading up to the war of 1965, that generated an understanding of border security as unstable and capable of radical change.

Through glimpses in the accounts here, we can see that there were dense accretions of investment in cross-border ties as safety nets in times of crisis. Through marriages, among other things, cross-border kinship was validated and strengthened in times of political violence and communal tension. The view from within these transnational kinship networks suggests that closure and a negotiated porosity exist simultaneously in single temporal periods, becoming visible in relation to one's perceptible social position, as marked by religion, gender, and class and refracted through the hierarchies of regional geopolitics. Residents with several-generations-old ties remain hopeful even as young men and women are frustrated by the hierarchical relations of value within which they find themselves embedded in their respective national borderlands. Cross-border marriages reoccur across generations *despite* the border, not because of a lack of awareness of it. "Generating relations amid multiple erasures, then, entail attending to these inheritances."[45] Shahida-chachi's reflection on the fraught nature of transnational intimacy point to this mutual ground of knowing and unknowing across generations, into which I too was pulled. I can't claim these kinship maps are complete or that making them legible supersedes the devaluations of bordering.

Taking seriously the spatial and historiographical practices employed by borderland residents makes visible a world made by transnational intimacy. Its values derive from the pressures inherent in kinship, an unequal pair of border regimes that demand performances of citizenship, especially of religious minorities, the discourses of national identity and neighborliness that seep into familial tensions. Bringing a transnational feminist lens to the study of bordering shows us how borders are not only processual and dynamic but also materialize via classed, gendered, and heteronormative logics within existing familial structures. Using relative intimacies to enter this field, we see that the borderland family is one site where gender and sexuality align in a particular way to give form to the world that bordering makes. Thinking through such intimacies gives us a way to locate the political economy of gendered mobilities in relation to one another, and to trace their connections at each scale, from the body to the national, through the household and the transnational. From hidden SIM cards to hidden daughters, in that story lies a different kind of biography of this border and its mediation of value in what should be near and what is far. How does one live, associate with, and narrate transnational intimacies *and* hierarchies that are deeply shaped by and continuously produce national distinctions? The next chapter continues to tell that story, turning to the fragmented mobilities of agrarian commodities.

4 Agrarian Commodities and the National Economy

Early on in my fieldwork, as I sought to understand the political economy of agrarian Lalmonirhat and Kurigram through the basic categories of landholding and crop cycles, Rafiq-mama forlornly explained: *"Amar simanta-ghnesha jomi, kono dam nei."* His land in Madhupur (Bangladesh), "pushed up against the border," was "worthless," prone to flooding and erosion in this riparian region. Despite the intense pressure on land in Bangladesh, such land had significantly less value than plots that were just a bit further "inside." Selling his land would fetch him little capital. Cultivating this land wouldn't be too profitable either, with the high costs of agrarian labor and resource-intensive cash crops like tobacco, corn, and potatoes. Mid-sized landowners like him leased out their land with sharecropping arrangements to cultivate rice, which ensured an annual supply of grain for household consumption as well as a fair amount to sell for cash. As I lived across the districts of Cooch Behar, Lalmonirhat, and Kurigram, the floodplains between the Teesta and Brahmaputra rivers, I noticed that border-lying plots on both the Indian and Bangladeshi sides would often lie fallow for one or two seasons each year. In a region that has recently intensified farming to three crop cycles annually (up from one, historically), with improved irrigation and genetically modified

12. Rafiq-mama inspecting his border-lying land in Madhupur village, Bangladesh, cultivated by sharecroppers.

seeds, this was a noticeable outlier.[1] Landowners claimed that it is better to leave land fallow than negotiate the multiple kinds of costs that come with farming land that is the target of border security, as described in previous chapters. Across the agrarian borderlands of northern Bengal, farmers pointed out that fertile land lay wasted, quite literally.

Krishi-kaaj (agrarian labor) in the borderlands has little *daam* (value, profit). The militarization of border control on the Indian side has driven land prices down on both sides of the border. Land most plainly foregrounds the question of value. Starting from this profoundly altered relationship, we can begin to touch some other skeins of agrarian and borderland political economy that unravel over space and time. While the increasing militarization of the border devalues border-lying land directly, and farm work more broadly, exacerbating the agrarian distress writ large across the region, farmers living with these conditions have nevertheless developed ways to attempt to leverage bordering into a resource for their own "marginal gains."[2] This chapter explores valuations and devaluations of bordering as rooted in agrarian political economy of land and commodity chains.

DAAM, ORTHO, CHAHIDA: DISTINCTIONS AS VARIETIES OF VALUE

Across northern Bengal, borderlands are agrarian production spaces, where people cultivate attachments to soil and home generated in regional political economic arrangements and through circulations of labor and commerce over extended periods of time. From this locus, I move away from thinking about borderlands as spaces of transit, marginal and disorderly areas, or as exceptional sites of contested sovereignty, including that of regulation.[3] Instead, this chapter dwells on ways in which urgent questions of contemporary agrarian distress, shared across much of South Asia, constitute borderland concerns (see also chapter 5). Peasant households on both sides of the border negotiate shared agrarian distress made more acute with the differentiated costs imposed by border security and surveillance. At the heart of these borderland concerns is how to make life meaningful, respectable, and viable amid a series of devaluations. The cuts of bordering accrue and make agrarian cultivation and commodity flows especially fragmented: what crops you can grow, how often you can access your border-lying fields, or the fluctuating rates of daily-waged labor which are hitched not only to the nationally determined minimum wage but also to local availability, where *local* is defined by a transnationally inflected supply/rate.

I deploy the historical anthropological method of *following the thing*, developed as a radical intervention in the economic anthropology of commodities in the 1980s. Breaking the static thingness of commodities, it is by following the "trajectory" of a thing that we get a window into the heterogeneous relationships that objects bring into being—that is, their "social lives."[4] Igor Kopytoff's notion of "cultural biography" has enabled scholars to conceptualize the multiple registers of value through which objects can travel, and the politics of commodity status itself.[5] I adopt this "things-in-motion" approach to ask questions about how and with what kinds of value agrarian commodities circulate across the agrarian borderlands of northern Bengal through the multiple distinctions of legality, nationality, locality, and under the constraints of border security. Doing so focuses our attention on the relationship between agrarian flows and varieties of value and how they constitute one another in the borderlands. I follow Priti Ramamurthy in refracting this method through a "feminist commodity chain lens," to track particularly how "gender and sexual ideologies structure relations and code value that is created, extracted, and distributed in commodity circuits" to transnationally accomplish the social reproduction and naturalization of national communities.[6]

Let us consider tobacco and ganja together. Respite and joy. Risky and riskier. Both crops with value in the leaf, born of tender care of every single plant. Tobacco is grown as a historical legacy of the Cooch Behar princely state and its embeddedness in early twentieth century global capital and trade. Ganja is a contemporary, perhaps fleeting, product of regional political economy, highly local and exclusively transnational. Tobacco takes over the landscape materially and visually for at least two or three months of the year. Its leaves are hung out to dry on rafters inside homes, on bare fields, and along village paths in between. Ganja may grow above the ground, but its presence is carefully shielded, sometimes by bamboo fences, grown in courtyards inside Hindu homes, or in back gardens where only trusted neighbors can see. Tobacco is an export of great local pride. Ganja is also a homegrown export, but it can be shameful for grower, trader, and consumer. Tobacco involves the whole family. When leaves are ready to harvest, children stay home from school to help in the plucking. Everyone gathers to put the leaves out to dry. Once dried, everyone sits together to arrange leaves into bundles. The household's fate depends on these stacks. Ganja disappears from the plant to tightly packed bundles hidden under the bed, behind sacks of rice and corn. It does not feature in household talk and only lurks in the margins of household budgets. A good sell is a bonus, the notes of cash tucked away, but a failure cannot be marked even in complaints.[7]

At first glance, bringing agrarian and borderland questions together exposes heterogeneous and even contradictory realities. The movement of people and goods, largely unauthorized by the state and thus cutting state regimes of border controls, is premised on the maintenance of national economies. Even though global economic flows, or "the licit life of capitalism" as Hannah Appel pointedly calls it, are rife with arbitrary and unaccounted transactions, smuggling is categorized as a sinister activity wholly apart in moral, social, economic, and legal terms.[8] Clandestine mobility, especially that of goods, has been analyzed as evidence of the transnational subversion of borders and of the strength of moral economies of borderlands. A robust body of anthropological work has sought to explain such activities in terms of local moral economies and cultural politics, looking to loosen the hold of statist conceptions of law and economy that criminalize the economic activities of often already marginalized peoples.[9]

While this true and invaluable—as the examples in this chapter also make clear—letting our analysis stop at this point leaves statist and national frames fundamentally unshaken. What states consider legal and what is socially licit is an important distinction, but it remains not only a defensive one—seeking to explain local moral economies in cultural terms—but also one hitched to a statist binary between legal and illegal. This line of analysis pays little attention to the boundary-drawing work of separation and distinction that occurs through the social lives of borderland commodity chains. That which illicit economic mobilities trouble— the national economy—itself escapes attention or explanation. Rather than thinking of *du-nombori* activities exclusively through the lens of moral economy, I suggest we think of the question of classification itself as a moral question of valuation and devaluation. What is this order of the national economy and from what forms of valuation and distinction does it derive? How do people know and understand *the* national economy?[10] Of what does the *national* economy consist? What are the different kinds of value, of which the law is merely one register, through which agrarian commodities travel, as they are considered in national security and economic frameworks?

In working through the answers to these questions over the rest of this chapter, I bring a feminist commodity chain approach to the study of regional political economy in the borderlands. The realm of the "national" is not disputed in these borderlands. On the contrary, the everyday transnational frame of reference, invoked by farmers and traders and discussed in peasant households, so clearly brings into view the ways in which hierarchies of value produced by bordering rely on and produce, rather than supersede, distinctions of the national. Nonetheless, such distinctions aren't simply there. They are made. As Anna Tsing argues, scale is "not just a neutral frame for viewing the world; scale must be brought into being: proposed, practiced, and evaded, as well as taken for granted."[11] Farmers, traders, border guards, and the police are busily engaged in thinking and performing these abstractions of the national, even when it is by taking it for granted.

Agrarian commodity chains, as we know from the classic work of Sidney Mintz and Tsing's more recent explorations, are particularly revealing as they embody transnational hierarchies and histories of colonialism and capitalism at every point and scale, as they rely on and produce value across a range of distinct registers. By setting the distinction of the border—in this national currency, market, economy; *here* not *there*— against these other distinctions, we see how value works across these registers. Borders and borderlands have been privileged sites for the study of economic regulation by states and the range of different actors that have claimed the right to regulate and thrive in the interstices of state regulation. "*The economy*," Appel writes, "is arguably the most privileged and political object of our unevenly shared modernity. Part of this privilege comes from the seriality of national economies, their comparability from one place to another *as if the same*."[12] Taking a similar ethnographic approach, I critically examine the naturalized container thinking invoked at any mention of *a national economy*. This fundamental distinction—one national economy from another—is necessary for comparability and requires processes of socio-cultural signification to appear natural and eternal. A series of related distinctions follow: simple identifications of here-not-there produce *relational* hierarchies of value in emplacing markets, quality, currencies. Nowhere are these processes more acutely on display than in borderlands, where the naturalness can be called into question because the highly tenuous work of producing these separations and distinctions is visible as an ethnographic object.

TOBACCO TRAILS

I followed Amal Barman at a brisk pace back to his house in Putimari (India), to begin a day of sowing *jati* tobacco (*Nicotiana rustica*). It was the 2014 *rabi* season and Amal-da had reserved his best plot of land for growing *jati*. Tobacco needed dry land that was not low-lying, as water collecting in the field was highly detrimental to the plant. Wanting to follow the crop from the field and in its journey through markets across the borderlands of northern Bengal,[13] I had volunteered to help with Amal-da's *chash* (both the verb, to cultivate, and the product, the crop) in the 2014 season. In between preparing the furrows in which the saplings would be planted and squatting gingerly to settle each sapling in, I chatted with Amal-da, his wife (and my good friend) Shyamoli-di, and their two sons. Both sons had been summoned from their migrant jobs in north India for this month of sowing to minimize the cost of labor. They were grumpy and working reluctantly, frequently scolded by Amal-da for being as inefficient and clumsy as me.

Amal-da sketched out the whole process for the farmer, explaining that he had chosen *jati* instead of *motihari* tobacco to cultivate this year because of the demand for *jati* by Bangladeshi traders in the previous year. "*Jobordast chahida chhilo* [the demand was strong]," he recalled, standing up and tipping his head to the side in emphasis. Running through the arithmetic of costs—which on the Indian side included the monetary, psychological, and labor costs of securing permission from the Border Security Force (BSF) for transportation—he confirmed that the Bangladeshi rate was profitable compared to what was being offered by traders in Dinhata, India. "Quite a good profit," he concluded, his words nudging last year's marginal gains into hope for this year.[14] This was the arithmetic of the agrarian economy in the borderlands: always already transnational. To farmers, additions on one side versus on the other represented the differences of two national markets, currencies, and the vagaries of border security taken together. Timothy Mitchell has argued that the idea of the national economy as "a system whose limits corresponded to geopolitical boundaries" was introduced as "a common-sense construct" by the state.[15] While he and others have richly showed how the "rule of experts" go about fixing this discursive object called the economy, equating it geopolitically to the *national* economy, in Amal-da's calculations we can glimpse how this "commonsense construct" is spatial-ized, made concrete and compelling in the everyday economic calculus of farmers across the borderlands.

I stopped short in my tracks with his words. Amal-da—by his own and all other accounts—was an upright if not overly nervous man. He had no *du-nombori* dealings and his wife and neighbors joked that they were doomed to eternal poverty, for Amal-da's fearful heart would turn away easy cash even if it came knocking on their door. When cattle smuggling was still at its peak, in the 2010–15 period, he was one of the few house-holders who refused to shelter cattle at his house, even for a single night, in exchange for cash payments.[16] Yet here he was hedging his agrarian bets on the gains from a transnational commodity chain that was *du-nombori*, in a matter-of-fact manner. His tobacco would have to be smuggled, in statist terms, across to Bangladeshi traders; his own payment would then come via *du-nombori* currency exchange channels. Over the years, I observed that he was not alone in his refusal to refer to the movement of tobacco in either direction as *du-nombori*. Nobody involved across the entire chain, whether farmer, middleman buyer/seller, or trader, Hindu or Muslim, described it as such. Rather than resort to the anthropological route of glossing *du-nombori* as contraband (and explaining contraband in terms of moral economy alone), I stay with Amal-da's shifting calcula-tions to understand what relations of value are encoded. Indeed, contrary to a presumed binary between agrarian and illicit economies in border-lands, there is a complex entanglement between the two, a framework that encompasses the virtuous and the illicit, the agrarian and the border econ-omies not as schematic opposites but comfortably coexisting.

From mid-April onward, the warehouse-lined stretches of Rangpur Road reek of tobacco. I had gone up and down this road at other times of the year without realizing what the rusty doors of the inscrutable tin structures concealed. Then, in the first full year I lived in north Bengal, this stretch of road—from Dinhata, India, toward the border villages, and in Bangladesh from the border villages toward Lalmonirhat—came alive. Vans and carts of various sizes could be seen crawling slowly toward Dinhata from all the nearby villages, busily loading and unloading their precious cargo from point to point. Sort, pack, load, unload, arrange. And then a throoooooow of a bundle from one stack to another. The stacks build up, reaching seven to ten feet high.

The same rhythm of urgency and reek of tobacco followed me from Dinhata and its surrounding bazaars to the Bibiganj *haat* farther south, famed since the colonial inception of the trade in princely Cooch Behar as a *jati* port.[17] As I entered, the hectic activity on the main street of the tobacco bazaar made it easy to forget that it was but five o'clock on a Sunday morning. The sounds and smells were overwhelming; tobacco farmers lined both sides of the road with their bundles laid out. The voices of farmers and buyers, traders and stockists steadily rose, energetically negotiating rates, while onlookers animatedly discussed the day's prices and deals. Buyers, having evaluated and snagged bundles of their choice before rival buyers outbid them, shouted franticly at their workers to load them onto vehicles. These ranged from cycle rickshaws to enormous trucks, depending on the quantity and destination (fig. 13). The two different varieties of tobacco historically grown and traded across this region—*jati* and *motihari* in Bengali—are sorted according to the kinds of buyers and routes of travel expected. The *haat* is almost exclusively a male space; all the labor of women and children drops out of view even as the entire household's capacity for labor is devoted to tending the tobacco harvest. The household and the *haat* produce value in this commodity.

On one of my first mornings at the Bibiganj *haat*, I parked myself next to the *haat-master* and his wooden desk. The pace was frenetic, the air was heady. Farmers must record here the details of what they are "putting up" for sale, while buyers record their purchases. Naturally, this is a hub of activity. Traders gather to share a smoke, discuss rates, and pass judgments on bundles displayed. Although there is an appearance of mere socializing, these discussions were vital to the value transformations, including the composition of price, taking place at this node of the commodity chain. The *haat-master* deftly kept up with his record-keeping and

13. Sorting bundles of tobacco onto different vehicles bound for different destinations at the Bibiganj tobacco *haat*, northern Bangladesh.

accounting, the gossip and smoke swirling about him, all the while making sure my cup of tea was never empty. As Mekhala Krishnamurthy has shown with grain heaps and Sarah Besky with tea leaves, buyers and sellers at these *haats* fold the production of quality into the measures of quantity.[18] In these borderland *haats* in Bangladesh, the quantities as well as quality of *jati* and *motihari* tobacco are layered quite literally with bundles from India.

In Bibiganj (Bangladesh) I accompanied Tofail Ali, a distant cousin of Rafiq-mama's, to the *haat*. He was a third-generation tobacco trader and a former *haat-master*. To my surprise I would find Bengali Muslim traders naming Marwari Hindu tobacco traders in Dinhata and surrounding markets in India and listing the rates being offered there. Careful distinctions of the quality and costs of different grades of tobacco were being made with references to place names that mark a transnational geography of tobacco trails across not only the India-Bangladesh border but also "jumping scale" into Southeast Asia.[19] Once I started following the discussions I realized that traders—most of whom were third- or fourth-generation—were discussing their deals between Dinhata (India) and Bibiganj (Bangladesh). Despite the official closure of trading routes and networks to the north into India, the other parts of the colonial trading routes and networks continue, extending southeast from this Rangpur division to Sylhet and through Chittagong to Myanmar.

Though dramatically reduced in volume compared to the decades prior to Partition, these clandestine deals that ensure the flow of tobacco across the Bangladesh-India border continue to be struck among trading families that have been dealing with each other for generations, since the rooting of tobacco in this region in the early twentieth century. Even as such deals continue between the generationally-associated traders, the families of Marwari Hindus had migrated away from Madhupur, Bibiganj, and the greater Rangpur region to the Indian side in the 1950s and early 1960s, while several Bengali Muslim families had relocated to the East Pakistan/Bangladesh villages. These intergenerational trading ties that persist despite demographic changes and migrations remind us of the extent to which mobility both connects and severs in the making of frontiers and markets.[20] Postcolonial bordering sets off processes of reshaping geographies of commerce, cultivation, and markets, not wholly unlike colonial interventions.[21]

Traders in Bibiganj actively discussed the prices and possibilities of bundles coming from "India," what they estimated those might cost, and who would supply them how much, incorporating them into their calculations. Amal-da's expected yield of six *maunds* from his *bigha* of *jati* tobacco would be a small part of these bundles. You had to be in the know to follow these references. I wasn't, so these were cryptic to me. All the more intriguing since place names that I recognized kept popping up in conversation.

"Can you explain to me what's going on?" I asked one morning.

"Ke kar shonge kena becha korchhe, tumi jene ki korbe? Ei to dekho na, chokher shamnei dekhte pachho tamak haat kemon choley. [What is it to you to know all that much about who trades with who? Look here, right in front of your eyes, how the tobacco *haat* works.]" Tofail Ali was gentle but guarded. Some of the connections that were obscured at the *haat* emerged in patches of family histories of marriage and migration in the homes of

these traders, stitched together in exuberant and wistful kinship recollections by wives and mothers (chapter 3 and 6).[22]

Traders' comparisons of the Indian and Bangladeshi tobacco markets suggests that the national economy does not entirely precede the agrarian commodity chain, whose unauthorized movement across national borders is illegal. Rather, "the commodity's circulation *made* the [national] economy" and its hierarchies of value possible.[23] Historians of colonial and anticolonial nationalism have argued that the conception of "the economy" acquired a spatial referent only in the late nineteenth century. What's more, the invocation of the history behind this geography of transnational trade suggests that the imagination of and traffic across these national markets coexists with multiple sensibilities of economic life.[24] In the late nineteenth century, the largest acreage of tobacco in colonial India was in Bengal province, followed by Bombay and Madras. In Bengal, the primary tracts for producing export-quality tobacco were Rangpur, Cooch Behar, and Tirhut.[25] A glance at the life and family business histories of these tobacco traders, whether Bengali Muslim or Marwari Hindu, make apparent the interconnections of mobility, trade, agrarian environments, and the cuts of border and nation-state formation. For instance, in Bibiganj, Tofail Ali, the oldest of eight brothers in a third-generation tobacco-trading family, recalled the changes he has seen in his own lifetime, from Pakistan times to the present. His father's business had been heavily invested in buying *jati* tobacco and sending it to Tinsukia in Assam of colonial India, a supply chain facilitated by the rail line that previously connected these *haats* across rivers and jurisdictional boundaries. With Partition, this business stopped abruptly.

The government of Pakistan viewed sending any commodity across the new border on what had been its regular commercial route (up until then) as economic treason.[26] Tofail Ali, his brothers, and other tobacco merchants of Bibiganj, now in their fifties and sixties, reminisced about the turbulent times in the 1960s when the Urdu-speaking police and border security force (then called the East Pakistan Rifles) of the government of Pakistan stationed in the border areas would not even accept any bribes and took harsh action against those found "smuggling national wealth" across to India.[27] Like *swadeshi*, the movement for home-produced goods, for anticolonial nationalists, commodity nationalism for the new postco-

14. Piling quality and quantity in a tobacco warehouse, Dinhata, India.

lonial states played a vital role in producing national territorial and economic space in concrete terms.[28]

The reminiscences of Bengali Muslim traders in northern Bangladesh
and Marwari traders in northern West Bengal echoed and overlaid each
other through my recursive conversations with them, as I traced their networks through the tobacco trading seasons of 2014 and 2015. The
enforcement of the border through the decades has not only geopolitically
severed but also literally ruined the road and rail infrastructures by
which the growers and markets across the region were connected (see
chapter 1). More recently, the advent of multinational company-con-
tracted cultivation of Virginia tobacco in northern Bangladesh has dealt a
blow to tobacco cultivation on that side of the border; on the Indian side,
acreage has remained quite steady.[29]

In their Dinhata trading office, the Agarwal brothers, fourth-
generation Marwari tobacco traders, claimed to know nothing about border-crossing tobacco, insisting that they did not solicit any supply from
Bangladesh. "We used to deal with them before— in British times—in fact,
in Pakistan times a part of our family used to still live in the Rangpur area.
But now we do business within India alone." And as if to redirect my attention, the older Mr. Agarwal began to list all the routes on which he sup-
plied tobacco from Dinhata. East, south, and southwest, *in India alone.*
Just as in Bibiganj, they boasted of their immense expertise in evaluating
and identifying the type, quality, and grade of tobacco leaves as evidence
of their position as a leading family in the tobacco business. They reclined
on the starched, white mattresses of their office, beneath the whirring of
old fans and the garlanded portraits of male ancestors, with burning
incense sticks sticking out from the edges of the heavy frames. The
Agarwal brothers basked in the accumulated and inherited wealth of a
colonial commodity chain.

The cavernous warehouses where they stocked tobacco and jute (fig.
14) were adjacent to this outer room. They insisted that they could tell
exactly where a leaf had been grown simply by touching and smelling it:
whether Bibiganj (Bangladesh) or Sitai (India), Kathalbari (India) or
Kaliganj (Bangladesh), they grew up with this geography of leaves and
markets.[30] On one occasion, the brothers instructed one of their staff to
bring out the samples to me. Holding them in their hands, they delighted

in flicking each leaf, caressing its texture, inviting me to soak in the smell. The shape of the leaf, its weight on the palm, the pattern of the veins, the aroma: these were all clues, they emphasized, to the source of the leaf and its value in the market. My incomprehension was so clear while their fingers and noses sorted distinctions. These mirrored exactly the "embodied expertise"[31] of evaluation that Bengali Muslim counterparts in Lalmonirhat also demonstrate. Although not tied to the soil as farmers are, each of these traders measured their own value, competence, and related socio-economic worth in the transnational tobacco trade in terms of their sensorial intimacy with the tobacco leaves and repertoires of knowledge regarding its treatment and curing.

These multiple and sensorial temporalities matter. In borderland tobacco *haats,* history is invoked as an alibi—"we have always been doing this"—against accusations of threatening national security and economy. But this is neither an unknowing nor a subversive breach of the national economy. For traders, the invocation of history is paradoxically the grounds to claim and perform expertise in determining the hierarchies of the national economic present: no one can better spot the differences in value of place-based *motihari* and *jati* varieties, now recast as "Indian" or "Bangladeshi" varieties, than those who have been handling these leaves for generations. While people try to sneak the bundles of tobacco past border security in both directions, traders ensure that they are spotted and evaluated according to their differences of quality, in terms of national currencies and markets, when they appear at *haats*. Such mediations allow the value—reflected at this point in terms of wholesale prices—to be momentarily stabilized and to vouch for the *distinctions* of the commodity: a leaf quality tied to place and simultaneously to a particular Bangladeshi *jati* or *motihari* season. Their work makes the value and visibility of commodities in national economic terms possible.

This range of distinct actors—from Amal-da to the Alis and the Agarwals—who deploy their embodied expertise daily to calculate profits and losses based on relational hierarchies of national distinctions points us also to a hitherto unacknowledged realm of economic performativity. Ethnographers have demonstrated that a range of socio-technical practices—GDPs, budgets, currencies, interests—have come to naturalize the national economy as a standard and modular form in a global context.[32]

Making each iteration comparable across the world rendered a colonial capitalist geography of extraction and underdevelopment into a neutral fact of unequal economies and their nation-states.[33] Here it is not the "rule of experts" but rather actors in the margins of the state—quite literally in the borderlands—who enact and produce the scale, space, and relations of the national rather than either being oblivious of it or resistant to it (in purely moral economic terms) through their work in transnational agrarian flows.[34]

Borderland and agrarian structures intersect to keep largely intact the hierarchical social relations that materialize through this commodity chain. Throughout these processes, encounters between the different kinds of actors and the commodities that circulate along a commodity chain "sort" one another out.[35] Gender and class intersect at each step to determine the value of labor and skill in the making of the commodity. Women and children whose labors are vital to the care and harvest of crop are sorted out of its market life and economic evaluations. Traders' engagement with tobacco—as they encounter a range of actors from farmers, small buyers, and middlemen to state civil and military authorities—sort them apart from all others, maintaining and reproducing their influential social status. In other words, the hereditary expertise that anchors the position of traders at the top of the capitalist stratification in this commodity chain remains secure through the cuts of postcolonial bordering.

Disaggregating the different actors and labors in these locally transnational tobacco flows thus reveals variations in value being produced, enacted, and embodied. In a region that used to be a major colonial hub for transregional commerce in tobacco, the enforcement of the India-Bangladesh border has severed tobacco growers from traders, production areas from markets. Despite the increasing militarization of the border and criminalization of cross-border movements, influential tobacco traders continue this now contraband commercial trade, albeit greatly reduced in volume, in both directions, with little damage to their social standing. For the upper-caste Marwaris on the Indian side, separating themselves from the middlemen and smaller traders (lower-caste and Muslim) who buy the tobacco from farmers (also lower-caste and Muslim) and then sell the stock to the Marwaris—sometimes even commissioned by them in advance—is what enables them to maintain this distance and ignorance about the "Bangladeshi" tobacco that may be a part of their own stacks.

On one occasion, I watched my friend Kader, a young Muslim man, estimate his purchases of tobacco from farmers across the Indian borderlands to sell to a couple of Marwari traders. A contractual bank worker by day and tobacco *paikar* (stockist) by night in Kathalbari, he took a break from his calculations to observe that this was perhaps one of the biggest changes in the tobacco trade in Cooch Behar. Kader is a third-generation small-scale tobacco trader, in addition to cultivating tobacco on ten bighas of family land; he had grown up going to the tobacco *haats* with his father every year. He recalls: "Earlier Marwaris would come and if they decided they would buy up the whole *haat!* They would take a look at the bundles and talk a little bit about the price—there were no phones in those days, so they had to come to the *haat* to talk to the farmers and stockists. They still go to the *haat* but we do most of their buying."

Kader—and others like him—do not view their cross-border business in tobacco as *du-nombori* or objectionable; this is a far cry from the outright morally condemnable businesses in cattle and various narcotics. The Marwaris, now located in India as law-abiding Indian citizens, have clearly shared their monopoly over evaluation—literally judging the quality and setting the price—as the price to pay to conveniently distance themselves from Bangladeshi suppliers, even as their trade and its hierarchies of value remain entwined with older transnational networks. This consolidates the bargaining position of numerous farmer-traders like Kader with the bigger traders on both sides, who need their brokerage to connect the supply-and-demand dots in the transnational tobacco trade. His socio-economic value as an indispensable link in the chain between farmers and traders and the inherent ambiguities in the trade means that there is no suspicion from the state authorities or other borderland residents in relation to this agrarian commodity. Tobacco's continued mobility as contraband does not undermine the national; rather, it solidifies the differences and hierarchies in value across the national.

GANJA IN THE GARDEN

In a meeting early on in my fieldwork with an Indian bureaucrat who had served in Cooch Behar district during the 1990s, I was quizzed about my observations on cows, bicycles, and ganja. When he saw how puzzled I looked about cycles and ganja and reluctant to talk about cattle smuggling, the meeting ended abruptly. He pronounced that I was not researching the "real things." Cooch Behar district allegedly held the dubious distinction of the highest bicycle sales in the state, all thanks to its flourishing cross-border economy. But in the northern Bengal borderlands, ganja was the boom crop at the turn of the twenty-first century.

Ganja is grown profitably on the Indian side exclusively for Bangladesh, as an unofficial export commodity.[36] When I first asked Malati-di, with whom I lived in Kathalbari, about ganja cultivation and trade across the border, she screwed up her nose and thought hard. "Some people do grow it, they say they need it for *pujo* [ritual worship]. . . . And then there is Ramesh, apparently, he has a big ganja business. . . . Other than that, where is ganja?" Her words came slowly, keeping pace with her thoughts, and turning the question back to me. Once she and I actively started looking for the cannabis plant on our walks to and from visits in border villages, we realized just how ubiquitous it was: inside the courtyards and back gardens of Rajbangsi homes, hedging narrow footpaths between Hindu neighborhoods: a plant here, a cluster there.

Now you may wonder why it is not grown in Bangladesh if it is mainly for consumers in Bangladesh. Intoxication of any kind is considered *haram* in Islam. In the Bengali Muslim religious morality that predominates in Bangladeshi society, growing ganja is socially inconceivable, even if the consumption of intoxicants has been steadily on the rise. This, however, has not always been the case. It is a sharp break from the colonial cultivation of ganja in the Bengal districts of Rajshahi, Bogra, and Naogaon, in what is now northern Bangladesh, by Hindu and Muslim peasantry alike.[37] On the Indian side, Hindu Rajbangsis, especially older generations, smoke ganja in their homes, characterizing it as akin to consuming various forms of chewing tobacco: it relieves the exhaustion and aids in the completion of hard agrarian toil. Indeed, elderly tobacco traders would remind me that *motihari* is grown for consumption as chewing tobacco in various forms, its demand first consolidated with a class of tea plantation workers in colonial times. With these comparisons, the cultivation and consumption of ganja *locally* within north Bengal as a regional entity is cast in terms of continuity with colonial practice.[38] Meanwhile the cultivation of ganja for sale to Bangladesh—in this current "export" avatar, as farmers joked—was explicitly articulated as a response to the postcolonial border's offering of a differentiated market and the devaluation of agrarian land.

I learned the most about ganja cultivation from Nirash Barman. My friend Shefali Barman and I were visiting her sister one morning in another border village to the east of Kathalbari. As we walked the narrow dirt path to their home, the plot of land adjacent to the homestead caught my eye because of the uncharacteristic bamboo fence that ringed it, making it difficult to look in, yet arresting attention to itself at once. Shefali and I tiptoed to peep over the fence and saw rows of lush cannabis plants, taller than us. Shefali flashed a smile, lowered her voice, and whispered with unmistakable pride: "It's my brother-in-law, he's very good at *ganja chash*, grows quite a lot of it, and then sends it to Bangladesh." Shefali and her sister were from a family that lived in a neighboring village in Bangladesh; Nirash Barman, as the *jamai* (son-in-law), was well connected. Later that afternoon, as the weight of a *polao-mangsho* meal settled us all into a comfortable stupor, Shefali persuaded him to tell me all about it. For research purposes, of course.

"Like tobacco, ganja has *onek rokom dhoron ar daam* [varieties of value] too," Nirash-da began, outlining the complex processes through which the care and cultivation of the plant had to proceed in order to secure valuable rates for the final yields. Rates, like for tobacco, varied greatly depending on the quality or grade. *"Chahida borabor achhe, tobe shobsomoy supply nai,"* he said: Precision, skill, and timing were vital to achieve these different qualities and to produce the supply for the "desire/market that was always there."

He had taken to growing ganja about eight years ago, when the BSF forbade the cultivation of jute in all the land that lay between the fence and the "zero line" and even in some of the plots of land adjoining the fence.[39] Nirash-da, a marginal farmer, was one of many affected by this entirely unlawful ban and needed to compensate for the damage to his annual income. "Half a *bigha* of land of mine lies fallow down there," he said, referring to the low-lying plot that was fenced out. "What else to do, I take a *chance* on ganja," as he described the skill-intensive and highly uncertain process of its cultivation. Crop booms, Derek Hall argues, provide insight about how small and marginal farmers reshape land uses and claims by bringing different orders of control to bear upon land.[40] Here in Cooch Behar, households redistributed their investments and risks across the land at their disposal as they were forced by border security to reimagine the very definition of land availability and value.

Like with tobacco, the farmer had to cultivate the desirability of the ganja plant, and had to inhere it with value; then value would be produced in the resultant commodity for the trader.

> Ganja plants start budding in Ashwin–Kartik months [September–November], this is when you can tell if it is male or female. These buds are everything; so you have to keep a watch on them. Once they mature and start drying in Aghryan–Poush [December–January], then you have to pluck them. Before that you have to trim the branches carefully to protect the buds—they should get enough light but not be burned. You have to watch over them every day! You also have to spray [pesticides] and give a small amount of *potash* [potassium fertilizer]. By Magh [February] you must cut the buds or else your plant will get spoiled, then it is all over. After we have cut it, we press it carefully and dry and pack it through Magh–Phalgun [mid-March].

Giving me a veritable demonstration as he spoke, Nirash Barman gestured to show how the buds are pressed between his palms, to be curled and compressed before being tightly wrapped to dry. His narration of the seasonal cycle of ganja cultivation closely resembled Amal-da's narration of tobacco cultivation, replete with references to pesticides and manure. Indeed, both men were similar in another respect: they were thorough teachers, insisting that I write down every detail, leaving nothing to my urbane eye and imagination. Over the course of this and several conversations that followed, Nirash-da explicitly drew out comparisons with tobacco. If its range of possible quality and requirements of skillful care were comparable to tobacco, its acute time sensitivity was unlike the other crops commonly grown in the area—namely, rice, jute, and potato. "If you leave your ripened rice or ready jute in the fields for a few extra days while you gathered the necessary labor to harvest it, no harm would come of it. But when it comes to ganja, this won't do. It's *khamkheyali* (moody)," said Nirash-da with an indulgent smile, as though speaking of an unruly but beloved child or cat. Typically, a healthy ganja plant, growing to six feet, yields about one kilogram of salable goods. And even that kilogram will not be of very much value if it has not been dried and treated properly, Nirash-da added.

Timing, pests, sun, police. There were many uncertainties that could ruin a ganja crop. It is considered a risky investment by those who invest time and money in a big crop (more than a dozen plants) that might be destroyed suddenly by pests or police raids. The few farmers who grow ganja plants over substantial pieces of land either invest in tin sheets or bamboo fences to surround the field. This is done so passersby can barely see the tops of the tallest plants, and growers can keep constant watch for raids by the police. The police, for their part, either accept bribes to turn a blind eye or insist on cutting down all the plants due to pressure from higher authorities. Nirash-da emphasized this riskiness and thus the financial gamble that ganja cultivation represented. "I don't have such intimate familiarity with the police that I can manage them. After taking such good care of these plants, if the police come, then that will be my ruin." Drives usually took the form of cutting down and burning ganja plants. Growers were never arrested, unlike in cases of other banned or contraband goods (cattle, other drugs and narcotics, consumer goods) where those transporting them could be and often were arrested.

Ganja cultivation presents a "dialectic between exposure and disguise, revelation and concealment," a feature central to the politics and practices of security regimes in relation to illicit flows.[41] Ganja as an export crop was undoubtedly *du-nombori*, for growers, transporters, financiers, consumers—for all involved, except those Rajbangsi householders who grew and consumed it. With this widespread social and legal consensus, growing ganja was possible only in particular spaces and not others, such as within or around the homestead. Consequently, even though farmers such as Nirash Barman clearly viewed it, and financially valued it, as one of their agrarian investments, as a plant it occupied an in-between position between a crop and a domestic garden (fig. 15). In the Bengal borderlands, the ganja plant's above-the-ground existence had to tread a careful line of not being visible and being physically spaced out enough so as to receive adequate sunlight and water. Nirash Barman's evaluations of land, crop, and investments has a careful spatial rationality despite his emphasis on chance and the position of ganja as a purely compensatory or diversified

15. Ganja plants being grown inside the courtyard of a Rajbangsi home with the *tulsi* plant altar in the right foreground.

form of activity, treading equally the gendered line between household women's domain and that of mainstay agricultural investment.

This has led to a pattern of fugitive farming in Indian border villages, where ganja plants are grown ubiquitously but in small numbers by impoverished Hindu households *within* their homesteads. It remains inextricably connected to other agrarian developments. It requires minimal financial expenditure, as the "medicines" (chemical fertilizers and pesticides) necessary can be drawn from the remnants of those used for the cultivation of other crops. Farmers can also have recourse to it when they find their land devalued due to militarization in the borderlands. Many farmers called it a "bonus", using the English word, grown in the spirit of additional or compensatory income. The border itself offers this opportunity for the taking. "Like land, labor, and capital in their own times," Jane Guyer writes, "risk now figures in price composition and capital accumulation, as both an addition and a subtraction."[42] As is amply clear with ganja farmers' calculations of price and value of their crop, risk is far more diffuse and difficult to identify or even quantify.

Ganja's cultivation is possible because it shifts into or around the Hindu homestead, and its agrarian labors of care come to be performed primarily by women. Rural homes are organized around a central courtyard with rooms for the family, sheds for domestic animals and storing biomass fuels and crops, and a kitchen and washing area arranged separately around its sides. Hindu homes, with Vaishnavism being the dominant form of worship among both Rajbangsi and other caste groups, typically display an altar with a *tulsi* plant in this courtyard (fig. 15). Women of the household are responsible for the ritual care of the plant, watering it and lighting an oil lamp by it in the morning and at sunset daily. Watering and caring of the homely ganja plants is added to this ritual. Depending on the direction of sunlight and the location of the particular house in relation to village paths, such clusters of plants are grown within the open courtyard space of a house or right outside the home, lining its walls.

When located in or immediately around the space of the home, ganja cultivation is often the initiative or enterprise of one or more women in the household, and its sale becomes an additional source of income to them in the annual calendar. Several women told me that they factored its inherent unreliability into their household financial planning, wagering that the income it generated could be put toward special expenditures and responsibilities. One woman, growing three plants in her courtyard, and extremely worried about the failing health of one of them, put it this way: "If these sell well, then that means all Durga Pujo expenditures taken care of. New clothes for the family, I can buy gifts even for my parents and my brothers' families. I won't have to put out my hand to my husband." In other instances, I learned that the additional income would often be further reinvested into more stable assets; women bought goats or chicken to raise with the money from the sale of their homegrown ganja. Feminist political economy has long emphasized the household as an institution critical to commodity production and circulation.[43] While a feminist commodity chain analysis emphasizes the constitutive links between production and consumption,[44] the case of ganja exemplifies how gender ideologies structure agrarian production and code value in distinct ways along the commodity's course. Ganja in the garden as a *bonus* breaks down multiple binaries: between a market and a household economy, licit and illicit economies, public and private spaces.

The ganja in the garden offers a rich case to think about *du-nombori,* its grammar of evaluation, the ordering and production of value close to home. Thus, among the portfolio of crops cultivated by borderland farmers, the crop that most destabilizes the moral order of being a farmer or household distant from the *du-nombori* border economy is actually to be found in and around the homestead. Here it sits among a range of garden plants such as vegetables, flowers, *tulsi,* and spices, which nourish the family and serve ritual and worship needs. On the one hand, it alerts us to how farmers try to distribute value across the land they own and harness all its productive possibilities—as border security lays waste to one piece of Nirash-da's land, he seeks to cultivate value from another border landholding. At the same time, the crops themselves figure as characters— *khamkheyali* (moody), *majhamajhi* (in-between). Occupying space between the home and the field, traveling across the border as a kind of national commodity, crops like ganja also constitute the borderlands spatializing and materializing value through relations of hierarchy.

The discursive absence of ganja stretched from its visible life above ground to its invisible and unspoken transportation across the border into Bangladesh. This plant, being unobtrusively grown through the Indian border villages, disappeared from sight and speech once it was harvested. Like tobacco, ganja's travels and transformations along the commodity chain "sorted" different kinds of value and actors out from one another. If the grower could be gendered female and spatialized as domestic, the trader-transporter was definitely gendered male, performed this work in the public and highly securitized spaces of the borderlands' paths, and did so entirely clandestinely. All the women who grew ganja insisted that they knew nothing about the *byabsha* (the business). Moving ganja across the border to Bangladesh is risky work, as it can be caught and seized by either the Indian or Bangladeshi security forces and police. Like cattle and the more organized cross-border economies, the men who provide the capital for the ganja business—buying large quantities with the tremendous risk that the goods might be caught in the process of transportation and all the money sunk before the buyer-partner in Bangladesh takes over liability— are not the ones actually transporting the ganja. Once grown and sold, ganja disappears into tightly packed bundles hidden under beds or behind sacks of grains to evade the prying eyes of neighbors and visitors and the occasional raids from tipped-off law enforcement agents. According to the popular stories recounted by locals and security force personnel, ganja travels under the cover of the night via ingenious ways. Bundles are frequently thrown across the fence and collected by carriers waiting on the other side; another popular method is for young men to swim across the border, carrying these bundles and covering themselves with *kochuripana* (water hyacinth).

Ganja reappears—in hypervisible form—in Bangladesh as much-displayed seized goods by the police and the Border Guard Bangladesh. A photograph posted on the official Facebook page of the Lalmonirhat District Superintendent of Police is representative of the visual politics of ganja above ground in Bangladesh (fig. 16). There is intense competition between these institutions in Bangladesh for the national prizes of seizure records and the corresponding allocation of limited governmental resources and accolades. Triumphantly posted on the social media pages of the district police (as well as similar pages in other border districts like Chapainawabganj, Kurigram, and Dinajpur), there is a clear compositional pattern to depicting ganja: the law enforcement officer responsible for the seizure poses either with what was seized or with the vehicle of transportation. Very specific details of the seizure appear in the captions, drawing viewers into the policing world and further fixing the borderlands as a site of anxiety in national interest. The ungainly bundles of plastic sheets wrapped tightly with rope, presumably to make them water- and airtight, thus enter into Bangladeshi media and state-mediated public discourse as morally condemned and socially devalued objects. While the police typically staged and took these pictures to post on their social media accounts, they occasionally invite journalists and other members of the local public to witness and further publicize this moment. I home in on this as a key framing moment in the commodity chain of ganja because it accomplishes two distinct structural and scalar functions.

Writing about the historical production of national economy and space in nineteenth century colonial India, historian Manu Goswami argues that studies of emergent national territoriality have failed to account for transnational flows and relations.[45] "The swadeshi movement accomplished the fusion of the abstract notion of a common economic collective with the particularized vision of the social body as specifically Hindu. . . .

লালমনিরহাট থানার মামলা নং-১৭ তাং-১০/১০/১৫ ইং। উদ্ধার-০১টি অটোরিক্সা সহ ১২ কেজি গাঁজা। উদ্ধারকারীঃ- এএসআই মোঃ নুরুল হক সরকার, লালমনিরহাট থানা।

16. The hypervisibility of "Indian ganja" in Bangladesh. Facebook posts by the Lalmonirhat Police on their official social media page display seized "Indian" ganja with the details of quantity, location, and the person arrested.

Commodities produced within the sacred space of Bharat Mata were endowed with a fetish value."[46] Considering the transnational agrarian commodity chains of northern Bengal, I extend Goswami's insights to the continued production of national economic space in contemporary post-colonial borderlands. What does it mean for citizens of Bangladesh to know that agrarian crops like ganja and tobacco cut across their national border at countless points?

First, the act of seizure thus dramatized transforms the ganja from a commodity in the possession of traders, traveling toward future consumers, into an object in the custody of the Bangladeshi state. Alongside possession, the commodity's characteristic shifts too, from objects of monetary potential into objects of shame and contempt that epitomize material, spatial, and moral contamination. But there is more to this step in which the ganja's value is transformed. It spatializes the Indian and Bangladeshi national economies in a way that is tangible and comprehensible to citizens and local law enforcement actors. In each instance of seizure, whether ganja is hidden inside a public transport vehicle or a truck carrying grain, the discovery enacts a kind of reverse commodity nationalism, alerting the public to the presence of *Indian* ganja in the *Bangladeshi* market, territory, and body politic. The visuality of ganja emphasizes the Bangladeshi borderlands as a vulnerable socio-moral space, rather than the border per se, as a space distinct from and prone to contamination from neighboring India. It establishes criminality as intrinsic to the borderlands (see chapter 5) and stages its economic life as a corruption of *jatiyo jibon* (national life). Agrarian crops—in this case, undesirable—seep across, their mobility threatening the national integrity of socio-moral space, society, and economy in Bangladesh.

Indian ganja as a seized object also spatializes and scales the Bangladeshi state.[47] For policemen in Bangladeshi border districts, seizures are polyvalent events. On a long, dull afternoon at a police station in Kurigram, when I sat poring over crime and seizure records in that border-lying *thana*, two policemen longed for "*du-ekta bumper phense-ganja sijar* [one or two bumper phensedyl-ganja seizures]".[48] *Bumper,* when attached to crops, is a bittersweet word across agrarian South Asia. It means an unexpectedly large yield, always a joy for toiling farmers, but also the danger of low prices. Like the *bonus* for women's household budgets, ganja's worth represents paradoxical gains in the margins. Ganja's mobility across the hierarchies of a producing "India" and consuming "Bangladesh" is a threat that can be harvested otherwise. This is a wish to notch a career highlight in the service of Bangladeshi national security by intercepting a consignment of smuggled ganja, emphatically nationalized as Indian. This professional wistfulness encapsulates how states accrue power, legitimacy, and concreteness in relation to illicit flows as much as in relation to the "licit life of capitalism."[49]

There is a distinctive gendered aspect to this statist self-fashioning. India's border security regime, guarding against the threat of Bangladeshi mobilities, genders these bodies and goods as masculine aggressors. Muscular Hindu nationalism, in its border security avatar, is to cut such threats down to size; bilateral ties hinge on an unequal relationship, where India is the *boro bhai* (big brother). Picturing seized Indian ganja creates a visual template for the Bangladeshi police and border guards to claim a cohesive, militarized masculinity in the role of a protector state and to be recognized as such by their citizenry. While India's militarized border security—indeed, national security regime—has developed in relation to the threat of external, neighboring aggressors, the same has not been the case for Bangladesh. In these instances the Bangladeshi state performs a South Asian militarized masculinity to its domestic audiences despite the official commitment to the story of a "friendly" border in regional geopolitics.

Furthermore, picturing the seizure of Indian narcotics in this way also allows the police to produce evidence of their superior work in policing the borderlands as compared to the BGB, the state agency dedicated to this task. Across Lalmonirhat and Kurigram districts, this was an emic concern, which the police repeatedly pointed out to me. It was an institutional "bonus," so to speak. Producing diligent reports and documentations of their good work enabled them to claim greater budgetary and other resources in national-level meetings on borders, drugs, and national security. Seized Indian ganja disaggregated and scaled the Bangladesh state from within and to its citizenry.

BEYOND MORAL ECONOMY

So what can agrarian commodity flows in the borderlands tell us about how national economies are produced? How do we understand the varieties of value that these commodities are enmeshed in? While I have chosen to write here about tobacco and ganja, I was tempted to write about maize and potato. Cooch Behar's maize crop, which the West Bengal government proudly counts among its bumper yield in 2015 and 2016, was enabled only recently through seed, technique, and daily wage labor from Bangladesh. Similarly, all the border-lying potato cultivation in Cooch Behar is enabled by daily wage labor from adjacent Bangladeshi villages; bumper yields of a highly perishable crop, in the absence of adequate cold storage in the national territory, means that rescue by clandestine routes is the only recourse for farming households. The hierarchies of value that maintain a differential exchange rate of national currencies, rates of daily wages for labor, and prices for different agrarian commodities are the distinctions on which borderland farming households rely. Instead of assuming a separation between contraband and agrarian worlds, asking how they are entangled through valuations and devaluations of the transnational agrarian economy of the borderlands can open these understandings.

While historians have examined such agrarian production from the viewpoint of legal and economic regulatory frames within global capitalism and ethnographers of borderlands have tended to approach these issues through the lens of illegality and moral economy, I have looked more broadly at the social, material, and gendered life of value and what transnational agrarian commodity flows spatialize. Tracing ganja through its travels across the borderlands shows us that the value of the plant-as-commodity transforms over the course of the commodity chain, and its social valuation shifts tremendously, too. Moral and material value are produced through its national identity and the visual aesthetics through which its presence is managed. Juxtaposing the case of ganja with that of tobacco brings together the discrete strands in the processes of evaluation as the economies of the agrarian and the national constitute each other. Considering these two crops together allows us to see the ways in which processes of evaluation arrange and classify commodities and people in relation to each other, beyond legalistic domains. It reveals the extent to which regional and transnational relations influence national space and scale everywhere. Risk is dispersed and mediated through relations of gender and class, even as farmers try to manage it in their calculations. We turn to the question of risk and how it is gendered in the agrarian borderlands in the next chapter.

5 Risk, Labor, and Masculine Becoming

"Let me tell you, *ye mitti hi kharap hain* [the soil itself is bad]. *Jo bhi rehta hain, do-nambari me phas jata hain* [Whoever stays here, gets stuck in the illegal business]." DK, a young male officer in the Border Security Force (BSF), spoke thoughtfully. We were sitting in the round visitors' enclosure of the Kathalbari border outpost and debating why locals, especially young people, got involved in *du-nombori* activities despite the crackdown by the security forces. Jaunty mynas chirped, a gentle breeze circled the open-walled round shelter, the bright flowers in the neat flower beds stood out in contrast against the lush green trees. Given that this space was inaccessible for locals, a site regarded with fear and tremendous resentment, I marveled at how calm it felt inside this meeting room. I had met DK early on during my fieldwork and found him to be unusually candid about the difficulties wrought by intrusive border security practices in the lives of borderland residents. He was considered a sympathetic officer by the locals, as he allowed women to smuggle small quantities of consumer goods, signed off on permissions easily for people to transport goods, and made the visitor's room marginally more open to residents. "DK *saheb* shows us some respect," people told me. On this afternoon in 2014, DK shared in his soft and halting

17. Young men hanging out by the riverine India-Bangladesh border in Madhupur village, Bangladesh, facing India on the other bank.

18. Hanging out in the evening in the quiet corners of the Kathalbari bazaar, India.

manner that he came from an agrarian background himself from the western Indian state of Rajasthan, also a border state, and thus had an appreciation for the hardships of rural borderland life. He observed that in the border villages of Rajasthan and even Ladakh, where he had previously been posted, poverty and the lack of development did not lead to *du-nombori* businesses of the kind that thrived in the Bengal borderlands. He concluded that here the soil itself was bad, corrupt, and corrupting.

In popular imaginaries borderlands are lawless places, criminal havens: in India and Bangladesh, this imaginary is evident in media discourses and mainstream social perceptions.[1] This type of narrative was common too among those who related to the borderlands from what one may loosely call the *desh ka suraksha/jatiyo jibon* (national security) perspective. College students in hostels in Lalmonirhat and Rangpur were mocked if their friends found out that they came from border villages. Residents were asked about their "hidden wealth" by co-passengers in public transportation when their destination was revealed. I found this criminalizing imaginary was acutely present among the border security and law enforcement agents posted in the borderlands on both sides. Trained to care about the geo-physical border and "national interests," members of these security forces and police are taught to regard the residents of the borderlands as a suspect population. In the BSF's eyes, the *du-nombori* businesses of the Bengal borderlands posed different risks than the border villages of Rajasthan, but here the "friendly" border also meant distinct conditions of delicate operation.

I smiled skeptically at DK's conclusion, impatient to engage him with further questions. But before I could, a trainee officer who had been sitting quietly pitched in.

Look, madam, look at the condition of *panditji's* [the priest's] grandson! Such a pious man. People come to seek his advice and blessings from near and far! He is so famous that even our officers come from headquarters to meet him. And his own grandson is a smuggler and a drunk. Sometimes we catch him with bottles of alcohol, sometimes with Phensedyl, sometimes with saris. And then whatever he makes, he blows on alcohol. Has the *panditji* been able to stop him? No! We have been telling him to send him away. *Dilli bhej do saaley ko!* [Send the rascal off to Delhi!]

Indeed, *panditji*'s fame was rivaled by his grandson's notoriety. The priest's grandson, a young man desperate for cash and prone to drink and smuggle, had "become a security threat," as one officer exasperatedly told me.

While this characterization of the profligate young man—smuggling whatever he could lay his hands on and then blowing his petty earnings on alcohol—might seem predictable, the characterization itself is highly revealing and introduces the central issues that concern this chapter. First, it elaborates on a theory of spoiling. In trying to understand what turned some and not all young peasant men into smugglers and wastrels, the BSF officers pathologize young men's struggles to accomplish a productive masculinity. DK shifted blame onto the space itself, its soil, the environment in which people lived and reproduced their material and social worlds. Second, the officers' characterization of the problem proposed a solution to this corrupt and corrupting influence of the borderlands. To cut these young men off from the border's smuggling economy required, ironically, another form of mobility: labor migration away from the borderlands. In sending *panditji*'s rascal grandson away to "Dilli," a capacious signifier for a migration destination in northern India, he could be saved from his lawless ways in the borderlands. Compelling him to live a life of "honest toil"[2] in this instance was akin to the distinctly colonial reformist idea of hard labor in prisons, or cultivating of virtue by moral discipline in the South Asian context.[3] It would both generate rightfully earned income as well as model that such livelihoods were indeed possible for other Muslim and Rajbangsi borderland youth—away from the borderlands. The note of brute force in the abusive last sentence is unmistakable. Of course, this "sending away" is a benevolent act, shown toward young men of families worth saving. Most did not enjoy such consideration.

In chapter 4, I described the spatial and intergenerational arcs of agrarian life and distress in this militarized landscape within which farming households make wagers on transnational crops, considering the relative value of land and labor at their disposal. Security regimes' pathologization of borderland masculinity as deviant unfolds in this milieu. Hanging out by the river (see fig. 17), reveling in the openness of the horizon and simultaneous closure of India (or Bangladesh) in the distance, I frequently found young men circling around profound questions of identity: *What if*

I were Indian and not Bangladeshi? The question fluttered, like the breeze, there for the taking, lingering on, with no clear resolution. I have many variations of this image: on the Indian side, looking out toward Bangladesh; with teenagers; with groups of men in their early twenties; or with mixed-aged groups as in the picture here. I chose this image to capture a recurrent moment I encountered: it is not necessarily one of conversation, more one of quietude. In this chapter, I center the reflections, decisions, ambivalences, jokes, and critiques of young Bengali men, as they contemplate such a horizon of relational value. It offers a different entry point to think about the (re)production of masculinity, risk, and value in the agrarian borderlands while in the shadow of the hegemonic narrative that criminalizes the space and their persons as wastrels and smugglers who deserve violent policing and social reprobation. I hope with this exploration, we can turn the lens back on DK's well-meaning diagnosis and examine how national security practices produce differentiated risks, fundamentally gendered, across a transnational and highly unequal terrain of mobilities.

The protagonists of this chapter are a diverse cross section of Rajbangsi and Muslim Bengali young men. I focus on how, growing up in the agrarian borderland, young men come to be gendered, classed, and nationalized subjects within a social, economic, and political context marked by a profound sense of marginality, little possibility, and tremendous violence directed at migrants.[4] Such a context is a transnationally produced one. They are not only a rural youth, marginal within their respective national contexts; they grow up also acutely aware of their relative prospects in comparison to their peers *across* that national difference. I juxtapose five portraits from the Indian and Bangladeshi villages with each other as well as in relation to the statist and normative social frames within which they are cast.

Using this method in the framework of a mobile ethnography draws out the ways in which internal and international migration and mobility within regions such as South Asia are connected phenomena.[5] The rural and working-class male migrant is cast as a threat to the city's and nation's modernity in India and Bangladesh, while the Bengali Muslim becomes the prototype of the border-crossing "illegal migrant" in mainstream Indian discourse.[6] While figuring this racialized fear and discourse of infiltration in India through the Muslim body (and particularly through Bengali Muslims in eastern India) has a long history, it has most recently come into prominence with the enactment of the Citizenship Amendment Act of 2019 and the National Register of Citizens in the neighboring state of Assam. With these developments, it is ever more urgent to take a transnational approach to examine the political construction of the male migrant as a security threat and locus of national anxiety in ways that allow us to reimagine the *connected* politics of migrant illegality across the region. These young men do not know each other, but in interweaving their decisions, trajectories, and rationales, I hope the "intimacies" of destinies and desires, experienced as the gendered and sexualized trajectories of separated nations as well as their citizens, will emerge across these pages. I follow Lisa Lowe in taking "intimacies" to be an analytical and methodological tactic by which to ethnographically counter the isolation of desire and experience, whether of individuals or communities, by national container-thinking. While an "emergent sense of intimacies," she writes, is "not explicitly named in the documents, it is, paradoxically, everywhere present in the archive."[7] While not referencing each other explicitly, the transnational intimacies of young men's desires and risks that cut across the borderlands make *varying* figurations of mobility possible.

SHOB DIKEI JHUNKI ACHHE

Bordering establishes a relationship between risk and value. In devaluing some spaces and some bodies, it makes risks profitable. *Shob dikei jhunki achhe* [there is risk in every direction/way]: young men shared this repeatedly, a conclusion, a lament, an angry critique, an expectation. For instance, the riskier it is to cross the border to transport goods or cattle, the more profitable it is, in immediate terms of cash payouts. In another calculus, with increased border security, it is too risky to cross the border often and so men may choose to stay away from the borderlands and take other risks to defer border crossing. Throughout my fieldwork, *jhunki* (risk) emerged as not only an emic but an epistemological concept. *Jhunki* operated on physical, economic, moral, and social registers. To be a farmer always means to live and work with a measure of risk. But coming of age with the expectations of a productive masculinity—knowing that whether you stay in the borderlands or whether you migrate you are likely to be a target of security and surveillance—produces an additional resentful dream, wherein success means risks do not have to be taken. It means reckoning with being rendered risky as a person. With mobility, there is a political ecology of risk in these agrarian borderlands: risk is seasonal, risk is contagious, risk is embodied.

Risk, in a classic anthropological exposition by Mary Douglas, is a socially or culturally constructed phenomenon. What is perceived as dangerous, how much risk is acceptable: such questions are products of social, economic, and historical factors.[8] While risk's productive aspects in association with speculation and finance capitalism has been the focus of anthropological study recently, risk's productivity in the borderlands of north Bengal is eminently material, embodied, grounded in the agrarian and in the hierarchies of regional political economy.[9] Across the world, those who work in what are branded as illegal or underground networks are widely considered to be criminals in statist and socio-legal terms. In north Bengal, it is the gendered criminalization of the borderlands and its young men as either smugglers and criminals, or predatory migrants in cities, that invites the violence of militarized policing into what is resolutely described as a "friendly" border. The lens of security, whether adopted by the state or by national publics, seeks to fix risk and danger in the mobile bodies of borderland men—lower-caste, Muslim, and laboring. I invite you to take a step back and consider the lens itself as an ongoing and expansive process of bordering. This view can reveal the deep cuts such bordering makes, and how it normalizes the more spectacular violence directed at the much-maligned figure of the "illegal migrant." Risk and masculinity constitute each other over the course of young men's lives in the borderlands. This chapter sketches out the interconnected domains and spaces across which young men struggle to gain respect and sufficiency, and leverage the risks they take for gains on better terms.

According to a report by Human Rights Watch, between 2001 and 2010 there was approximately one fatal shooting by the BSF every four days along this border.[10] The Indian and Bangladeshi human rights organizations that assisted in the documentation of this report have kept counting; the fatalities have continued to accumulate in the decade since, even with the use of nonlethal weapons by the BSF.[11] Even though the numbers stun, they say little about the nature of the uneven societal cuts of militarization.[12] While Bangladeshi citizens figure as the majority of victims in this tally, the count of Indian citizens is significant, too.[13] In telling the story of the priest's grandson, the officers casually described how he is occasionally taken to the border outpost and given "a good beating" to "bring him to his senses." They referred to his good fortune in being let off with this relatively benign gesture as a courtesy to his family. On another occasion, DK emphasized his concern for the "innocent" borderland residents by describing how he had "made the screws tight" for "the border boys." This innocuous comment covered for sinister methods: the use of nonlethal weapons to scare and perhaps injure, not kill, during vigilant policing at night. "Does it seem a bit emptier here [the Indian border village] these days? In the shops, in the usual hangouts?" he asked me on one occasion. "As soon as these boys realize business is slow they will spend some time waiting, then when their cash from the season dries up they will go off to Delhi. That is what I am waiting for!"

The BSF's violent policing and the credible threat of that violence literally emptied the borderlands of its young men. It is no exaggeration that it is good fortune to be let off: in the borderlands of Kashmir, young men are detained, interrogated, tortured, legally ensnared, and disappeared by the same BSF alongside a mesh of other security forces.[14] Much is written about the difference between Indian and Bangladeshi border security regimes in terms of the imposition of a nonlocal and linguistically unfamiliar force on the Indian side contrasted with the Bangladeshi side; however, in Bangladesh, the same border guards and other security forces are not quite so friendly and benevolent in the borderlands of the Chittagong Hill Tracts or towards Rohingyas in the borderlands along Myanmar.[15] For a more capacious understanding of the conditions of possibility of border violence we must, therefore, look at how the fiction of a friendly border thrives in the India-Bangladesh borderlands even as violent policing, disguised as benevolent and necessary for the reformation of borderland masculinity, draws on practices in other geographies of national security.

The criminalization of borderland young men and the project of remolding this deviant masculinity is both specific to the militarization of a friendly border and a part of broader currents of depeasantization and immiseration in which agrarian youth across South Asia struggle to stay afloat. While the heteropatriarchal norm of success and maturity as a man is to marry and support his family (wife and children, parents, and in many cases, unmarried siblings), this is barely attainable in the marginal agrarian household that is typical of these borderlands. Meanwhile, with growing consumer desires, agrarian or other daily waged labor is unattractive to young men, while salaried jobs are rare. Across South Asia, migration and remittances have come to play a big part in "an individual's progress along an idealized trajectory towards mature manhood," and as Caroline Osella and Filippo Osella argue, "male identities are dialectically related to dominant essentialized notions of how *successful mature* men should be and behave."[16] In the Bengal borderlands, migration out of the village is less of a "coming of age ritual"[17] and more a stage in the accumulation of capital necessary to marry, repair homes, and start a long-term business in or close to the village. Success as mature men increasingly means not to undertake frequent risks, of which migration is certainly one.[18] What, then, makes the borderlands of northern Bengal risky spaces for young men? How are the risks and notions of safety and danger gendered under the sign of national security, especially as they intersect with heteropatriarchal standards of respect and desires? In the pages that follow, I explore what risks appear in the lives of young men in these borderlands, how they relate risks in different domains and times of their lives, and through what social idioms of aspiration, satisfaction, and dignity they navigate these risks.

SHOBUJ

Shobuj disappeared from Kathalbari (India) to "Dilli" while I was living there. He was twenty-two when I first met him in 2014, the third of seven brothers in a Muslim family with very little land. *"Byabsha kore* [do business]," he said about himself and his four oldest brothers, his glance clearer than his words. He looked up momentarily from the lit screen of his phone, as we sat by the closed shutters of a shop in the Kathalbari bazaar. The five older brothers were determined to ensure that the youngest two completed all levels of school.

"I was fifteen and I was still studying in school," recalled Shobuj of his first foray into "business." "I didn't ask for it. One night, my brother, who worked in the cattle business, couldn't go, and he sent me as his replacement. I had to transport a pair of cows all the way up to the border. Came home at dawn with cash in my hands. That's how I got entangled."

Hanging out with Shobuj was not easy for me. I joined him and his friends as they hung out in the quieter and darker corners of the bazaar a few times, but this made us all uneasy. I was intensely aware of how out of place I was: each time someone walked past us they did a double take. An incredulous "Sahana, what are you doing here?" would pierce the dimly lit space.[19] So, each of our conversations was patchy—veering between jokes, social commentary, and intense personal reflections—and they often ended abruptly. We understood that I was being judged for being where I should not be and equally for being in the company of someone I had no reason to be with. Shobuj and his friends, a mixed group of Rajbangsi and Muslim boys, were acutely aware of this devaluation, though Shobuj did not share their defensive swagger. He fell quiet when they boasted of their accumulated nightly or monthly earnings in comparison to that of a particularly disliked primary schoolteacher, who never lost an opportunity to throw a barbed word their way. "You are the dirt of Kathalbari. Unless you leave, Kathalbari's environment will never improve." The schoolteacher practically spat out these words against the betel-nut-stained walls of the bazaar complex, as he walked back home with vegetables in one hand and stew meat in the other.

Shobuj's parents are elderly. His two older brothers, who have married, must now stay engaged in the border's economies to earn enough cash to keep their households running. Keenly aware of how cash flows from the *du-nombori* border economy and the transition to being a householder with financial responsibilities can become entangled, Shobuj had quietly remarked numerous times that he did not want to marry until he had found a "stable" source of income for himself.

One afternoon, I accompanied Shobuj and his friend as they bought their goods—cosmetics for one of them and a large carton of Lays potato chips for the other—from wholesalers in Dinhata. They grappled with the different scales at which *byabsha* unfolded. They were going to transport these items across the border to their "partners" in Madhupur (Bangladesh)

themselves. We sat in the back of a shared vehicle with at least twelve people stuffed in on this last leg of public transportation to where the road
ended, so to speak, in Kathalbari. Shobuj raised his voice above the wind,
motor, and passenger chatter: "What I do is petty business [*khuchra
byabsha*]. I don't have the capital for anything bigger than this." He joked,
"if I could just go to the *bank* and say, 'give me a *loan* for my group, please'
that would solve all my problems." His friend knew that I was well
acquainted with the women's self-help groups of the area, as I often
attended their meetings and accompanied them to the banks. He chimed
in: "Yes, why don't you get help us get a loan. *Amrao swanirbhar hote
chai!* [We also want to be self-sufficient]!"

Their joke referred to the darling of the developmental world: the
microfinance model of women's self-help groups that receive loans for
individual or group enterprises. While much has been written about this
in Bangladesh, in West Bengal it is held to be a successful paradigm of
developmental intervention, providing capital to women to encourage
small-scale enterprises and financial independence.[20] By focusing exclusively on women, however, it puts rural men entirely outside this system of
financial networks. Across the borderlands, young men compared the differences they learned about between credit systems in India and
Bangladesh and the ways in which they impacted gender norms, family
relations, and women's expectations of men.

Turning serious over a cold drink of Fanta at the Kathalbari auto stand at
the end of our ride on Rangpur Road, Shobuj continued. "I don't like *bakir
byabsha* [business of credit/debt], it's very complicated to recover money
from Bangladesh, my networks are not so strong. So, I only do straightforward transactions—chocolates, chips, creams, all in small quantities. That
limits me, but I don't like this in any case." His friends left the *mishtir dokan*
(sweets shop), and strangers came to share our bench. Shobuj retreated into
an intensity that even the loudest buzzing flies could not disturb. "A boy got
shot in the arm, right next to me, while we were swimming across the river
[to Bangladesh] in the darkness of the night with plastic-wrapped bundles
of ganja. That boy is still living with pieces [of shrapnel] in his arm."
Gesturing to the back of his arm, Shobuj looked past me as he spoke. "This
happened two winters ago and I became afraid, afraid of my life. So, I
stopped this business of the night. Now I only do this small stuff."

The risks of border security cut very close to the skin.

After about a year of such petty business Shobuj had concluded that it was not profitable enough to provide the necessary capital and he would have to seek such income elsewhere. The allure of *kancha taka* (cash) is tremendous for teenage boys and young men. On either side, you could spot a boom—seasonally, during the monsoons or with specific commodities when a particular route was "open"—by the groups of energetic boys in new jeans and sunglasses, hanging out in the cool music or gadgets shops of the villages, their smartphones luminous in the darker alleyways and bazaar corners. But while this *kancha taka*—belittled as easy money— buys some of the accoutrements of youth masculinity and allows them to be stylish for a while, it seldom consolidates a transition toward "mature masculinity."[21] Booms eventually bust, and no sooner than these young men and their households start enjoying the cash, they are without any. After they try their hand in the various businesses of the border economy, young men often decide to take on the risks of migration. The Indian BSF understood the temporality of this economic desperation and operationalized it in their strategies. In order words, they intended their unsparing security practices to make it too risky for young men to remain engaged in *byabsha*.

In 2015, I came back to the Indian side from the Bangladeshi side to find that Shobuj had vanished. His friends told me that he had migrated for work, but no other detail was known. Even his family had a hazy picture of his whereabouts, and not even a phone number to reach him. He clearly did not want to be found. When we met in the bazaar in his old hangout half a year later, he was a shadow of his cheerful self. He had spent a bit more than six months working in a garment factory outside Delhi. Shobuj insisted that it was a reasonably comfortable life given the labor required—which he compared to the hard, physical labor on construction sites and brick kilns. Yet the fatigue from weekly targets of production and long hours of monotonous work were imprinted on his face.[22]

This embodied transformation, the hardening and darkening of young male bodies into tough manly ones through hard toil—for example, sowing, ploughing, *mazdoori* (waged labor)—was unmistakably related to the violence and risks wrought by border security on young male targets. Shobuj's portrait of decision-making around livelihoods makes amply clear that "Dilli" and the borderlands are connected economies with money and multiple forms of value flowing in both directions. People earn in one to invest in or further interests in another: these are critical to certain kinds of "inter-articulations" of value.[23] Such a connected calculus of risk and danger that stretches spatially across these locations makes the conceptual boundaries between formal/informal, legal/illegal, place of origin/work questionable, particularly in relation to mobility. This connected geography of risk in becoming a successful and mature man in the borderlands surfaces "scattered hegemonies" of gender, class, caste, and the hierarchical value of the national.[24] Shobuj felt safer in industrial work than in the multiple kinds of risks—financial, social, and physical—entailed in working in border businesses. In both sets of economic relations, he is fungible labor and his decision is made in a visceral confrontation of the violence inherent in both border violence and the factory floor. Now that he was a "migrant" and not a "smuggler" or a "wastrel," he had stopped hanging out with his old friends. We met by day. "*Baire kaaj kortesi* [I'm working outside]," he'd say, to anyone who asked what he was up to these days.

Shobuj refused to answer my questions about fun in the city, giving the impression that no part of his experience as a migrant was enjoyable. Both in India and Bangladesh, I found that migration was lauded by few; it was a necessary evil. New and veteran migrants across the borderlands emphasized that migration was risky.[25] This disposition is at odds with much that has been written about the urban-oriented aspiration of South Asian young men and the liberatory dimensions of migration experience. Instead, it echoes the profound ambivalence that Dolly Kikon and Bengt Karlsson find more recently among indigenous migrants from India's northeast as they leave but remain "stretched" across multiple places.[26] For Bengali Muslims, this stretching is fraught and exhausting and needs to be understood more specifically. As borderland Bengali migrants—both Indian and Bangladeshi—are repeatedly attacked in locales across India with allegations of being "illegal migrants" and their vulnerability is exploited, their identities are collapsed into the "Bengali Muslim" figure. Internal differentiations—especially that of nationality—sharpen ever more.[27]

ALAM

> The good students leave the borderland as soon as they can
> and go inwards for further studies.
> —Farukh, undergraduate in Lalmonirhat College, from a border
> village, Bangladesh

Alam Hossain is one of those who have not left. "We have to try our
chances here. *Lekha-pora* [education] is not for people like us. We neither
have any *boro bhai* [patron] nor that much money that we can buy a job.
Only education will not fill up your stomach. What else to do—you must
feed your *bou-bachha* [wife and child, shorthand for household]. Must
keep trying here. Being scared will get you nowhere. Have to use your
brains and understand how things work."

Alam dwells on the ends and means of education for unconnected rural
poor like himself while we sip watery tea in his family's tin-walled home
in Bibiganj (Bangladesh). He was the black sheep in his family, or so he
was presented to me by the rest of his family. His older brother Ashraf ran
a small *paan* (betel nut) shop just by the auto stand in the village and kept
phones with Indian SIMs that people could use to make and receive calls
for a small charge. I had been directed to his services once when my Indian
SIM was not working, and we had struck up a lively friendship. Since it
was very close to the Rahmans' house where I lived in Bibiganj, I would
frequently walk over after dinner to eat a *paan* and join in the *adda* (informal discussions). There was always a handful of men and women from
that neighborhood, sitting on a wobbly old bench, eating *paan* and
exchanging local news. The radio's crackle in the background had been
replaced not so long ago by a mobile phone's broadcast of radio programs
and songs. Occasionally someone coming to use Ashraf-bhai's phone service from further afield would give cause for more excited discussions.

Ashraf-bhai had never left the greater Rangpur area of northern
Bangladesh, but rattled off names of northern Indian places with much
élan. It was his party trick; regulars in the *adda* at his shop pushed him to
perform for our collective amusement. With a flash of his *paan*-stained
teeth and a flick of the sweat on his brows, he always indulged. They were
not well-known towns; I didn't recognize most of the names. Ashraf-bhai

explained that the callers on his Indian phones were men from Bibiganj living as migrant workers in these places. They would call to speak to or leave messages for their family members. As I got to know Ashraf and his family, he always spoke of his brother Alam apologetically, saying that he wasn't doing so well. Ashraf was determined to persuade Alam to leave Bibiganj and head to "Dilli" with one of the many good contacts he had developed through his phone business. One evening, he held up a small, now old-fashioned blue Nokia phone in his hand and said, "My friend in Siliguri has been there for so long that he has become a labor contractor now. He is all settled there. He tells me repeatedly that I can call him any time and send Alam. He has given his word to take care of him."

But Alam was not going to be sent thus—clandestinely crossing the border to India. It was several months after hearing about him that I finally got to spend some time chatting with Alam alone, at a distance from his family's judgments. We stood on the village path in front of their house, talking while he washed his auto. No sooner than I had broached his brother's designs, he lashed out in protest. "Why go to do *bideshe golami* [servitude in another country] when I can do something here? If I have to take *duniyar jhunki* [all kinds of risks], I might as well as take them here, sitting in my own home."

Alam's pragmatism about the economic prospects in/of the borderland rang out sharply, especially since "servitude in another country"—that is, labor migration—is one of Bangladesh's most precious exports. Alam was not referring to India alone, although stories of migrants working in India are plentiful. These stories can be about the charms of the country or the hardships of getting by as an always-suspect "illegal immigrant," depending on the speaker and the narrative context. Belying the Bangladeshi national economic story of migration as a pathway to development and progress,[28] Alam insisted on choosing his risks and hardships in the borderlands. He dropped out of school in grade seven to earn money to aid his landless family. A decade later, he tells me with unmistakable pride, he is the proud owner of two electric auto rickshaws, one he drives himself, and one he rents out. It has been half a year since he spent four months in prison on charges of "smuggling Phensedyl." While Alam insists to me—as he did to the mobile court that sentenced him, accompanying the police inspector making the seizure—that he was unaware of the contraband goods in his Lalmonirhat-bound vehicle, it is an open secret in the village that Alam's swift economic gains came from ferrying drugs along with passengers from the border villages to Lalmonirhat. Alam managed to extract his seized vehicle from police custody after his release, and has been working long hours to pay off the loan with which he purchased the second vehicle.

The borderlands of India and Bangladesh are full of Alams. It is a place that the young with promise leave; therefore, the young who remain, by that circular logic (recall DK, the BSF officer), are considered to be *bokhate* (rotten) by both state and society. The burden of this alleged dangerous criminality located in the space of the rural borderland rests on the shoulders of young men like Alam. Those who remain or return, like Shobuj and Alam, and try to eke out a living in these agrarian borderlands become the prime targets for security forces and law enforcement agencies— namely, the BSF in India and the Border Guard Bangladesh (BGB) and district police in Bangladesh.

Stories of such young men demand a departure from dominant paradigms in the scholarship on youth in South Asia. First, these are accounts in which we find aspirations largely delinked from education; indeed, they are linked to a cynicism regarding education.[29] Second, these accounts turn away from an urban orientation to attend to bitter critiques made by Muslim, lower-caste, and laboring men in agrarian contexts. They call to be taken seriously for how they relate to work, worth, and aspirations from their situatedness in those contexts.[30] Third, while precarity has been widely established as the pervasive condition of the workforce in liberalized economies,[31] following the spatial geography of risk as sketched out in the lives of agrarian borderland youth, as they move between various sectors of informal and sometimes illegal economies, takes us across rural and national borders. In Alam's pithy analysis of his predicament, *bou-bachha*—that is, the gendered pressure of advancing to a mature and productive manhood—frame his necessity to keep trying, to take risks for marginal gains. This grates against criminalizing discourses, especially toward poor communities, which make invisible and sever the individual from his social and familial ties. The normative pressures of productive masculinity drive the necessity to earn and contribute to the household, to become economically fit for the observance of adult social roles of being a husband, a father, a good son.

Categories of gender and age have multiple lives—scholarly, political, and developmental. Compromised of a range of international donor organizations such as the World Bank, UNDP, and national NGOs, the developmental sector in Bangladesh has focused overwhelmingly on women's empowerment, particularly making them income earners. In South Asia, the production of a successful masculinity hinges on the simultaneity of economic productivity and social responsibility.[32] Furthermore, income generation alone does not equal social status. Young men in the borderlands struggle to make their work meaningful. These struggles intersect with the heavy weight of surveillance at the borders, which single out male bodies as especially suspicious and criminalize economic activities in and across the borderlands.

Karim Islam, an old student of the Kathalbari High School in the early 1980s, had recently returned to it as its assistant head teacher. When I went to meet him, he pulled a great many files out of the official steel almirah to confirm that the "peak time" for dropouts in this high school is between grades six and eight. The high school serves roughly fifteen thousand people across two *gram panchayats*. "I can say, on average, girls between the ages of thirteen and seventeen, especially from Muslim families, get married and leave school. *Chhelera na ele amra dhore ni—Dilli othoba du-nombori*. [If boys stop coming, then we assume that it is either Delhi or the smuggling]." As I pored over the numbers of dropouts by year, class, and gender, which he had written out for me, he continued speaking; this matter was clearly close to his heart. "There are plenty of talented students here, it's sad that many of them don't get a chance for [higher education in] their future. The good parents remove their students as soon as possible and send them to Dinhata." The age/class vulnerability for dropouts and the account of negative influences on students matches to a startling extent with those furnished by Karim Islam's counterpart in the Madhupur High School in the adjacent Bangladeshi *union parishad*.[33] Echoing his Indian colleague, unknown to him, Tofajjel Hussain exhaled deeply as he despaired at the number of dropouts and early marriages, despite "countless awareness programs by BRAC and RDRS."[34]

Paribesh [environment] plays a big factor here. In class seven, eight, boys start with a hidden smoke behind the school walls. Before you know it, a cigarette leads to ganja, trying out Phensedyl, *mod (*alcohol). Problem is that everything is available here in front of them. Soon they need to make quick money to buy chips, sunglasses. Once you have a girlfriend, you can't ask your father for money to buy her a lipstick, can you? Selling these things is an easy way to earn. The poorest boys *joriye pore* [entangled] first. It would not be such a problem if India were not right beside us here.

Alam dropped out of this same Madhupur High School. Seventy-eight percent of Bangladeshis live in rural areas. Driven and aided by international organizations like the World Bank, UNDP, and UNESCO, Bangladesh has made considerable improvements in the level of primary education since the 1990s; however, rural high school dropout rates remain high compared to urban areas.[35] In India, too, the gains made in educational levels since the 1990s, as seen in the visible emergence of an educated youth, have been highly unequal, varying across regions along extant lines of social inequality, including caste, religion, gender, or class.[36] Border villages on both sides have lower levels of education than their respective state or national averages. With neoliberal restructuring and state disinvestment, education does not translate into salaried employment for most. It requires existing channels of socio-political capital, as Alam astutely indicated. In recent decades, districts of northern Bengal in both India and Bangladesh have come to be well-known sources of seasonal migrants within their respective national territories.

BOKHATE CHHELE ("THE WASTREL")

Discourses of contagion and criminality manifest in gendered categories of intervention. The *bokhate chhele* (wastrel) is one such gendered figure. In the newspapers in Bangladesh as elsewhere, reports of deaths, accidents, and thefts are the ordinary stuff of daily news. In this usual inventory of minor and major calamities, *madok drobyo* (narcotic substances) have secured an exalted place, and consequently also in the life and imagination of Bangladeshi society. As I read the papers daily through 2015, *madok drobyo* appeared everywhere: in villages and cities and the highways in between, outside schools and in public parks.[37] They were transported in ingenious ways, from ambulances to police vehicles, and even by model members of society like judges and the offspring of parliamentarians.[38] Seminars on drug addiction held in Dhaka are widely reported in newspapers and telecast live on national television. In one such event, organized by the *Daily Star*, a researcher reported: "Two lakh bottles of Phensedyl enter Bangladesh every day while Tk 220 crore is spent on them annually." He added that the consumption of Phensedyl had increased ten times in the last five years. The one constant in such stories was the source of origin in the geo-body of the nation: the borderlands. Phensedyl, ganja, and alcohol from India, and Yaba tablets from Myanmar, are reported to be pouring into Bangladesh from all sides. The sense is of a country under siege; neighboring countries are "insidiously destroying the youth."[39] Headline after headline forwards the same message: *Jubo samaj* (youth) is under attack.[40] The sense of siege is rendered in gendered and nationalist terms in Bangladesh: a more powerful and militaristic neighbor wages a covert war to render its youth (gendered male)—that is, its national asset and resource, in World Bank developmental lingo—impotent, wasted, and worst of all, dependent on Indian drugs.[41]

Indian drugs are not only targeting youth with addiction but also turning them into criminals. Nation-centered analyses make this connection clear, spatializing the borderlands as dangerous, and borderland youth as especially vulnerable and dangerous. "About half of the five million drug addicts in the country are involved in crimes," said leading Bangladeshi anti–drug abuse campaigner Arup Ratan Choudhury in a seminar in 2013.[42] This discourse and social anxiety about the corrupt and corrupting borderlands are not only deeply felt in the borderlands where "targets" are located, they are also actively produced by a range of actors from within. In northern Bangladesh in 2015, a fifteen-year-old girl boldly asked the superintendent of police of the border-lying district of Lalmonirhat (Bangladesh): "There are a lot of drug addicts in our society and there are a lot of drug-sellers in these borderlands. How do we stop them?" The superintendent was in her school as part of a drive to reform "vulnerable youth" in which the district police was reaching out to students in high schools, colleges, and madrasas.[43] To the hall full of about a

hundred fourteen- to eighteen-year-old schoolgirls, he described a familiar "type" of social miscreant, the "*bokhate chhele,*" or corrupted male
youth. "He resembles a dog," he began, as giggles rippled through the
room, "with heavy chains and bracelets around his neck and wrists."

> He has streaks of color in his spiky gelled hair, cigarette in his fingers or
> dangling out of the corner of his mouth as he stands leaning sideways, fash-
> ionably. That's the *bokhate chhele* standing around outside your school, on
> your route back home, trying to impress you. They usually take drugs; often
> they have some drugs on them, selling them. [As the girls giggled nervously,
> not used to such frank talk, the police officer continued bluntly.] I usually
> beat them up when I catch them. After that, sending them to court only
> means that they will get out on bail or by giving money. So, I shame them.
> Sometimes I even call their parents and shame them and their parents
> together.

He went on to boast that his team, instructed to show no mercy toward
corrupted youth, had picked up thirty-six *bokhate chhele* between the ages
of fourteen and twenty-eight from the streets of Lalmonirhat. "Now I need
your help to catch more of these *bokhate chhele.* Together we have to make
them stand up straight, not fall over. We have to do this for a better society,
for our country! Will you help me?"

The police chief's metaphors tapped into idiomatic Bengali moral lexicon about *nijer paye darano* (standing on your own feet). His invitation
encouraged the students—all drawn from either Lalmonirhat or surrounding border villages—to fix their gaze toward their peers, brothers,
neighbors in this criminalizing fashion. His contention that they would
have to be reformed—with deterring violence, if necessary—echoed his
Indian counterparts in the BSF. Across the postcolonial world, projects
labeled as "community policing," such as these, have been championed
and funded as the kind of liberal reform necessary to strengthen the
police-public relationship. In Muslim majority countries like Bangladesh
this is an integral part of the enormous funding that the American and
British governments have poured into strengthening and militarizing a
range of security and law enforcement institutions as part of the global
war on terror. Policing and reforming borderland men—and the invitation
to vigilant citizenship *within* the borderlands—taps into a normative language about a *proper* heteropatriarchal social order. This includes the

humiliation, devaluation, and violent punishment of a male subject framed as deviant. As a form of what Foucault theorized as "pastoral power,"[44] the police chief taught and invited peer youth to surveil and incarcerate more of their fallen friends for their own sake and in the *national* interest.

Alam fits exactly the description of young men on the watchlist of the Lalmonirhat Police, which under the superintendent's energetic leadership has made it their mission to cure the border-lying district of its primary social malaise, a *noshto jubo samaj* (corrupted youth). Dangers, threats, and contagions are never disembodied. As scholars of policing have noted, albeit primarily in contexts of urban inequality, policing in the contemporary late capitalist context normalizes a shift in state efforts from the production of and investment in social goods toward defining and subsequently managing "security" concerns.[45] In such a framework, danger and threat are in young male bodies that are criminalized and pathologized as the "*bokhate chhele.*" None of the interactive sessions that the police organized in high schools mentioned the agrarian crisis, disadvantageous trade agreements between India and Bangladesh, legal prohibitions on industry in borderlands, or neoliberal economic policies pushing more and more people into precarious forms of labor. A discursive framing that focuses on their risk-taking behavior as evidence of delinquent, immoral, and failed masculinity, actively *frames out* young men's rationales and efforts to reproduce social and familial roles and responsibilities.

SALAM AND REHAN

It was past nine o'clock at night and while the other shops in the row were all pulling their tin sheets down to close for the day, there was still a buzz of activity under the bright white light of CFL bulbs at Salam's shop in Madhupur (Bangladesh). As with Shobuj, it would have been difficult for me to hang out with Salam and his friends if it had not been for this shop. It was a proper site, a status, and a statement loud and clear: Salam had matured. Wooden shelves were stocked with bulbs, and electrical wires, nuts, bolts, and other hardware goods lined the walls. However, the best-selling commodity was invisible: prepaid mobile phone recharge. In a dog-eared notebook, Salam wrote down the date, every phone number, and the recharge amount. An agent from the telecom company checked these accounts every fortnight. Customers stopped by frequently, while young men between sixteen to thirty years of age stood around in small groups, chatting, looking at Facebook on their phones, and playing songs on the desktop in the store. On this day, while I waited for Salam to finish adding up his accounts for the day, there was another person in the store, sitting alone and muttering to himself under an unkempt head of hair. He attempted to talk to me, but his slurred words and unfocused eyes made it clear that he was intoxicated; each time he spoke, the others at the store cast sidelong glances, nudging and winking, gesturing toward me to ignore him.

Most of the time, Salam was accompanied by his closest friend, Rehan. Salam had presented Rehan to me as what was socially considered an oxymoron: he does *du-nombori byabsha* (contraband business) but he is also a *bhalo chhele* (good boy), he is responsible and he is disciplined. Rehan belied the equivalence between *du-nombori* and *bokhate* (wasted). Together, Rehan and Salam told me about the intoxicated man.

> SALAM: I hope you won't mind him, *apa* [he says apologetically as soon as their backs are turned]. What can I say, he is a really sad story. He is a college graduate.
>
> REHAN: He even had a job with a medical company in Lalmonirhat! He was intelligent, but now under the influence of Phensedyl addiction he is ruined.
>
> SALAM: I heard that even his wife has left him.
>
> REHAN [IN A DISPARAGING TONE]: Of course, that will happen, he is *bekar* [useless/unemployed] and still spends money on all this!

Salam's and Rehan's narrative, and their reflections on their own resolve to not be useless or unruly, framed their indignation at the man's fall from self-sufficiency. The Phensedyl addict's failure was not merely his own individual ruin as a *bokhate chhele*. He was thought to be useless and disruptive and a more significant failure as an adult man because he was unable to fulfill his duties as a productive husband, father, and son.

Salam declared that he himself was wiser after a brief stint in a steel rod manufacturing unit in Dhaka and a clandestine pleasure trip to Delhi with relatives working in the construction industry there. He had decided that the hard life of a migrant worker, whether in Delhi or in Dhaka, was not for him. Rehan's entrepreneurial activities in the border economy emerged from his responsibilities as the oldest male child in a recently impoverished family. He was from a family previously of relative wealth, who had lost most of their land in recurrent floods. Rehan was determined to save up money to buy new land. Narrating his life, he noted how one could not count on the government in Bangladesh unlike across the border in India, where he believed state assistance was available. He recalled that in 2004, in the worst flood of his young life, all the family received was four bundles of tin and 2,000 BDT from the district administration. He was convinced that had this been India, the state would have given them a new house. Rehan's sense of self in the world was constituted by being a Bangladeshi, particularly in contradistinction to being Indian, and what life chances that offered to him. The understanding that he could only be a temporary migrant worker in India, not a rights-bearing and welfare-claiming citizen, further strengthened his resolve to be self-sufficient in Bangladesh. Salam, too, had compared prospects based on national identity after his trip to Delhi. Had he been born an Indian citizen, working as a migrant within that national territorial-economy might still have made sense. As a Bangladeshi, a Bengali Muslim, the risks of clandestine mobility were not worth the potential opportunities in India, he concluded.

One evening right before dusk, as the pink and orange sky exploded into the water-filled rice fields of Madhupur, I sat with Salam and Rehan.

"*Krishi-kaaj korte chao* [Do you want to do farming at some point]?" I asked.

Rehan gave a dismissive snort. Eyes twinkling, he hitched up his lungi to dart into the domestic vegetable patch beside which we sat, plucked the leaves out of the ground and held them up to me. "Can you tell what *shaak* this is? Even if I don't farm myself, I am a farmer's son. We are farmers." Having made his ties to the soil clear through the leafy greens which I couldn't correctly name, he shared his aspirations.

Like Shobuj, his "target" was to muster enough capital to invest in cultivable land that would be adequate to feed his family and then to invest in a more stable business. "*Barir bhaat,*" said Salam almost wistfully, "*ke na khete chaye* [who doesn't want to eat rice of one's own home]?" Despite a rejection of agrarian labor, there is a strong affective and material tie to the agrarian space and to land, as noted by several recent ethnographies of migrant youth across agrarian South Asia.[46] *Barir bhaat* (rice grown in one's own land), as opposed to *kena bhaat* (rice purchased because one either lives in a town or is landless), is both economical and a source of sustenance. But in Salam's words and Rehan's bodily reaction to my question, it was clear that it had a much deeper value for a virtuous masculine ideal of the providing householder.

In a society that has been deeply scarred by 1943 and 1974's devastating famines,[47] directly caused by colonial and postcolonial wars, the "politics of food" connects agrarian political economy squarely to the geopolitics of aid and deep rooted existential questions around socio-cultural identity, as Bangladeshi economist Rehman Sobhan has powerfully argued.[48] The famine of 1974 is supposed to have started in Northern Bengal—Rangpur district, to be specific, which was one of the worst areas affected. Besides these historical famines, *monga*, a regular seasonal famine, plagued this area until the recent advent of *boro-dhan*, a high-yielding and drought-resistant variety of paddy grown in the *boro* season, which can provide essential food for the otherwise deadly Kartik month. If Sobhan's intervention is necessary for us to comprehend the politics of food and starvation in the 1970s, this history is vital for us to grasp the force of the virtuous dream that continues to animate masculine becoming in northern agrarian Bangladesh: to seize the risky profits of the border's *byabsha* to provide for *barir bhaat* within the borderlands.

Grinning, Rehan continued:

Can you keep running around like this forever? . . . If you have brains you can manage to make a living right here in the borderlands; those who do not have that presence of mind are the ones who migrate. I did chocolates business for a long time. I used to send chocolates to Dhaka, supply to Chowk bazar. Then I also sent cumin for some to Chowk bazar. . . . Just a few days ago my *maal* [contraband goods] worth two lakh taka got seized at Rangpur junction. It was cumin in a pickup truck. It was a big loss, but we've told the Dhaka party. . . . You don't have to have money to do business—Can you do business with only money? You see, if people can trust you only then can you do business well.

Rehan's aspirations emphasized principled self-sufficiency, working the discourse of corruption in government jobs to their advantage. Having an income was a source of agency and necessary means to meet overbearing social and material ends that ranged from immediate survival needs to more medium- and long-term monetary needs, such as money to renovate homes, marry, invest in land, or other commercial enterprises. Alam, Salam, and Rehan are all peers in the group of borderland youth: staking a claim, generating a social value to the money to be extracted from the borderland economies. Their navigation of risk from both the economic and legal aspects of their enterprises within the border economies was a matter of pride and a source of self-affirmation. Echoing Alam, Salam and Rehan are steadfast in their refusal to migrate. These questions resound between urban ghettoes and rural homes as young men consider their options of movement, considering the multiple dimensions to risk. Salam's caress of the leafy greens stubbornly gesture to dreams of nonagrarian livelihoods that are, in fact, in the service of reproducing their peasant identities.

HASHAN

In one chat, Rehan had memorably declared, "Not everyone is able to do this business, you must be a bit of a don first." I was reminded of this flavor of masculinity, a macho risk-triumphing heroism about the aptitude for sticking it out in risky border businesses, as I listened to Hashan Ali, who had been a toiling migrant worker for many years. Dwelling on his life choices Hashan spoke seriously: "My wife says if so many people can earn staying here, why is it that we can't fill our stomachs here? She is from another border village, and all of her brothers are involved in *byabsha*. She thinks I am stupid for working so hard in Dilli."

I first met Hashan when he was on a brief visit during the month of Ramzan to his home in Kathalbari (India) from "Dilli," where he worked on construction sites. Twenty-six years old at that time, and from a landless family, he had been working away for most of each year for the last six or seven years—first as a bachelor, later with his wife, and then together with their three-year-old son. In speaking of his experiences "away," a shorthand for migrant destinations outside the rural homeland, he established his "rural cosmopolitanism"[49] through an easy familiarity with the geography of the megapolis: rattling off names of neighborhoods (older residential ones as well as new ones on whose construction he has worked) and boasting to an impressed audience of neighbors of the ease with which he knew how to traverse the city using the swanky Delhi Metro. We exchanged notes about food in northern India, the Hindi names of vegetables, our favorite public places to visit in the city of Delhi, and shared jokes about Bengalis' difficulties with gender conjugations in the Hindi language. It was clear that he had worked hard to accumulate social, cultural, and economic capital from his labor migrations over an extended period. He had ensured that despite his absence in the village, the fruits of his hard labor were visible in the material investments that resulted from his remittances—new clothes for family members on festive occasions, an electricity connection obtained off the grid with a bribe, and finally, the skeleton of a new home being built.

Enough to gain a wife, these incremental material gains were not enough to keep his wife happy. Najma, Hashan's wife, admitted her dislike of life in Delhi in a separate conversation. Not knowing anyone there and unable to go anywhere outside the shanty in which she stayed to cook and take care of their son, she felt captive. She described her days as spent mostly crying and feeling resentful as she kept hearing via phone calls how much cash the men and women of the neighborhood had made in various border *byabsha*. She argued that they needed to stay at home so that their son could attend school in a stable environment, now that he was almost old enough. For Najma, the city was an oppressive place of immobility; the borderland, despite its surveillance and limits on civilian movement, was enabling precisely because of its collective joys and sufferings and surprising gains. Four months after Ramzan, Hashan was back in Kathalbari with his family. He was dressed in a new white vest tucked into a pair of blue jeans when he came into his neighbor's kitchen. I was there helping make puffed rice over a smoky hearth. Hashan rubbed his sleepy eyes open; I joined others (his neighbors) in teasing him about sleeping until so late in the day. I asked if this was a brief visit. "I don't think I'm going back soon—I'm doing some *byabsha* here now. The very night after I came back I earned Rs 2,200 and since I've been back I've already made over

10,000!" he said, expecting the numbers to be self-explanatory. He was clearly not keeping his risky work in the cattle smuggling business a secret, but rather willing to make a case for his choices. Toil, as Anand Pandian writes in the context of southern India, has a place of great virtue in agrarian societies. It works "as a lever of moral and material advancement."[50] But chance and accident invariably have their way, making clear moral valences in toiling paths connecting the present and the future practically impossible. With Hashan, too, "honest toil" and the "crooked path" were not so obviously distinguishable, and he was drawn back through the differentiated risks and gains of bordering.

Najma's hopes had been realized, her faith in the border as a gainful resource vindicated. They were getting their "*peter bhaat* [sustenance]" in the borderland, from the borderland, even if not from the land itself (as was Rehan's target), but getting closer to that goal. We might view young men like Hashan, then, as "being on the margins, but in the norm"[51] in their choices for illegal means of earning but in service of heteronormative masculinity, which in this agrarian borderland context is squarely to save to invest in the stability of land, the material maintenance of a home, and the reproduction of an intergenerational household. To be clear, they are no Robin Hoods, nor self-fashioned bandits bearing the burden of resistance to state or capital in any organized, collective fashion. Yet in insisting on a right to earn from the illicit border economies, despite the multiple forms of violence and harms inflicted by the state's criminalization, there was a boldness of aspiration for financial futures that gave meaning to their return to or refusal to migrate from the "corrupted" space of the borderland.

In 2015 Rajnath Singh, the Indian Home Minister of the right-wing Bharatiya Janata Party, made announcements about putting a complete stop to all cattle smuggling at the border to Bangladesh, and officially placed pressure and responsibility on the BSF to do so by all means necessary.[52] At about this time Hashan left his well-established position with a labor contractor in the construction industry in Delhi to return to the borderland. "*Mahajaner kacche amar number chhilo to, barey barey phone kortese amake* [the person in charge had my number and he started calling me repeatedly]," he said, the enthusiasm and energy irrepressible in his voice and smile. "So, I heard that *byabsha* was picking up, not very much, but better than nothing." Hashan had joined the cattle business.

When I worried if he and Najma were concerned about the risks entailed in *du-nombori* by night—and especially so for this explicit target of the BSF's violent security regime—Hashan scoffed, barely concealing his impatience. "*Jhunki* is in everything. I am always careful, but if something happens after that, then it is in my *naseeb* [fate]. I think that while carrying heavy loads, unimaginably heavy, up the scaffolding of buildings, ten stories, twelve stories, and I think it is *naseeb* here at night at the border." Pausing thoughtfully, he added: "*Jai hok, ekhon shooting order mana ase*" [in any case, at present *shooting order*s have been stayed]—unless we directly attack the BSF they will not shoot."[53]

Hashan could be seen, then, to be merely capitalizing on the bodily risk that he would have to undertake in any setting where he chose to work. However, in the borderland increased risk equals increased profit in a way that is unlike the construction industry. This point was starkly made by a local and part-time life insurance agent, in one serendipitous conversation we had while we were planning the sessions I would teach in a borderland village school where he also taught. He rattled off numerous examples that established a link between the increased sale of life insurance policies in the border villages to families with members engaged in the illicit border economy and the number of shootings by the BSF as border control became more violent since the late 1990s. His point was to prove the extent to which risks to life are deeply felt and incorporated into the financial thinking among border households today. Hashan's assessment—"no risk, no profit"—laid out the commodification of risky labor.

Hashan's Rajbangsi neighbor, a middle-aged farmer in whose courtyard we were sitting, chimed in to defend Hashan's nightly activities as no riskier than a whole range of other activities in the agrarian borderland. He spoke matter-of-factly, the gruffness of his words in stark contrast with the gentleness with which he fed a pair of goat kids milk from a syringe. "One night, a few years ago, a huge lot of cattle being chased toward the border trampled over my *jati* tobacco field. It was completely destroyed! I found out who the *mahajan* was. I could have gone to the police. But I didn't ask him for compensation because I didn't want to get involved in all that *du-nombori* business. *Simanta elakaye thaklei jhunki achhe* [there are risks when you live in a borderland]. Will I stop cultivating my fields because of that?"

His question laid bare the naivete of my question and raised a far more complex understanding of differentiated and dispersed risks that underlie even conventional agrarian activity in these militarized borderlands, seemingly disconnected from *du-nombori* businesses. The accretive and expansive cuts of bordering make such distinctions in an agrarian borderland increasingly untenable (see chapter 4). Everyday decisions of risks and gains reckon with these hierarchies of value as they are continually calibrated across connected domains of marriage, crop cultivation, masculine becoming and provision, neighborly trust, and intergenerational kin intimacy.

PEACEKEEPING AT A "FRIENDLY BORDER"

The Indian and Bangladeshi states insist that this is a friendly border between two friendly and equal neighbors, and take great pains to showcase such exemplary peacekeeping to their domestic audiences.[54] But dead bodies keep turning up inconveniently. The politically vicious question that is forced upon our discourse time and again, whether in the Sonoran Desert or the Thai jungles, or here by the barbed wire in the blooming grass (*kaash phooley kaanta taar*): whose fault is it when bodies of migrants show up dead? Their appearances pose extraordinary challenges for the living, ones that cut through the somewhat stable arrangements of moral order and national categories of risk and threat through which the government of borderlands proceed. I want to conclude this chapter's discussion of the relationship between border violence, a transnational geography of differentiated risks, and masculine worth with a pair of deaths, both caused by the BSF, a month apart from each other in 2015.

On a soggy July morning, after a night of blinding rain, a group of Madhupur men came to summon Rafiq-mama before we had finished our morning cup of tea. They were in a hurry and they were tense; they refused pleasantries and snacks. A young man in the neighboring village had just breathed his last breath, succumbing to a gunshot from the BSF as he tried to receive Indian cattle. Rafiq-mama was among the elders of Madhupur called upon for informal *shalish* (mediation) in interpersonal disputes, whether over love or land, and this morning they were being urgently called for their counsel on what to do next. We rushed to the man's house. His parents and wife, numb with shock, were unresponsive to the questions of a Lalmonirhat journalist who had just arrived. "Are you going to take this up as *manobodhikar mamla* [a human rights case]? Are you going to ask our government to take this up at the bilateral level? *Ei lash ki amader mene newa uchit* [Should we accept this corpse]?"

The final question was as political as it was practical. Refusing to accept the corpse was a tactic of drawing the government's attention and calling for it to take responsibility. Yet no one in the family was in a state to answer these difficult questions. State violence in the security regime of the India-Bangladesh border cannot hide itself. Yet in separating its targets, its rationale, its actors, and its occasions based on identity, such as gender or nationality, it obscures its coherence and fractures political solidarities and subjectivities. As the assembled group of older men confirmed in the dark room of the tin-walled, mud-floored home, this was a poorly resourced and landless household. The parents of the deceased had been sharecropping Virginia tobacco that season, and he had two younger siblings working in the garment industry in Dhaka. The deceased had spent several years in "India." "*Ish, Indiaye thaklei parto, ei borderey byabsha korar jhunki....* [If only he had stayed in India, this risk of doing business at the border ...]," trailed off Rafiq-mama's lament. Though unspoken, I thought everyone was mulling over the risks chosen and those forsaken, like Rafiq-mama.

Local Lalmonirhat and Rangpur newspapers recorded the incident the next morning with a tired monotony, buried in the bottom left column. It wasn't remarkable enough to merit a picture. There were no takers for a defense in his death; after all, this was a "friendly" border and you had to really be in the wrong if a protest was to disturb the peace.

Neither had there been for the case of Achhanur Hoque, a sixteen-year-old resident of the adjoining Indian border village of Balatari who was shot and killed as he was transporting a pair of cattle through the night. I was in Madhupur when this happened, and was called by his cousin, Kader, who I knew well. (It could have been Hashan too, I thought.) "*Ki kora jay, kaw to? BSF dhorte parto, poolishe dito, marlo keno?* [What can be done? The BSF could have caught him, handed him over to the police, why did they shoot him?]," Kader asked.

Angry words, and a search for answers that we both knew would probably be futile. Trying to be helpful, I suggested that we could urge the local
elected political leaders to lodge a complaint with the police. "*Tomar
dorod hosse* [you are feeling sympathetic] but you know the whole reality,
the law, and the truth. What can we do for him, you tell me," said the
elected head of the *panchayat*, rather bluntly, when I rang him later that
day. "It *was* at night, he *was* hustling cattle, and the BSF caught him. We
know that is wrong, that it is *du-nombori*. If I protest this, if I take this up,
I will lose all *naitik adhikar* [ethical right], the BSF will not listen to me
on anything else. As it is, they [the BSF] pay us [elected local politicians]
such little importance. You know how it is," he concluded with emphasis.

Juxtaposing the questions that the Lalmonirhat journalist considered
posing to the Bangladeshi government and the questions that the
Kathalbari *panchayat* head determined he cannot ask of the Indian government brings out the tensions around responsibility, and ultimately, the
value of life across a regional political economy of bordering. The juxtaposition shows that it matters which side of the border you are on. It deter-
mines what questions one can ask, socially and politically, about the legitimacy of border militarization. For risk, too, it matters where you are, since
to be a successful man is reduced exposure to taking risks. Uncertainty,
marginality, and possibility: each of these social constructions radiate
through some form of risk.

Analyses of militarized border security widely use Giorgio Agamben's
conception of "bare life" to describe its violence, positing security forces as
"agents of exception" with the power to decide between life and death.[55] It
is an episteme of violence in which the visuality of bordering is spectacular: dead bodies at the border fence are the expected, abject outcome of
this brutalizing force. When faced with state violence, such frames are
relevant and tempting. The state and media invite us to focus on the
simultaneous abjection and criminality of these dead bodies—disheveled
and wounded, with bare feet and a machete ornamentally placed by the
body—to make their crime and violent death make sense *in relation to* the
picture of uniformed men of both countries congenially keeping peace
at this friendly border. To radically question these limiting frames—
including their colonial visuality—and alter the very terms of discussion of
the relationship between risk and violence in the lives of young border-

land men is to begin by asking what is at stake for them *in their terms*. Here, I have tried to offer a different route to reckoning with the questions left in the wake of dead bodies at the border, one that reimagines the horizons of risk and value that young men face. Across a regional political economy, risk is nationalized even as the pressures of masculine becoming in a distressed agrarian world are interwoven with the risks introduced by militarization. A spatial geography of risk emerges in which migrant work in the construction or manufacturing industries, petty labor in local villages and towns, labor in the agrarian economy, and working in variously organized border businesses are intertwined, as borderland young men consider them as a set of choices. Juxtaposing these portraits is *to see* a different kind of spectacular picture emerge, *to hear* about an intimate and dispersed geography of risk.[56] Depeasantization, migration, and immobility are structural and material conditions that are constituted transnationally across these borderlands.[57]

6 Dwelling through Mobility and Unsettlement

Standing by the wooden doorframe with an *om* and a swastika carved into it is Amena Bibi, a matronly Muslim woman in her late fifties.[1] With two recently married sons and two teenage daughters, Amena-khala manages a full household with a firm hand in the Bangladeshi border village of Bibiganj. Most of the family was out on this day that I was visiting, and Amena-khala told me we had a couple of quiet hours to talk. As I finished my first cup of tea I asked if I could photograph the house. Amena-khala agreed, but stiffened ever so slightly as she followed my gaze when I stepped out from the dark room to the sunlit porch. I smiled at the bottle of shaving cream occupying the niche in the wall designed to hold idols, a common feature of Marwari mansions designed to display Hindu religiosity (fig. 19).[2] That seemed to put Amena-khala at ease again, though neither of us mentioned it. As we walked through and around the house, there were visible incongruities between the built structure and its present occupants: the *oms* etched into every carved door, the niches in the wall meant for Hindu idols, the private well at the back for drinking water unshared with Muslim neighbors, and the remnants of a marble-tiled pedestal for a *tulsi* plant in the courtyard.

19. An old Marwari house in Bibiganj, Lalmonirhat district, now home to a Bengali Muslim family with whom the Marwari family exchanged properties in 1962.

Amena Bibi's husband was a tobacco trader, and so was her father-in-law. When I gently asked about the migration history and resettlement of her husband's family from the Indian border town of Dinhata to Bibiganj, concerned that this might be a difficult topic to discuss with a new acquaintance, Amena-khala readily provided a brief account devoid of descriptive detail. She said that in 1962 her father-in-law had exchanged his property, including warehouses and their family house, which was just outside Dinhata, India, with a Marwari family of Bibiganj with whom they were already acquainted through the tobacco trade of the region. Though new to the area, the family was wealthy and sought a marital alliance with Amena Bibi's family after the 1965 War, as her father was a respected imam at the local mosque. Amena declared rather matter-of-factly that her father-in-law died of a broken heart soon after her marriage and the *sangram,* the 1971 war.

Indian manush chhilen [He was an Indian person]. The business did not pick up like it had *oi deshe* [in that country], and he was never comfortable in this house. *Ekhane mon bosheni kono din* [his heart never settled here]. Then we were in India during Joy Bangla [the Liberation War of 1971],[3] we left behind everything in this house, and went to stay with their old acquaintances in a place called Dinhata. But it was not the same there—my father-in-law *mela koshto paisen* [suffered a lot] through those times. *Sheshe, moner dukkhye mara gesen* [at last, he died of a broken heart].

My attention to the visibly Hindu past of the house, which despite the exposed brick patches and peeling layers of paint still bears the marks of its Marwari builder, seemed like a diversion to her narrative rather than its key. Amena-khala spoke quite unsentimentally about the nearly year-long refuge they took across in the Indian borderland during the Bangladeshi Liberation War of 1971, like almost all families in the then-East Pakistani border villages. However, her account of how her husband's family came to live in this house centered dislocation, not settlement. This house, that house: belonging and identity were deeply felt through property, material structures, and conditions. The description of these compounded dislocations connected place-belonging with personhood, resettlement with suffering, and migration with an irreparably broken heart. Occupying "this house," a large brick-and-mortar structure that was a rarity and a luxury in rural northern Bengal of the 1960s, "his heart never settled." For Amena's father-in-law, home and dwelling, identity and citizenship had never aligned.

Her father-in-law had gone from being an Indian citizen to a Pakistani citizen, with the exchange of properties and transnational migration, but he had remained "an Indian person," in Amena's words. In her narration she used the language of blood to make kinship with a deep cultural identity, naturalizing and decoupling it from a bureaucratic identity of nationality. This would seem like a perfect example of what scholars of transnational migration and diasporas have studied extensively—"cultural identity" as distinct from bureaucratic nationality or citizenship.[4] However, while these assume difference in terms of physical and cultural distance, postcolonial refugees do not figure in these discussions. Not only did they migrate short distances to neighboring countries—an overlooked feature of contemporary refugee movements[5]—in post-Partition South Asia the migration of religious minorities to become majoritarian citizens was premised on the assumptions of cultural belonging, not difference.[6] The material and affective dissonance of this premise rippled through countless borderland families like Amena Bibi's, taking on enormous political significance over generations.

Bureaucratically speaking, this was a "voluntary migration" at a historical juncture where, as a Muslim resident of India, Amena's father-in-law chose Pakistani nationality. Joining thousands of Muslims who were migrating for a variety of reasons, they were deemed to be *muhajirs* (refugees) and embraced as bona fide citizens in East Pakistan. By the end of the 1960s, two decades after Partition, even conservative estimates suggested that 1.5 million Muslims had migrated from West Bengal to East Pakistan;[7] about 5 million Hindus were officially estimated to have left East Pakistan for India (including West Bengal, Assam, and Tripura) in that same period.[8] Unlike in the case of the western India-Pakistan border, these migrations and displacements were not spatially and temporally concentrated but occurred "sometimes in trickles and sometimes in big waves."[9] For example, in 1951 the Pakistani census counted 700,000 Muslim *muhajirs* in East Bengal, of whom two-thirds were thought to be from West Bengal. Prior to the 1965 War, the government of India estimated that in eight days of January 1964 alone, 70,000 Muslims fled across the border to East Pakistan.

Yet, Amena Bibi's father-in-law's experiences of migration, (re)occupying home, and belonging are not legible in terms of the official statist or analytical categories we have to understand the lived experiences of either being a displaced refugee or a postcolonial citizen. I was deeply moved by the statement that he was "an Indian person," not least because it was not unique: numerous others in the Bangladeshi borderlands used these kinds of references to describe themselves or others to me. "An Indian person" was a reference ostensibly to a particular migration history, but something much harder to grasp exceeded the itinerary of this journey from one nation-state to another. Was this a reference to previous citizenship? An attachment to a place? A stubborn ethnonational sense of self, refusing to be replaced by current national identity? Taking seriously this story of an enduring and profoundly *unsettled* experience of dwelling as a Muslim citizen first in East Pakistan, then in Bangladesh, a series of questions followed. Even in Amena-khala's brief account, the picture that emerges is of a succession of wars and political decisions that entailed numerous partitions and migrations, not a singular even if lengthy process. Over these three decades—from the early 1950s to the late 1970s—Muslims and Hindus migrated and settled across the border *in relation to* one another. What role did the states play in managing or recognizing these migrations? How do these migrations and resettlements in short distances across the border—that is, *within* the borderlands—trouble our understandings of home and the relationship between displacement and (re)settlement in citizenship and refugee regimes in the postcolonial world?

To answer these questions, this chapter draws on a particular genre of stories in the borderlands: migration histories. I present three microhistories of migration within the borderlands of northern Bengal through the 1950s to the 1980s: Bengali Muslims who moved to East Pakistan, having exchanged properties with westward-moving Bengali Hindus, up until the early 1960s; Bengali Muslim marginal peasants who were displaced by episodes of religious violence to East Pakistan in the early 1950s; and Bengali Hindu migrants from Bangladesh who moved to India as self-styled "refugees" in the post-1971 years. These histories illuminate different aspects of dwelling through mobility and unsettlement. It assembles and reads a material archive of dwelling through mobility in a transnational frame of reference: exchanged and reoccupied homes, tin trunks of documents, treasured household possessions (such as agricultural tools), itinerant objects, and community buildings of religious significance.

Despite the richness of cultural and scholarly work exploring the varied experiences of Partition, the dominant assumption is that historical events related to the origin of the postcolonial nations—1947 and 1971—are "known" and the gaps that exist can be filled in within these "known" nationalist master narratives. The year 1947 is about India and Pakistan; the year 1971 is about Pakistan and Bangladesh. Borderland migration histories fundamentally challenge this epistemological order by forcing open and leaving unsettled "the memorial relationship between 1971 and 1947."[10] In doing so, this genre is central to understanding the "recursive recalibrations" of citizenship and belonging in postcolonial South Asia as they manifest over generations.[11] Even while exploring the political fractures that come with refugees rebuilding lives, historiographical work has focused overwhelming on questions of citizenship and territoriality, tracing the centrality of refugees to these postcolonial regimes.[12] These assume the categories of citizen, refugee, and foreigner to be fixed, with who-fits-where as the main arena of political struggle. Amena-khala's story about how she and her family came to live in that house, the story's shifting meanings over generations, and its discussion within the family exceed these categories. Mobilizing a transnational feminist view enables us to see that the national identities of "Indian," "Pakistani," and "Bangladeshi" become meaningful *in relation to* one another, serve different purposes, and shift intimately, geopolitically, and affectively over time.

DWELLING

Sipping tea in Amena-khala's home, as the delicious smells of the meal she was directing while talking to me wafted into the room, we looked around the walls of the old house. This is the only home her children have known, growing up unambiguously as Bangladeshi. Marrying into this *muhajir* family—and the exchanged house—Amena herself shares little of the heartbreak and memories of an elsewhere with her husband and in-laws. The question of dwelling has been central to understanding material conditions of life possible in relation to mobility and violence as well as subjective and existential experiences of belonging and identity.[13] In Bengali, the verb and noun forms *bashati* and *bash kora* refer to "dwelling" in terms of a physical structure or as affiliation to a location or place. Indeed, feminist interventions have argued that in a wide range of contexts, "home" is more than an affective place of longing, nostalgia, and belonging in any straightforward way.[14] Nicole Constable's work on domestic workers' transnational migration illuminates the experience of "being at home but not at home" in both the states they migrate from and to.[15] Arguing that in post–civil war Sri Lanka, returning to homes from hiding or displaced peoples' camps was a political act of possibility, founded on imagining particular political futures, Sharika Thiranagama urges scholars take points of reference for the phenomenological experience of displacement and refuge as an empirical question instead of assuming the nation-state as a lodestar.[16]

The multiple senses of home and dwelling are key to the contradictions that migrants experience in estrangements and attachments simultaneously held. Following Thiranagama's caution against universalizing conceptions of being stateless or a refugee, while considering the dialectic between legal and experiential modes, the case of dwelling as a refugee-citizen in the postcolonial borderlands of India-Pakistan/Bangladesh shows that displacement does not necessarily mean statelessness, just as being a recognized citizen does not amount to being a thriving resident "at home."

Adopting "dwelling" as an analytic attunes us to a subtle range of verbs with which people on the move negotiate and inhabit fraught relations between personhood and locations, multiple belongings, and modes of recognition. Dwelling—what and where it means to be *at home*—are enduring and eminently political questions. Nationality and legal protection within the Westphalian state system came to be constitutive of the socio-legal category of the refugee in the foundational moment of the Geneva Protocol and the apparatus now referred to as the international refugee regime in the years after World War II.[17] These categories of "citizen" and "refugee" are dominated today by "the national order of things" and the international refugee management regime, within which the camp is the unquestioned topos of the post–World War II world.[18] The millions displaced in South Asia contemporaneously were not recognized as refugees in the 1951 Refugee Convention, since they were not viewed to have suffered a loss of nationality.[19] Instead, India and Pakistan developed what Cabeiri Robinson has called "the regional refugee regime" with its distinctive rehabilitation policies.[20] Disrupting the linear progression expected of refugees, from the disorderly movement of displacement to the stasis of citizenship and resettlement, this chapter lingers on unsettlement, the vexed relationship between dwelling and mobility. Dwelling means residence, a legal category as well as a physical structure. But to account for this transnationally held, embodied sense of place through mobility and not despite it, we must investigate how migrants relate their own experiences to state categories and ask what is at stake for this ongoing relationship between territorially contained national identity and dwelling practices around which oral migration histories cohere.

By centering the figure of the refugee—whether in Europe or in South Asia—the history of twentieth century decolonization and transition from colonial empire to postcolonial nation-states can be imagined as a history of the "renegotiation of the relationship between communities and the territories they inhabit," especially through documentary regimes.[21] Vazira Zamindar's scrutiny of the state categorization of "domicile" challenges avowed commitments to secular citizenship. She shows how "'doubtful' and 'disloyal' [turned] into critical categories for transforming markers of religious community into citizens of new nation-states."[22]

However, there is a danger in focusing on the state alone as the sole guarantor of citizenship and taking the state's documentary regime and refugee rehabilitation schemes as the anchor for politics and political subjectivity. The paperwork available to track the state-in-action in this respect pertains to only a minute fraction of the cases of cross-border migration, particularly in the eastern borderlands. In contrast to the bureaucratic category of domicile, "dwelling" opens up the lived and lively aspects of citizenship as materially, socio-politically, and affectively potent. Given the high political stakes of being recognized as refugees across the war-torn Global South today, the historical ethnography of borderland refugees in South Asia has wide relevance for our understandings of the relation between refugees and citizens and a hierarchy of migrant pasts, where some trajectories can be subsumed within nationalist narratives and some must be arrested, denied, or violently attacked. In centering the figure of the refugee outside the camp, the presumed role of the state or international organizations in citizenship and refugee regimes can be rethought beyond this locale.

In Amena's telling of her father-in-law's migration story, it becomes clear that to fully grasp the stakes of these histories of migration, refuge, and belonging we must approach "the work of storytelling both as a memory practice and as an ethnographic genre."[23] These "stories about stories," often told by the women in households doing the innocuous family talk that women are perceived to do, participate in rather than simply reflecting changing domestic and regional geopolitics by surfacing unresolved issues, disobedient emotions, and audacious political imaginations.[24] Dwelling, then, is not only about inhabiting particular places and properties but about inhabiting historically shifting political positions. These articulations change across generations and may come to grate against one another. At each juncture they are politically charged; with every telling the categorical boundaries and (in)stabilities are tested. Borderlands are sites of historiographical contestation, where the politics of remembering and forgetting, of constructing teleologies and trajectories are germane to the cuts of bordering.[25] Bengali Hindu and Muslim residents of these borderlands worked—through decades and successive generations—to order the mismatches of present location and imagined communities, citizenship, and belonging. These histories, attachments, and estrangements make the lived categories of "refugee," "migrant," and "citizen" both more porous and more variable than a statist view would permit. Mobility was—and remains—key to this order.

ESTRANGEMENTS AND ATTACHMENTS

At a distance from urban or administrative centers where professionals opted for India or Pakistan and exchanges of property were administered by the states, numerous small farmers and petty traders all along the Bengal border sought to exchange their homes, landholdings, and assets through the 1950s and 1960s. These were people who left their side of the emergent borderland out of cumulative experiences of persecution, quite often out of fear for their dwindling economic and social well-being.[26] As Md. Mahbubar Rahman and Willem van Schendel found in their research in the Rajshahi district of Bangladesh, "many of these borderlanders settled not far from their old home, in a neighboring district that was now in the other country. And unlike many refugees who moved from more 'interior' places to cross the border and settle down far from it, border refugees often maintained contacts across the border, with relatives and friends who stayed back."[27] In other words, people chose to migrate the shortest distance to remain in a familiar region, but on the side of a border where they would be in the religious majority. Their migration and settlement within the borderlands hinged on the aspiration to *remain mobile* across the border.

The vagaries of this aspiration and the entanglement of cross-border attachments with estrangements became most clear to me through the migration history of Fazle Rahman's family. Like Amena Bibi's husband's family, they had exchanged properties to migrate to East Pakistan and Rafiq-mama introduced them to me as a "distinguished Indian family" in Madhupur. It was the month of Ramzan in 2015 when I first visited Fazle Rahman in his sprawling home in Madhupur (Bangladesh). He had recently retired as a principal of multiple high schools in northern Bangladesh. This was the first Ramzan of his retirement and bemoaning that he was not busy enough, he invited me to spend successive afternoons recording his family's history. Although I intended to focus on his family's migration to East Pakistan, the way in which the matter came up in our conversation was surprising.

It was the week in which a landmark Indo-Bangladeshi joint survey was taking place in all the enclaves of northern Bengal, simultaneously on both sides, to collect enclave residents' decisions on citizenship.[28] The local newspaper that day carried a story about a Hindu family in an Indian enclave in Bangladesh that made the difficult decision to permanently move to India, even though they had never set foot in that country before.[29] Fazle Rahman picked up the day's newspaper and pointed to the picture of a peasant family looking tense, the men in their *lungis* and *gamchas* with stony eyes, the women with saris pulled over their heads, clutching their children close. *Here is a picture of agony*, he gestured, overcome with emotion.

Invoking a comparison with this ongoing exchange of enclaves and the election of citizenship, Mr. Rahman visibly shuddered as he recalled what a tortured decision it had been for his father to leave their now-Indian border village, the neighboring Kathalbari. What was most difficult, he remarked, was *the way* in which he left. Hanif-daktar, his father, had been well known and well established in the Kathalbari *gram panchayat*. He left with almost his whole family, without telling many people in the village in which he had lived his entire life.

You see, if everyone came to know, then they would try to stop him and make him change his mind. Besides that, my father was very uneasy about this move for another reason. He was a village doctor, always surrounded by people. Certainly, someone or the other would catch hold of him and say 'take me with you.' How could he take that responsibility? So, he kept very quiet about it—all the finding out [about properties in East Pakistan across

the border], negotiations, and preparations—didn't let anyone find out. I
was a student, a young man then, so I would come across [to East Pakistan]
and fix everything. I came many times. I had friends coming too—together
we got admitted to Rangpur College.

.   .   .   .   .

Once he came over to Madhupur, [Hanif-daktar] didn't know that many
people here, and he kept to himself. The village already had a doctor. He
would see patients mostly at home. Sometimes he would get called to the
bazaar or to someone's house. He would try not to go away because there
was a lot of theft in those days, and we didn't really know who to trust or
whether people would want the best for us. It was an extremely poor area,
and we were all trying to make get enough money to make the foundations
bhite paka [concrete] to avoid robberies.

As he spoke, his narration swung between contrasting emotions: his
eyes glinted and he smiled when he spoke of all the clandestine crossings
he undertook to "fix everything" and the group of friends with whom he
became a student in a well known institution in Rangpur. But in the next
moment his back stiffened and his face became somber as he spoke about
his father. About fifty years after the migration, the carefully arranged
exchange still sounded like an estrangement, the gift of Pakistani citizenship overshadowed by the tremendous socioeconomic uncertainties of
changing residence through *badli* (exchange).

Even when elective, these migrations were not entirely voluntary and
were always accompanied by an experience of profound loss, whose contours shaped the way these migrants settled and socialized in their new
nations of choice in the decades that followed. Anthropologists studying
conflicts and wars have argued that studying movement amid violence in
relation to place calls into question the strict boundaries between "forced"
and "voluntary" migration, a cornerstone in distinguishing migration
from refugee studies.[30] Mr. Rahman suggested that although they were
not forced to move, they were forced to decide, to stay or move, thus
underlining the false hope offered by such a liberal language of choice. In
Mr. Rahman's accounts, the emphasis was on the uncertainties—social
and economic—after they had migrated to what was becoming the borderland of East Pakistan.

I had six sisters, all unmarried. Abba did not broker any relations in India afterward. We used these marriages to make new *sagai* [relations] here. He was well known and respected, so people even in this new place helped and vouched for him. He only made friends with the local elders and important people in the village. We were also very close to the others who had come from India, they would always support Abba in any matter.

Contrary to the episodic displacement caused by riots or violent attacks that have marked our understanding of Partition-related displacements, whether in South Asia or elsewhere,[31] for exchangees the process of moving and settling entailed layers of familial discussions and partitions. Like Amena-khala's own marriage, these became projects without clear resolutions, located in the margins of emergent national difference. Marriages making new relations held the ambitious promise of turning "the unknown into the known."[32] Social and economic relations derived from trust. Although exchangees often did not move more than twenty kilometers away from their older residences, there were immediate concerns of safety and well-being at play. An overwhelming number of exchangees married into other exchangee families and socialized with families like theirs.[33] Solidarity and interest groups formed out of economic cooperation; local mosques and community affairs developed around figures who took leadership and public positions of national allegiance. During the tense hostilities of the 1965 War, which saw border areas come under the vigilant observation of the Pakistani armed forces and East Pakistan Rifles, these families found that being referred to as "Indians" or "people from India" was socio-politically disadvantageous. On the other hand, when the pro-India tide swelled after 1971, the same referents were positive.

The experiences of Mr. Rahman's family pointed to the element of competition; existing residents of the Madhupur region, fellow Bengali Muslims and putatively equal Pakistani citizens, belonged to multiple interest groups, stratified by class and labor interests. The state may have declaratively embraced the new migrants as Pakistani citizens, but in the borderlands of Lalmonirhat and Kurigram districts,[34] those newly arrived found it challenging to work out what that meant at interpersonal and structural levels. In East Pakistan, these Muslim migrants were not necessarily celebrated as "homecomers" in the way that many Bengali Hindus migrating to West Bengal were heralded in Bengali public discourse during this

period in the 1960s. Many of them, especially those without much propertied wealth, struggled to establish social status and ties.[35]

ANNOTATING A TIN-TRUNK ARCHIVE

On the very first afternoon of recording his family history, Fazle Rahman
pulled out a large tin trunk from under his bed. In it, neatly organized,
were all his documents and state-issued certificates (fig. 20). One folder
for all his bank documents. Another plastic folder, brittle and cracked,
held certificates: school graduation certificates from the Indian board of
education to the *muhajir* or refugee certificate issued by the government
of Pakistan. One afternoon he wanted me to examine the Indian school
certificate carefully; on another afternoon he compared the Indian school
education he had received to the one he had helped build in independent
Bangladesh. When we looked at his refugee certificate (fig. 21) together,
he chuckled. He pointed to the reason for migration: "forcibly driven out
of India."

"In those days they wrote that for everyone, it's not that they asked us
what our reasons were. We needed the paper so we had to go and get it."
He swiftly moved on to talk about the economic implications of the division of families. In the lengthy decision-making that Mr. Rahman
described, his father considered the impact of their migration on friends
and kin associated with him. This shaped what Mr. Rahman portrayed as
acts of care for others, even in their own migration. Many—Hindus
looking toward India and Muslims looking toward East Pakistan—
had disagreements within the family. Brothers opted to split the hitherto
joint family rather than move all together. Daughters who were already
married were left behind. Individuals would cross the border illegally—
sometimes by bribing irregularly posted border guards—to scout out the
land and property in question. They actively sought to stay beneath the
radar of the state and wider public scrutiny. In securing these transactions, their network of friends who had already exchanged and migrated
assisted them and greatly influenced their decisions on whether to remain
or to move. Many families, rendered religious minorities in their places of

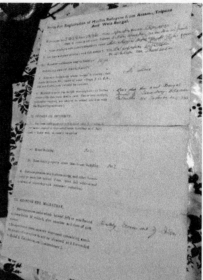

20 (Left). A tin-trunk archive, stored under the bed, with refugee paperwork issued by the Government of Pakistan.

21 (Right). Mr. Rahman's refugee certificate.

residence, wagered on staying with their extant businesses through these decades. They lost everything when capital and assets were confiscated under the Enemy Property Acts, passed by both India and Pakistan in 1967. Thus, "Partition refugees were also defined based on their relationship to property in each of the new states,"[36] in ways that foreground the constitutive role of class in the legislative formulation of refugee protection.

Mr. Rahman held up the Pakistani-state-issued refugee certificate. "We were called *muhajir* here and the government was very helpful. We left our *boshot bari* (ancestral residence) and became *nagorik* (citizens) here." Although residents in India at the time of Partition and therefore "Indian" by birth, citizenship in the new nation of India had not arrived fully formed in their lives. Conversely, while secure in their status as citizens in East Pakistan, Rahman's choice of words subtly suggests that being residents somewhere was not the same as living at home. They had moved from dwelling in a *boshot bari*, a physical home, a lineage, to dwelling in a status, stable but hollow.

State narratives, in contrast, homogenize migrants and emphasize their own role and involvement in managing refugee mobility and resettlement more than the narratives of self-reliance told by migrants themselves.[37] In northern Bengal, the presence of the state was certainly felt in providing labels with which Muslim migrants could classify themselves and others for the limited recognition that was forthcoming from the East Pakistani state. In a larger sense, the states did provide the systemic pressure to induce people into making these choices of citizenship. Yet, not only do the terms of these migration histories in the borderlands of northern Bengal decenter the state, they also depart sharply from the paradigmatic experience of Hindu refugees crossing the border to India.

Scholars writing about Hindu refugees in West Bengal and Assam have emphasized the political importance of refugee mobilizations and organizing to engage the state in shaping policies and party politics.[38] While exchangees were Hindus and Muslims—indeed, they were interdependent in exchanging with each other—the historical and popular record is dominated by the experience of *a* quintessential refugee: Hindu, upper caste, and male.[39] Shelley Feldman argues that this "exclusion of and silence from East Bengal" is not accidental but reflective of the nationalist narratives that dominate studies of India, Pakistan, and Bangladesh. To engage this silence as a form of feminist critique is not simply to recover particular histories but to provoke a conceptual reorientation.[40] The nostalgia for *chhere asha gram* (the left-behind village) that frames Hindu refugee identity and proliferates in West Bengali cultural representation and iconography is insidiously cast as secular universal experiences of displacement in the twentieth century.[41] This kind of nostalgic attachment to a lost *desh* (homeland) and yearning for an impossible return was completely absent in the narratives of Muslim exchangees to Pakistan.

For Fazle Rahman and his family, the estrangement with "India" at the scale of national belonging was refracted through a slow rupture in ties with their Indian relatives, culminating in a dramatic choice of life and death during the 1971 War.

All of us fled to India during *Joy Bangla*—except Abba. He was adamant. He said that when he left Kathalbari [India] he had sworn that he would not set foot on Indian soil again, and we just could not persuade him. He was sleeping in the afternoon; the Khan *sena* [the Pakistani army] came with Biharis from Lalmonirhat. I had come just that morning to see him. We had got news in India that some neighboring houses had been burned down, so I had come to check on Abba and our house. We had hidden our cycles and some other things in that pond [pointing to one next to his house]. We had seventy-four pumpkins at that time—I asked him if I should take some of those. He scolded me, saying, '*jahan bache na, kumra nitey chao?* [Can't save our lives and you want to save pumpkins!]' But he made me take a sack of grains. He sent me away immediately and was very worried. They would especially target students, so he forbade me to come again.

In a tone of bewilderment, he described the chaos through which their lives turned topsy-turvy in the country to which they had migrated and painstakingly rebuilt their worlds. I, too, was startled by the revelation of Mr. Rahman's father's death and the suddenness with which it appeared in our conversation about the 1960s.

"But Abba refused to come with us. He had been so hurt while leaving India that he would not break the vow of no-return." For a generation of Muslim migrants, hurt and death came between being denied their lives as "Indian" and embraced as "citizens" in the East Pakistan borderlands. Under duress, Mr. Rahman's father refused to migrate to India, however temporarily. This "mute condition of restraint" was transnational dwelling as immobility, at home nowhere; a kind of duress that Ann Stoler—via Frantz Fanon—describes as "a form of power that slashes a scar across a social fabric that differentially affects us all."[42]

This refrain about Abba's refusal punctuated Fazle Rahman's memories and mediated his own relation to "India" and all his relatives on that side. His father had left behind a brother, two sisters, and several cousins. Although Mr. Rahman was acquainted with them all, he neither crossed the border to visit them nor made any effort to keep those connections alive. The Enemy Property Act of 1967 had made maintaining contact with "enemy aliens" across the border an act of treason and thus fraught with danger.[43] "They have all become strangers now. So much has changed there. India has become *ojana* (unfamiliar) now. *Tumi khoj koro* [You can go look for them]."

At the same time, Fazle Rahman was a *muktijoddha* (freedom fighter). He had joined the Bangladeshi resistance right after his father was killed. In the afternoons that followed, we spoke in great detail about his experiences of fighting in the war and his nationalist dedication toward Bangladesh, to which he devoted himself in his subsequent career as an educator. His telling of the past, of the soured relation with India *and* with Pakistan—to which host-turned-enemy state he had lost his father—was irrevocably shaped by his identity as a freedom fighter.

Amena's declaration of her father-in-law's death by heartbreak after migration from India no longer seemed so metaphorical or melodramatic as it first had. Citizenship was hardly bureaucratic and national belonging was always geopolitical, material, and affective all at once. As meanings of mobility shift over the course of one's life, with marriage, death, and aging,[44] so too do these attachments. Belonging in these distinct registers could—and did—shift dramatically in relation to the subcontinent's tumultuous politics.

HISTORIES OUT OF (NATIONALIST) TIME

Though lumped in the same category of *muhajir* by the East Pakistan government, the contrasts between Muslim *badli kora* (exchangees) and *colonir lok,* Muslim refugees who settled in state-designated colonies, were vast and significant. The exchangees decided to migrate to East Pakistan after considerable deliberation and making practical arrangements, particularly to protect propertied wealth; *colonir lok* were displaced overnight in episodes of religious violence in the simmering years after Partition. One had property to exchange and protect and social capital with which to do so; the other had meager properties that were abandoned or destroyed and thin social networks and resources. Decades later, the exchangees have built social status and political capital over a generation in independent Bangladesh; the colony inhabitants continue to stand on shaky grounds of political identity and belonging. One spoke of their "India" past unabashedly and sought me, the Indian Bengali, out, with volumes to say; the other is shamed for being "anti-India," with a migration history no one cared to lament or memorialize in contemporary

Bangladesh. I only found it by accident.[45] It was with a place name on an auto route between Madhupur and Lalmonirhat—"Itepotha colony"—that I began to inquire.

Marginal peasants, the Muslim families of the colonies were spread out over lower Assam and the eastern margins of the Cooch Behar princely state at the time of Partition and were caught up in several localized incidents of religious conflict in the early 1950s.[46] In my interviews with families across three such colonies in Lalmonirhat district, Bangladesh, I was struck by the absence of a *single* event or day of violence that was shared by all those displaced, of the kind that dominates our understanding of Partition-related violent displacement in South Asia or elsewhere.[47] Instead, those forced to move told me "those days cut into our minds," referring to a period of time. They were multiple and highly local but nonetheless "critical events."[48] These ranged from disputes over the price of grains in the market to participation in local fairs, or existing relations of wage work. In incidents that have not merited official designation as riots in either nation's histories,[49] people spoke of their displaced parents being paralyzed by fear as homes and barns were set ablaze and their neighbors pressured them to go to Pakistan, which they were told was their place as Muslims. "*Oi dingular resh mone kanta-tarer thekeo dharalo* [The memory of those days cuts sharper than the edge of the barbed wire fence]," said an elderly man in an especially difficult interview.

For many, the details of their family's violent displacement and journey across the border, which frequently involved multiple stops before finally settling in the colonies, was not simply a matter of knowing or remembering correctly.[50] For these families, there was not a tin-trunk archive full of records to support claims and stories; oral histories did not annotate extant documents. Narrating the inherited history of his family's displacement, Shakib, a middle-aged male resident of one of these colonies, charts his complicated relationship to each of three postcolonial states that have attempted to exercise national territorial claims on the region that he calls home. "I am Bangladeshi, I was born here in Pakistan times, but my forefathers were Indian." "*Shunechhi* [I have heard]," he continued, tracing his father's family's steps: "First, they came to Kurigram—just across the border. Then the government gave us land and arranged seventy to eighty households to settle down together by forming colonies. Like this *colony*—

at the beginning it had only *shottor ghor* (seventy houses). Now that has grown in number, like our own family. Everybody in this *colony* was from Assam, Cooch Behar, Alipurduar, Goalpara, Dhubri."[51]

This "*shunechhi*," which prefaced the oral histories I recorded, was pointed. It did not simply mark the mode of inheritance and transmission of personal history: oral. This *shunechhi* could function as an alibi against accusations of antinational feeling. *Shunechhi* put hesitation on record. Whether in India or in Bangladesh, borderland residents were particularly suspected of being disloyal, too close to the neighboring country by way of transnational kinship and histories of migration. After all, it was quite likely that they had been on the other side at some point, as indeed these stories make clear. In 2016, the resurgent nationalism of the Awami League led to the drafting of a law that made disputing the "facts" of the genocidal war or in any way sympathizing with Pakistani perpetrators a punishable offense.[52] In India, the vilification of the "illegal immigrant" made synonymous with the Bangladeshi Muslim had gained popularity within a Hindu nationalist imagination. In this way, migration histories had the potential to become subversive footnotes to nationalist history, shaking the iron cage of *shothik itihash* (correct history).[53] The nationalist affiliations—perceived, attributed, or claimed—that migration histories suggested was a matter of tremendous and abiding political contention. Whether in India or in Bangladesh, migration histories that do not serve nationalist accounts are dangerous. Borderland residents tread these margins every day, navigating this side and that side, deeply aware that sides may shift. This dwelling through mobility aspires to transnational ties through various kinds of cuts across the border, not its closure.

Age, gender, and the authority of witnessing assumed significance in these "arrested" migration histories. Describing the status of resistance stories in the Tibetan community's dominant current of history in exile, Carole McGranahan suggests that "arrested histories are not so much erased or forgotten as they are postponed and archived for future use."[54] Unsurprisingly, I would be frequently advised to seek out old men as authoritative storytellers. On one such occasion, I waited as residents of a colony chased after a *murubbi*, an elderly man, one of the few surviving members of the original set of colony families who, they insisted, could tell me his "eyewitness accounts of real history." On this day, my presence became the occasion of a small storytelling gathering. As the elderly man prepared, his sons, daughters-in-law, and neighbors debated whether or not he would actually be able to remember and recount the history "properly." As we waited in the heat outside his thatched-roof and mud-walled house more than sixty years after the homestead had first been built in that spot, he broke into tears. "They [Hindus] set fire to our homes. We left in fear."

> At first, we all came to Tiktiki [in Lalmonirhat district]. We came completely empty-handed, not even a *hari-kula* [utensil] in our hands. We had fled, leaving our homes behind. Then when we heard that the Pakistan government was giving land in these colonies to those who came from Hindustan, we came here. There was nothing here—*khali jongol* [only jungle]. There was just one resident house, of Halim *saheb*. He was the *jotedar* in the area.[55] The *sarkar* [government] gave rations for some time. There was nobody of your own here. But since we were given *thakar jayega* [space to live], we had to live. We started farming with borrowed *jontro* [tools] from Halim *saheb*. Somebody called *chacha*, someone *mama*, someone *dulhabhai*, in this way we all came to live together [as kin]. People started marrying each other in the *colony*.

My fieldnotes could not keep pace with the detailed discussion of the borrowed farming tools and other shared household objects; in that moment I had not grasped the value of these implements in the social history of this refugee settlement. Unlike most other displacements and refugee protections of the twentieth century, there was little ambiguity or contestation about the nature of political relations with the postcolonial states: there was no question of return to India, unlike the case of Kashmiris in Pakistan[56] or Tibetans in India,[57] nor did they have to struggle for recognition as citizens as with the continued case of Biharis in Bangladesh.[58] Sharing these histories were not "commemorative events"[59] that dramatized the political valence of collective memory, where individuals remember against the nationalist grain or at odds with singular nationalist stories of displacement.[60] In these recollections, *thakar jayega*, an uninhabited and so-far uninhabitable place to live, became a place to make a life. Refuge came from the kinship that sprung up in these colonies, the hospitality they received from local residents.

These stories and remembrances index a rather perfunctory relationship with the host government, the state by which they had been embraced as new citizens. Instead, families emphasized the harsh struggle of surviving amid absolute poverty and the socioeconomic ways in which they were born again to become rooted among their immediate local communities. These "dissenting memories" have not become histories, neither nationalist nor subaltern, in any of the postcolonial states.[61] So, while local historiographical efforts, for example, painstakingly documenting the *sangram* in the Lalmonirhat Jadughar (Museum), have fixed their compass to finding a place in the Bangladeshi national imaginary, there is no place for these colonies in that history. Instead, other kinds of struggles and idioms of dwelling were foregrounded, ones that were absent in the narratives of propertied exchanges. Frequent pauses and long silences expressed the embarrassment that many displaced families felt when they recollected the destitution of those days. One recalled:

> We came and cultivated rice here after clearing the forest—buying seeds in Durakuthi and Lalmonirhat. *Tokhon khub obhab* [those days were of scarcity]. It was a struggle to keep ourselves fed. We used to work as daily wage workers in the homes and fields of the local resident landowners, like the home of Ganga *dhani*. There were days when we had to make *ek powa chaal* [250 grams of rice] last for two days for six of us. Pakistan government gave us wheat to cultivate, but we were not able to make it grow here. So then we stopped and grew jute instead. But there was a lot of theft in those days. When we would leave our bundles in the water, they would get stolen. What could we do? We didn't know that many people, how could we start a fight about all this? . . . *Ki koi, ekhane bash korte mele kosto korsi amra* [What can I say, we struggled a lot to settle here]. It was not all happiness.

Settlement came in the classic agrarian form of clearing land and cultivating it.[62] Members of these families spoke in detail about what crop they had grown in the initial years, how they had borrowed implements to collectively clear the forest, worked in groups to prepare individual plots, suffered from low and sometimes failed yields, and taken desperate measures to tackle hunger. With these narratives of toil and deprivation, they highlighted their self-sufficiency, underlining that they were not needy refugees dependent on the government dole. The simple *"bash korte"* [to live or settle here] conveys a range of complex processes of translation and endurance in the margins of difference. Claims to land and belonging were forged through this arduous process of getting to know the land better, of teasing yields out of this intractable soil, of enduring an unknown social geography and transforming it through new relations of labor and capital. Dwelling meant making this place habitable and their own: these material and affective ties were stubbornly local. To the soil—and time—of Pakistan in which those struggles of transformation and endurance and a material future had been made possible.

Although I found that members of borderland families down the generations were well acquainted with their respective family history of migration, in the colonies, people were reluctant to reminisce. When my presence prompted collective recollections, not least because I was an Indian Bengali, they would frequently lead to heated debates. Ethnographic thick descriptions were hard to come by; Renato Rosaldo's question in the context of comprehending the connection between grief and rage echoed: "Do people always, in fact, describe most thickly what to them matters most?"[63] Refugee life invariably entails multiple temporalities;[64] these histories grapple with this under the weight of a normative temporal (and political) progression between mobility and settlement.

I am still startled when I think of the time an uncomfortable son admonished his father: "*Oi juger alap ei juge korle to cholbe na* [You cannot talk of those times in these times]." This objection pierced the collective that had gathered beneath a shady mango tree, remembering, listening, questioning, and even laughing together. Everyone fell silent for a few minutes and the storytelling session lost much of its energy after the man left. Such a prohibition signals the profound instability that time brings to place-making.

The prohibition—*you cannot talk of those times in these times*—lingered as a question for me. "Those times" and "these times" are historical moments, but also physically located and socially marked places. The time-place referred to is that of East Pakistan, which bears an odd relation to the time-place of Bangladeshi nationalism today. Moreover, colony residents are situated awkwardly to that time-place of East Pakistan which leads, invariably, to the 1971 War. An explanation came unexpectedly a few days later. One evening after a day of interviews, I was watching TV with one of the colony families. A nationally popular freedom fighter had died, which was reported on all the news channels. Suddenly, the grandfather in the family (who we thought was dozing) spoke up: *"Ke polaye ke thake, ke ba jane* [Who ran away, who stayed, who can say]?" I exchanged a puzzled look with Rupsha, the teenage daughter, who was sitting beside me. "What do you mean, *nanu?*," Rupsha asked. After a few more cryptic statements, the old man explained that he and his peers in the colony, all able-bodied men at the time of the war, ran away and hid for weeks in some neighboring villages that were considered to be safe. "Everybody, all young men ran to join it [the 1971 War]. We didn't want to fight. Pakistan *sarkar* gave us a place to stay here, but now everyone said we are Bangali, we have to get rid of the Pakistanis and have our own *sarkar*." To claim no part in the war for independence is a matter of great shame in contemporary Bangladesh. Residents in these colony villages were reluctant to speak of the circumstances leading up to the war and the development of the nation thereafter, often saying they had forgotten.

Having suffered for being Bengali Muslims in India and with no particular cultural attachment to the growing Bengali nationalist movement in East Pakistan, this group of migrants in the 1950s did not readily identify with the anti-Pakistan upsurge. The "gift of citizenship," as Mimi Nguyen has powerfully shown in the case of American liberal empire, commands an eternal debt for "the precious, poisonous gift of freedom."[65] The promise of freedom accrues its own debts and attachments in postcolonial South Asia. Colony residents felt alienated by the popular support for India as a place of refuge, having been violently displaced from there once already. In the political landscape of independent Bangladesh, they identified with Ziaur Rahman and his party's anti-India stance. As Bangladeshi and as Muslims, they wanted to mark their difference and distance from India; however, their allegiance is shaped by a material history of dwelling. These experiences lurk beneath the surface, as "cracks in the national story."[66] In the present volatile political climate of Bangladesh, this group of citizens is at an odd relationship with the dominant arc of nationalist history.[67] As these discussions drew me into local and contemporary politics through a series of assumptions that linked citizenship to identity and loyalty—including mine—it showed the extent to which identifications between places and people are vexed political issues with recursive lives *across* generations. Regional geopolitics is not a rarefied field of high politics but in fact intimately grounded in these everyday risks of admitting to and narrating migrant pasts.

A FUTURE PLACE OF REFUGEE-CITIZENSHIP

If the people of the colony dwell as Bangladeshi citizens through an unspeakable migrant past, Hindus who clandestinely migrated from Bangladesh to settle in the Indian borderlands *after* 1971 describe themselves as *shoronarthi* (refugees).[68] This identity, however, is not one that is bestowed upon them by the Indian state. "Illegal immigrants" according to Indian law, which marks March 1971 as the cutoff date for migrants from Bangladesh who are eligible for citizenship in India *as* refugees,[69] these Hindus from Bangladesh have long sought to differentiate their migrations from other "illegal immigrants"—read, Bengali Muslims—by performing what I suggest we think of as refugee-citizenship as a form of futurity. The stakes of this differentiation have become urgent in recent years, with the Hindutva underpinnings of the Modi-led Indian government, under whose auspices the search for the "illegal migrant" has intensified across the country.

At the same time India has constitutionally amended the basis for citizenship in India with the enactment of the Citizenship Amendment Act 2019, transforming it from a secular category to a religious one.[70] What appears as a crisis of secular citizenship—with the potential exclusion of millions of predominantly Muslim and lower-caste groups alleged to be "illegal migrants" and the promise to accelerate the inclusion of Hindus persecuted in neighboring countries—is in fact possible because of a long history of slipperiness between the categories of refugee, citizen, and migrant. It is in this context that we must ask: What is the substance of this "hailing" as "*shoronarthi*," in Althusserian terms, in the name of a category without legal recognition? This speculative relationship with refugee-citizenship among Hindu migrants in the Indian borderlands as well as aspiring migrants among the Hindu minority in Bangladesh can be read as an effort to legitimize their physical place and presence in Indian territory despite their clandestine mobility. The "performative force" in this hailing is an imaginary and paternalistic relation with the state.[71] This refugee-citizenship, however, is all but settled.

I was back in the Kathalbari bazaar (India) after some time in northern Bangladesh in February 2015, which included some visits to the colonies discussed above. The opposition alliance, led by the Bangladesh National Party, had launched a countrywide blockade in January, protesting a year of what they alleged was undemocratic rule by the Awami League, which had forced elections and swept into power in January 2014. Even the international media picked up on the ongoing political violence in Bangladesh, framing it as an undemocratic suspension of the rule of law and simultaneous rise of Islamic fundamentalism.[72] Borderland residents in Kathalbari were certainly abreast of news in adjacent Lalmonirhat and Kurigram districts. Dilip Barman, a man I knew only as a friend of Malati-di (with whom I lived in Kathalbari) and who cycled past our house four times daily from his house in the neighboring village to his shop in the Kathalbari bazaar, was most vocal in his interest. In Kathalbari, Dilip-da is the secretary of the temple committee and the keeper of a *dashakarma bhandar,* a popular store for items of Hindu religious practice. He had migrated to the Indian side as a teenager in the early 1980s with his family, and spoke of his childhood memories of the 1971 War with a mix of bitterness and bravado. His favorite story was of hiding in a ditch by the side of the road in Lalmonirhat, caught in the firing by Pakistani soldiers upon fleeing Bengalis while freedom fighters fought back. Each time I heard him tell the story, always in his well-worn *dhuti* and sleeveless vest, his sacred thread visible over his protruding shoulder blade, he would drop down to his knees and duck his head. Sometimes the bullet would graze his ear, sometimes his hair.

Dilip-da usually ignored me, which I concluded was because I had never taken up his invitation to attend the regular gatherings in the temple. Over the previous winter, on at least two occasions, I had skipped the *kirtan* and *katha* (music and discussion) and had slipped in to join Malati-di for the delicious hot meal they served at the end. So, when he stopped by one morning to ask me to meet him in his shop, I was mortified at the thought of being told off. His shop was the site of a daily gathering of a particular network of Rajbangsi and other lower-caste Hindu residents—all of whom had migrated from across the border at different points of time over the last few decades.[73] Conversations about temple activities, comparative prices of food items on both sides of the border, politics, and local news all bled into each other. As we sipped tea, he had pointed questions for me regarding Lalmonirhat during the forty-five-day-long national blockade. "Has any Hindu temple been attacked? What about one tucked away behind Goshala Bajar?" When I confirmed that I had not heard of any attacks, he seemed almost disappointed and continued probing. "What about Hindu homes? Any temple within villages?" I reiterated that I hadn't heard of any such incident but admitted that did not mean that there had been none. I remember feeling nervous at being quizzed, especially in the presence of several other elderly Hindu men, locally venerated for being pious and moral leaders in the Rajbangsi community.

I had barely begun to answer these questions as gathered residents (almost always male) began to offer stories on these subjects, both attacks on Hindu religious sites and on practicing Hindu men and women, from their own repertoires. Nobody spoke in the first-person narration of personal experience; nor did they speak to me directly. This was another instance of something I had marveled at and noted in my fieldnotes several times: their voices echoed each other as if collaborating to tell a story whose denouement they all knew. Narratives of dwelling (*bash kora*—literally, to dwell), past and present, are common subjects of daily discussion; unlike with the Muslim migrants, they were neither about properties and exchanges nor about the physical toil of agrarian cultivation and settling land. By contrast, these accounts of unsettled life as minority citizens in Bangladesh and postmigration life as putative refugee-citizens in India centered on religious practice and the material conditions and structures for those practices. Their relationship to the national territorial space of India is most emphatically premised on being *Hindu* refugee-citizens; caste distinctions are noticeably absent.

The question of property is particularly contentious in Bangladesh. The Hindu minority has a fragile relationship to land and property, after what has been described as state-sponsored land grabs and the dispossession of minority citizens in the loss of agricultural and homestead land under the guise of enemy property laws dating back to Pakistan times.[74] While some would invoke their "birthplace" (*janmasthan*) fondly, it was never

22. The Hari Temple at Kathalbari, Cooch Behar district, its scaffolded spire in the background, expanded by Rajbangsi migrants from Bangladesh, shares a wall with the Kathalbari madrasa.

devoid of the violence they experienced there. There was no nostalgia for a return, nor was the "*desh*" a rural idyll of the earlier generation of dominant caste Hindu refugees, perhaps made most famous in the films of Rittwik Ghatak.[75]

The emphasis on *bash kora* forces us to expand our understanding of dispossession as not only an individual's propertied loss but also the impossibility of inhabiting a physical space as a religious community in material and spiritual practice. A comment on the absence of religious freedoms and pluralism in Bangladesh was implied by a contrasting emphasis on the flourishing activities and plans of the Kathalbari Hari Mandir, to which most of them were devoted. The Hari Mandir was both a community of worshippers and a physical structure that brought the Rajbangsi community together in this part of the Cooch Behar borderland. The temple with its small courtyard, abutting the bazaar and located opposite the Kathalbari mosque, seemed to be perpetually under construction (fig. 22). It was always humming with people and plans: they shared responsibilities to collect funds, maintain the temple and its yard, and organize monthlong daily religious gatherings accompanied by meals (*bhog*). "Having come as refugees, we found *shanti* [peace] here at last," said one middle-aged couple at the end of a *kirtan* session. We sat in a dimly lit corner of the temple courtyard, talking through the buzz of surrounding voices and the clink of cymbals as they were put away for the night, and looking at the bright lights of the temple itself in silence. *Here* was the Hari Mandir, this community of Hindu migrants and Hari *bhaktas* (devotees), this Kathalbari bazaar, this India.

This level of organized activity, bolstered by voluntary labor as well as financial support, was relatively recent, Rajbangsi elders recall. In 1971, when the Kathalbari *panchayat* area was host to thousands of refugees fleeing the war, this temple was a mere shack, a small tin shed at the edge of the bazaar. It was only with the increase in the number of recently settled Hindus, who had escaped religious precarity in a state-declared Islamic Bangladesh (1988–2005), that their enthusiasm for the collective and public observance of religious rituals resulted in the expansion of the Hari Mandir. Understandably reluctant to discuss either their clandestine journey across the border or settlement in the Indian borderland, they were eager to talk about their life as *shoronarthi* and that they could "observe religious practices in comfort." Stories of dwelling in discomfort stretched out roughly between 1971 and present times and conjured a gendered geography of belonging. The border marked a territory where Hindu women were unsafe (girls could not travel to college in district towns alone, women could not observe rituals or festivities in public spaces in the village) and Hindu men were emasculated (men could not press political, economic, or social claims, or suffered workplace indignities in silence). This narrative of persecution and appeal to the masculinist protector-state of India is reproduced over generations across these borderland villages. In the precincts of the Hari Mandir devotees spoke of their migrations from Bangladesh and arrivals and settlement in the Indian borderland with the collective pronoun *amra*, "we."

In contrast to the collectively mobilizing, rights-claiming political subject of post-Partition West Bengal,[76] we see a different kind of political performance and claims-making. The freedom to be anonymous in the ordinariness of a citizen seemed to be ultimate aspiration; this ordinariness was no unmarked quality, as it hinged on becoming a part of the religious majority of India. Even as these stories located these migrants as rightful residents of Hindu *Bharat,* they also produced margins of difference. They inadvertently dated their migrations through references to political events and figures in Bangladesh as well as West Bengal. On the other hand, the emphatic descriptions of ritual life before and after, emphasizing caste specificities and separation from Muslim neighbors, set them apart from local Rajbangsis. In candid moments, migrants from the 1980s and 1990s admitted their initial shock when they found that there was no "Hindu sweet shop" in the bazaars of the borderland villages. Commensality of Hindus and Muslims was not a feature of life that they had expected, and they grudgingly accept it as a feature of the India they were living in, not their Hindu nation of their imagination where they had sought refuge.[77] Rajbangsis in Madhupur *union parishad* (Bangladesh) told me they wanted to "*Hindu deshe shoronarthi hote chai* [become refugees in the Hindu nation of India]" and would refuse to believe that the Kathalbari (India) temple shared its wall and tube well with a madrasa (see fig. 22). The longing and belonging to a Hindu homeland actively articulated in this way constituted a group identity that straddled the border in what Peggy Levitt and Nina Glick Schiller theorize as a "transnational social field."[78] Even in their longing they performed this speculative citizenship—to take refuge would be a necessary step toward absorption as citizens. They believed that they would belong culturally, even as their conceptions of religious life and community were clearly shaped by the experience of being minorities in Bangladesh.

The attitude of local Rajbangsis and those who migrated in the legally recognized period (between Partition and 1971) toward these self-styled "*shoronarthi*" also illuminates how the performance of speculative citizenship is clearly mirrored in the validation it receives, both structurally and institutionally. I was instructed in this by Gopal Ray, who retired as the secretary in a border *gram panchayat* in the Dinhata subdivision in 2015. He and his family had migrated to the Indian side in the early 1950s from Kurigram district. He spoke proudly and passionately about the assistance he and others in local government have provided to "Hindu *shoronarthi.*"

> At that time [when he had migrated] it was the government who registered us as citizens. The condition of Hindus in Pakistan! You cannot imagine! Especially the torture toward our women. Do you think it has got better now? Of course we must help those [Hindus] who escape this torture and come here out of fear. We at the *gram panchayat* have made voter cards for so many people over the years. What can we do? It is our duty to help them, we know how it is there! Earlier it was easier, just a letter from the *pradhan* was enough as a certificate of residence. But it has become harder these days because the Election Commission and the Block Office wants to see birth certificates, your father's documents, your mother's documents.

The acquisition of documents as a step to citizenship is not a matter of mere legality: both Muslim and Hindu migrants employ the same means, with very different outcomes. Speculative citizenship is a process in which the claim to refugeehood is an essential step in becoming a citizen-subject. This mode of speculative citizenship and language of political claims-making was vindicated with the landmark proposal of the Modi government to grant citizenship to religious minorities seeking protection in India from Pakistan and Bangladesh in September 2015.[79] Graphic stories of forced marriages and the rape of Hindu women by Muslim men during Partition riots, the Liberation War of 1971, and the decades thereafter were recalled, repeating and reinforcing the tropes in Hindu refugee narratives that I heard in the Hari Mandir and the Kathalbari bazaar. These are telescoped into a perpetual state of siege against Hindus in Bangladesh, thus standing as evidence of their status *as* refugees. "Home" for Bengali Hindus migrating from Bangladesh to India is articulated in terms of the nation as a necessary step toward attaining recognition and citizenship in its territorial boundaries, even as it materializes through localized everyday practices. It is important to note, however, that their self-presentation in the category of "refugees" is not a desire for relief and rehabilitation from the Indian government, as is the more familiar use of the term in eastern India. This form of "hailing" the state legitimizes their legally questionable presence in the geo-body of the Indian nation as deserving *ought-to-be* citizens in social eyes. Second, and of pragmatic everyday significance, it allowed them safety and protection in their respective new locations as they settled in the Indian borderlands. As Indian border security practices intensified from the late 1980s, this self-fashioning was vital for negotiating the surveillance of the Border Security Force *as well as* the surveillance of neighbors, that is older residents of the region among whom they sought acceptance and sympathy.

RECURSIVE LIVES OF MOBILITY AND UNSETTLEMENT

In contemporary South Asia, borders are the locus of exclusionary nationalism, stitching majoritarian cultural claims to citizenship and belonging. Paying attention to the reproduction and circulation of stories about migration *within* borderlands sheds crucial light on the horizons of possible claims in the present and the politics of history—that is, what stories are silenced, and which kinds of self-fashioning have cachet in a particular political climate. Building from the emphases in this genre of storytelling, the chapter uses "dwelling" as an experiential category to push against the legalistic focus on domicile and residence that undergirds South Asian postcolonial citizenship and refugee regimes. *How* borderland residents render their own—and the region's—histories of demographic change, as they attempt to align residence with senses of belonging and bureaucratic citizenship, illuminates the constitutive contradictions in the categories of citizen, illegal immigrant, refugee, and foreigner, through which the postcolonial states attempt to align territory with desired communities.

Such a vantage point allows us to see the obscured histories of inequity and instability that lurk beneath the certitude of categories. To be sure, I do not mean a redemptive history to add to the collection of postcolonial refugee histories. The material traces on the landscape of layers of dwelling practices—like the well in the backyard, the borrowed tools for farming—and the affective charge of transnational ties question the binaries of displacement/resettlement and refugee/citizen. The politics and struggles of dwelling offer powerful insights to the scales at which belonging and home—as existential and legal but also affective and material conditions—are made and remade and how these assessments of legitimate ways of living as "refugees" or as "citizens" shift over time.[80] Following how borderland residents engage with scalar units such as village, community, state, and region keeps us close to their reference points for dwelling—consisting of refuge, rooting, and *continued mobility*. Perhaps these histories of mobility and dwelling through *un*settlement can offer some clues to the unraveling of citizenship and securitization of borderlands as spaces of suspected foreigners in contemporary India and Bangladesh.

Epilogue

JAREENA'S RELUCTANT MOBILITY

Headaches and dull pains in her legs kept Jareena awake for several nights. Even the last resort of an expensive *bodi* (pill), quite likely to be a generic painkiller, had not brought any relief, either physically or psychologically. Tucking into a *paan-supari* to alleviate some hunger and some stress, the shared gestures of a comforting daily ritual of sociality for Jareena and her friends (fig. 23), she complained that she could not take a rest. She had borrowed from three different microcredit lending organizations—for subsistence, emergency medical, and other household expenses—in the Bangladeshi border village where she lived. She was desperate for the weekly cash necessary to pay the interest due to these lenders. "I have to go to Balatari (India) tomorrow, there is no other way." When I asked if she could take a rest, should the money be arranged somehow, she held my hands, tiredly, looking somewhat conflicted. "There's no point. I have to go. I've taken an advance from Altaf. . . . I'm going to work in his potato fields this week. Now that I've already taken the money, if I don't go, he'll be very angry."

Jareena revealed that she had agreed to work at a lower than usual daily wage rate for Altaf, a farmer in the neighboring Indian village of

214

23. Jareena and her friends after a long day's waged work in "India."

Balatari, in exchange for a small advance that he'd given her in Indian currency notes. Women like her were paid a lower daily wage rate than men in any case. When I pointed this out, indignantly, I was promptly told that it was courtesy of the border and "India" that they were getting any *hajira* (daily wage) at all. Without that wage-labor, "*amra kamla khati* [we are daily workers]" simply for food and some grains at Bangladeshi landowning households, for such arrangements of care and maintenance had been "fixed" for generations between families in rural neighborhoods.[1] Jareena's cousin, who was an informal money changer in the borderlands, had given her a good rate, so she gladly took the deal. But now this debt of labor added to her pressures, for she had to cross over to work in the fields every day for the rest of the week, risking the border turning hot and dangerous, as it periodically did. She felt caught between the risks and promises of the border and the demands of the debt collectors who came to her village from town centers like Dinajpur and Rangpur. Bordering fixed the difference of national and gendered labor markets, bordering was the outside of a feudal agrarian economy, bordering was inside of a transnational neoliberal lending circuit, bordering was the stitches in a patchwork household: bordering cut a thousand times, each time entangling Jareena in the lives of others, in different relations of value.

The next morning, at the start of an excruciatingly hot day, I accompanied Jareena and two of her friends from her home as they walked toward the border. They each carried in their hands a *gamchha* and a full-sleeved men's shirt that they could slip on over their cotton saris to protect their bodies from the scorching sun. Food and water would be provided by the households they worked for. I urged them to rest often in the shade and drink water frequently, as we walked the trail through the fields toward "India." They teased me for being so worried: "If you're so concerned about us, the next time you come from *Amerika* you should bring us each a pair of those *dhopka* [thick and clumsy] sandals you wear." Doubling over with laughter at this unflattering description of my footwear, they joked that they looked good to run in, in case they needed to escape from the Border Security Force (BSF).

We stopped about two hundred meters away from the *zero point*, as the borderline is called in local parlance. Two plainclothes Border Guard Bangladesh (BGB) personnel sat at the bend of the road on a bamboo bench, smoking cigarettes, and watching this path toward India. "*Salaam, saar,*" said Jareena respectfully, "we need to go today. How is the border?" After a pause, "*Thanda* [Cool]?" With a brief and demure exchange, Jareena and her friends carried on, not wanting to be delayed. I lingered, hopeful for a chat, eager to seize the opportunity, knowing how rare it was. After quietly looking at the backs of Jareena and her two friends, gradually becoming smaller as they zig-zagged through fields that were hard to identify as "Indian" or "Bangladeshi," the BGB officer was the first to break the silence. I had been curious to know what he was thinking, but I did not dare ask. When he spoke, his words came as a surprise.

"Did you see the news? Those pictures! Uff, you have to turn away. They are not human anymore, have become skeletons," he said, giving an even more graphic description. After this, he went on, "You see Bangladesh is a poor country. There will always be such cases—What else are poor people to do? They have to find a way to fill their stomachs somehow. Now India is a huge country and it is all around us. That's why I don't stop them when they go. I just say be careful. If something happens to you there, we cannot go in there to save you. Just run and somehow cross back over the zero line at the very smell of trouble."

The pictures he was referring to were those of mass graves of Bangladeshi and Rohingya migrants discovered in the jungles of the Thai-Malay borderlands or washed up on Thai shores near its border with Myanmar. Bangladeshi newspapers on that day, May 3, 2015, and for a few days at that time, were flush with these reports. The horrific pictures were front-page news in all national and local papers in a country that capitalizes on migrants' remittances but is reluctant to recognize them as anything other than workers out of place. As I have been arguing in this book, using the India-Bangladesh borderlands as a vantage point, across the world postcolonial nation-states and publics (including in borderlands) are deeply invested in autochthonous discourses that distinguish migrants from citizens.[2] The BGB officer's commentary, as he stood watch over this theater of duty, grounded structural inequalities and geopolitics in Jareena's cut across the border, connecting her fragmented mobility across this border to the newly exposed corpses on another, neighboring migrant trail.

·   ·   ·   ·   ·

Jareena is not alone in this reluctant mobility, the trip that she was dreading but had to take. Across the world people are faced with decisions they are reluctant to make about the risks, distances, costs, and gains of clandestine mobility. In beginning and ending this book with women's stories of mobility across the agrarian borderlands of northern Bengal, my hope is to underline that gendered and classed bodies do more than merely bear the marks of mobility profoundly unequally. The gendering and nationalizing of bodies, interwoven, produce the very hierarchical relations of value through which bordering unfolds over time, space, and imaginaries. Jareena—and Rani, with whose wedding arrest and continued life of clandestine mobility I began the book—and the many others who have filled these pages, are cross-border wives, separated daughters, commuting daily wage workers, neighbors policing each other, Rajbangsis fiercely brandishing signs of Hindu identity, Indian on paper but Bangladeshi at heart.

Feminist scholars make legible the multiple forms of women's (im) material labor that undergird political economies of production, transnational care, commodity chains, and reproductive units, whether of the family, ethnic community, or commercial establishments.[3] Building on that work, the transnational feminist approach to bordering in this book centers the relational hierarchies—whether of men and women as daily wage workers, of India and Bangladesh as separated markets and economies, or of Bengali Muslim masculinity and mobility as a national security threat counterposed with the vulnerability of Bengali Hindu women— which are constitutive of the devaluation that takes places at multiple scales. Bordering, I hope this book has shown, does not simply have an effect on gendered bodies and relations; rather, bordering itself is a transnational and hierarchical relation of value that becomes concrete through a range of gendered mobilities and immobilities. Contemporary forms of clandestine mobility, then, are not at odds or in a paradoxical relationship with bordering regimes, as is commonly depicted and theorized. They constitute one another in a global system of capital accumulation and gendered racial and class formation. As Radhika Mongia writes: "The very development of the nation-state occurred in part to control mobility along the axis of nation/race," under the British Empire and as a prelude to the postcolonial national.[4] This is the historical and sedimented view offered from the agrarian borderlands of northern Bengal: like a thousand tiny cuts expanding over land and rivers, memories of generations, identities of families, the sleeping nights and working days of rural neighborhoods, deforming and reforming conceptions of space and region. Not a spectacular scar, a definitive event, an infinitely memorialized wound, but a slow, ongoing, and accumulative sharpness; of being with and coming apart.

There are important political and ethical stakes to telling the story in this way. Over the decade of my fieldwork and writing this book, the political debates around migration, borders, and neighborliness have grown shriller in postcolonial South Asia. The answer to who can or cannot be a citizen in India and Bangladesh has become horrifyingly narrow at the cost of minority communities, including those who have lived and belonged to these lands for generations: caste atrocities against Dalits,[5] lynchings of Muslims suspected of eating beef or cow slaughter in India,[6] defiling idols during Hindu religious festivals in Bangladesh,[7] and the systemic statelessness induced through the National Register of Citizens process of verifying citizenship in the eastern state of Assam are but some of the choice highlights.[8]

In Modi's India, Hindu nationalists have attempted to monopolize the substance of the national, be that of territory or identity, and especially of history, recasting it in terms of a singular Hindu homeland, with far-reaching transnational consequences.[9] The militarization of the India-Bangladesh border has long been a bipartisan political issue in India, receiving steadfast governmental support long before the Modi government won a national majority in the 2014 election. However, since then the border has been co-opted as a rigid marker for Hindutva's exclusionary container-thinking in a twofold way: it represents the natural cohesion of the national, a naturalness perceived to be under attack from the mobilities of people and goods across the border, and it symbolizes a separation that is naturalized as a religious difference. In Bangladesh, too, a struggle pitting secular citizenship against political Islam has intensified;[10] it has come at the cost of shrinking democratic space, many lives, and has strengthened the impunity with which the ruling government wields security forces and law enforcement agencies to silence journalists, the political opposition, and activists.[11] It is not a coincidence that in both countries, national history has become a site of national security: state-sanctioned singular versions serving ideological ends are militantly propagated and celebrated, while any debate or dissent can be cast as seditious, against national interest. In the quicksand of these developments, the figure of the migrant is rendered abject and desperate at best and a criminal security threat at worst. As disobedient transnational connections past and present remain the visible seams at the borders of nations, what can this story of a thousand tiny cuts across the borderlands of northern Bengal mean?

A militarized security regime to uphold the sanctity of borders and the hierarchical relations of value in a capitalist nation-state order relies on and exploits the asymmetries of power within regional political economy. But to represent borderland mobilities through the prism of state security regimes is to be afforded the limited choices of victimhood or resistance. In *A Thousand Tiny Cuts* I have refused to narrate spectacular acts of violence and border killings, of which there are many, or gloss these transnational lifeworlds in the borderlands in terms of moral economy alone. Instead, I have searched for an altogether different language with which to narrate and reckon with the depth and expanse of devaluations that bordering brings to the agrarian ordinary news cycles. Following feminist ethnographers of political violence, looking to grasp "intimate geopolitics,"[12] I have allowed myself to be led by the ideas and terms of value that the Rajbangsi and Muslim residents of northern Bengal grapple with: they are neither victims or heroes alone but lead complicated lives. In telling such a story of bordering, transnational households and familial relations are centered as the capacious site at which we can see the interplay of multiple scales and domains of power.

This is vital for two reasons. First, it historicizes our present "crisis of citizenship" in South Asia, attempting to provide an answer to a perplexing question: "How did we get here?" Concerns around exclusionary citizenship and the fragility of legal and bureaucratic status have long been central to the life of borderland residents. Jareena's reluctant mobility, the microhistories of exchange in the 1960s, the tenuous practices of cross-border kinship, the anxieties of agrarian livelihoods and households across northern Bengal all foreground different ways that citizenship is never lived in a singular register nor as a historically stable category. *A Thousand Tiny Cuts* holds space for the range and ordinary eventfulness in which the national becomes tangible in the understanding of identity, economy, and citizenship precisely through transnational mobilities and connections.

Through the decades of decolonization and postcolonial nation-state formation across the world from the 1940s to the 1980s, refugees have been widely considered a problem of the Global South.[13] In the twenty-first century, as new imperial wars and occupations, border conflicts, and strident nationalisms impel refugees by the boatloads to wash up on the shores of the Global North, it becomes ever more urgent to historicize and politicize the figure of the refugee in its particular historically constituted contexts. An ethnography of borderland mobilities shows that being a citizen comprises distinct and interlocking layers of identity and recognition that do not always align, and certainly not in the same ways over generations. How people inhabit these categories and how political subjectivities and communities are forged in relation to them are not as straightforward as indicated from a statist vantage point; neither are they bureaucratic or legalistic struggles alone. These continue to have tremendous significance in regional geopolitics today in influencing what communities might expect of nation-states and how states respond to such claims and visions of inclusion. The citizen-subject, in practice, is linked not only to rights and claims and a transactional relationship with the state but also to social idioms of kinship, hospitality, and social recognition that are marked by deep histories of mobility. Moving beyond laws and bureaucratic complexities, attention to the multiple aspects to dwelling illuminates how *being a citizen* is conceived, enacted, challenged, and defended across historical junctures and as a mode of placemaking through mobility.

Second, my account of bordering aims to de-exceptionalize borderlands and its residents: they are central to the formation of the "national," a relation of value that attaches itself to security, identity, economy, and territory. The tiny cuts of bordering are ongoing, and have birthed national borderlands as particularly disconnected and remote spaces. These spaces, separated and nationalized by the end of the twentieth century, are suitably underdeveloped to be reframed as threatening sites of national security, needing the militaristic and developmental attention of their respective states to be properly settled. In October 2021, the Indian government declared that the remit of the BSF would be extended to areas up to fifty kilometers from India's international borders, an increase from the existing jurisdiction of fifteen kilometers. Overnight, the entire district of Cooch Behar, and several others in eastern India, became designated borderlands, sites of national security. Meanwhile in Bangladesh, since the exchange of enclaves in 2015, the state has been actively incorporating land and people into the fold of the national, through intensive presence and forms of "sovereign atonement"[14] that reinforce the borderness of these borderlands. A story told from the borderlands shows most clearly how political economic questions of land, resources, and the exploitation of labor are routed through the lens of national security regimes in our contemporary world. The cuts of bordering separate and debilitate such that solidarities are hard to imagine. The fraught intimacies and unruly connections that flicker across the pages of this book dare us to think, question, and organize value beyond the "national."

These queries—and this choice of storytelling—are in part inspired by transnational feminist critiques of methodological nationalism. Migration scholars have themselves been guilty of methodological nationalism, naturalizing the nation-state while describing transnational processes and lives and engaging in normative policy debates over the usefulness of migrants and refugees to national polities.[15] In the study of South Asia, I find that methodological nationalism persists by taking borders as self-evident demarcations and focusing on statist processes of resettlement or the experiences of migrants on one side or the other, resulting in "partitioned academies."[16] Studying the cuts of bordering through an analytic of relationality surfaces the heteropatriarchal discourses through which the mobility of people and goods are nationalized and differentially valued as threats. As regional histories and global master narratives of security threats collide in the insistence on a "friendly" border, this book names and describes militarization beyond spectacular structures and violence.

Borderlands are not incidental locations for twentieth-century violent displacements throughout the decolonizing world. The narration of migrant pasts in such postcolonial borderlands does not simply affirm or contest national imaginaries. They reveal the instabilities of the very categories of citizen-refugee-foreigner and the national territorialization of people and places. In choosing to tell the story of fragmented mobilities across the borderlands of northern Bengal through a focus on an ordinary eventfulness, *A Thousand Tiny Cuts* emphasizes that what is considered "national" is never purely so. In postcolonial South Asia it is inevitably transnational, sedimented with multiple attachments and even multiple estrangements. At stake is to strive towards a "national consciousness," which in Frantz Fanon's caution "is the only thing that will give us an international dimension" to counter the violence of the postcolonial national.[17] I do not hope or suggest that the national can be overcome or done away with; that would be naïve. However, this ethnography of bordering does show how profoundly unjust, naturalized, and consequential differences, such as that of the national, are unstable relations, still becoming. In recognizing our transnationally-constituted "national" categories, we must imagine more just, redistributive, and equitable ways of being in relation to one another. As the people of northern Bengal know only too painfully, but also with great lightness and hope, there are many ways to be friendly neighbors.

Acknowledgments

I have long waited to write this part and now it feels so inadequate to acknowledge the years of collective efforts behind this work. I hope that everyone who features in this book (and countless others) recognizes and enjoys their stories in this work even though I have used pseudonyms for people and places. I remain humbled in their friendship and hope I have done justice to the complicated worlds that they welcomed me into and guided me through. My research and continuing engagement with northern Bengal would not be possible without the love and support of those whom I call Malati Barman and her family in Kathalbari, the Rahmans in Madhupur, and Kader in Balatari. I hope I can bring you, my transnational borderland kin, together someday. Many thanks to Badsha Alam of the extraordinary organization Arshinagar in Lalmonirhat, and to B. D. Sharma, Md. Habibur Rahman, and T. M. Islam for enabling my fieldwork at crucial junctures.

I have been blessed with the most exceptional mentors; they have always been there to discuss ideas, offer all manner of support, and share the perspective that there is a world outside the professional academy. A very long time ago, a class in the literature of diasporas with Nilanjana Deb at Jadavpur University sparked an interest in ethnography and derailed me from becoming a book historian. I thank her and my teachers at Jadavpur University for making all kinds of imaginative leaps possible. This book has grown from a doctoral dissertation at Yale University, where I was fortunate to have the mentorship of K. Sivaramakrishnan and Inderpal Grewal. Shivi demanded extraordinary standards not only intellectually but for honesty and humility in scholarship. Thank you for always being available to read, discuss, and advise, with infinite kindness and generosity. Inderpal Grewal's scholarly impact is staggering but I have learned equally about politically engaged feminist work inside and beyond the classroom from her. Thank you both for being such inspirations.

At Yale a great deal that I learned from Aniket Aga, Jafari Allen, Kamari Clarke, Narges Erami, Dipti Khera, Liz Miles, Sara Shneiderman, and my brilliant cohort of 10 Sachem informs this book. I am grateful for the love, drinks, and gossip that Marleen Cullen and Connie Buskey brought in coping with American academia. Kasturi Gupta, Piyali Bhattacharya, and Tariq Thachil made New Haven home, to my surprise. Samar al-Bulushi first became my housemate and then steadily my all-round partner; much of this book has traveled through conversation with her. To the many musafirs of the South Asia studies community that I was lucky to cross paths with, I raise a hot cup of masala chai: Chandana Anusha, Priyankar Chand, Rohit De, Nihav Dhawale, Karine Gagne, Bhoomika Joshi, Vatsal Naresh, Edie Remnick, Jacob Rinck, Sahar Romani, Swapna Sharma, Tanmoy Sharma, Anurag Sinha, and Ali Yawar.

The fieldwork on which this book is based was funded by grants from the Wenner-Gren Foundation, the Social Science Research Council, the National Science Foundation, and Yale University. I am thankful to the Harvard Academy for International and Area Studies at Harvard University and the Watson Institute for International and Public Affairs at Brown University, which provided the privileges of calm space and time to write and resources for the book manuscript to develop. My thanks to Bruce Jackan, Kathleen Hoover, Natalie Gutkowski, Sarah Besky, and Vazira Zamindar for making these spaces hospitable and generative. At Harvard, Ajantha Subramanian enabled critical scholarship, nurturing community and solidarity across groups and hierarchies. I am grateful to have been a part of the stimulating Political Anthropology Working Group. The Atelier community at UC Press is a most precious gift and Kevin O'Neill, editor extraordinaire, is astounding in his commitment and ability to gather people. It has been an honor and pleasure to think and develop this book with my special crew—Kaya Williams, Keisha-Khan Perry, and Alix Johnson. My thanks to Kate Marshall at UC Press for championing this project, selecting excellent reviewers, and supporting the book through all the stages. Thank you to the two reviewers of the manuscript for their time and care in providing constructive engagement.

Over the decade of researching and writing this book, many people have nurtured it with ideas, inspiration, and all manner of counsel and engagement. Many thanks to Nosheen Ali, Sunil Amrith, Anjali Arondekar, Firdous Azim, Narges Bajoghli, Amahl Bishara, Shaheen Bhai, Mona Bhan, Gunnel Cederlof, Sukanta Chaudhuri, Nusrat Chowdhury, Jason Cons, Samir K. Das, Antara Datta, Swargajyoti Gohain, Radhika Govindrajan, Sondra Hausner, Annu Jalais,

Mohamad Junaid, Khushi Kabir, Naveeda Khan, Noora Lori, David Ludden, Catherine Lutz, Ammara Maqsood, Duncan McDuie-Ra, Rimple Mehta, Deepti Misri, Anu Muhamad, Negar Razavi, Sharika Thiranagama, Arupjyoti Saikia, Banani Saikia, Nethra Samarawickrema, Aditi Saraf, Dina Siddiqi, Svati Shah, Sabrina Shamshad, Suchitra Vijayan, and Ather Zia. For generously reading drafts and offering marvelous comments, I am indebted to Attiya Ahmad, Sarah Besky, Steve Caton, Jason Cons, Jatin Dua, Ilana Feldman, Ieva Jusionyte, Kartik Nair, Kevin O'Neill, Jim Scott, Willem van Schendel, Sara Shneiderman, and Ajantha Subramanian. In Singapore, where this book was completed, I am grateful for the comradeship and support of Sneha Annavarapu, Andy Chang, Roselyn de Fabroa, Sidharthan Maunaguru, Yasmin Ortiga and Vineeta Sinha.

I would never have got to this point without my writing companions. I wrote the dissertation over a wonderful, energizing yearlong exchange with Farhana Ibrahim, well before the pandemic moved us all online. Across births, losses, pandemics, and changing time zones, Samar al-Bulushi and Meghna Chaudhuri have been steadfast, anchoring me with support, *adda,* and co-working hours; our rendezvous online have been the most precious refuge. In various writing groups and exchanges over the years, Hayal Akarsu, Radhika Gupta, Kartik Nair, Kalyani Ramnath, Sayd Randle, and Madiha Tahir have made writing fun and inspired me with their brilliance. I am so grateful to you all.

Friends before and beyond academia—Shirsha, Karubakee, Meghna, Ani, Deepti, Fahad, Bhavya, Jayant, Kartik, Rachel, Zoheb, Barbara, Insiya— have sustained me across time and space with their love, lightness, and distractions. Thank you to my sisters, Naini and Doel, for their unflagging devotion and work in keeping our families together through difficult times. Thank you to Asa and Jan for their open welcome, loving home, and sharing the joys of Benareby.

I owe everything to my parents; it seems silly to even attempt a thanks. My mother Malabika followed every day of my fieldwork with tenacious interest, scoffed at the offer of payment for hours of interview transcriptions, and circled many parts of the draft manuscript that she thought could be better written. I miss my father Prabir dearly; even when he didn't understand what I was doing, he was always so encouraging and concerned. I could potentially write a whole other book with the cuttings he made from English and Bengali newspapers of what he thought relevant to my research. I know he'd be so happy to see this book out in the world. I am lucky to have been raised by my maternal grandmother, Banee Sirkar, a fierce woman who challenged numerous social norms, forging a life through war, displacement, and extraordinary losses. Her commitment to public service and faith in the power of storytelling shaped me deeply and continues to inspire. How can I ever thank Martin Mattsson, who makes everything possible and better? All-round champion partner, I cannot imagine this project nor the tangles of life without his companionship and calm, loving support. I completed the dissertation while pregnant with our daughter Tara and wrote this book while learning to be a parent to her. She cares little for the book, though she didn't mind the pictures. On her first trip with me to the place I call Kathalbari in this book, she loudly asked, "why are there soldiers here?" and then, more loudly, "why do they have guns?" Indeed, questions we should all be asking.

Notes

INTRODUCTION

1. In India *panchayats*, clusters of villages, are the smallest units of government with elected representatives. Their equivalent in Bangladesh are *union parishads*.

2. Sartorial choices were important: over time I learned to distinguish Indian prints from Bangladeshi ones on the cotton saris that most women in these borderlands wear. Chapters 2, 3, and 5 discuss sartorial performances with regard to the intersectional values of gender, class, and nationality in establishing one's identity.

3. Cricket matches are a volatile border issue in subcontinental South Asia, where people's true loyalties are said to surface. Cricket mediates cultural nationalism through a particularly virulent celebration of heterosexual masculinity. For an analysis of ethnonationalist masculinity centered around cricket cultures in South Asia, see Hossain (2019).

4. I take postcolonialism to be an imperial legacy and the hegemonic consolidation of the nation-state form across vast parts of the decolonizing world, including South Asia. The postcolonial national, as Nandita Sharma writes, "far from ending the violent practices and relationships of colonialism, marks the ascendancy of the national form of state power and its reliance on *nationalist subjectivities,* national forms of exclusion, and kinds of violence that nation-states carry out" (2020, 14–15).

5. Van Schendel (2005), D. Hussain (2013), Cons (2016), D. Chowdhury (2018), Sur (2021).

6. Value has been a central anthropological concern and anthropology has made an important contribution to pushing beyond economistic understandings of value and the view of humans as rational, profit-maximizing actors. Broadly speaking, there have been two strands: a Marxist-inspired one, which takes labor as the source of value (e.g., Mintz 1985); the second takes desire or exchange to be the source of value (e.g., Appadurai 1986).

7. Ferry (2013, 19), Graeber (2004).

8. Strathern (2020, 2; emphasis mine).

9. Ferry (2013, 25).

10. See Ghosh (2022a) for a photo essay foregrounding the materialities and sensorial experience of militarization in these agrarian borderlands.

11. Rajbangsis are a linguistic, ethnic community historically centered around the erstwhile Cooch Behar princely state and the broader region of northern Bengal that is now within northern West Bengal and lower Assam in India, Rangpur division in Bangladesh, and southeastern Nepal. They are the second most numerous Scheduled Caste group in West Bengal, while in Bangladesh they form a part of the Hindu minority. Unlike the Namasudras in West Bengal, the Rajbangsis do not self-identify as "Dalit." For accounts of Rajbangsi caste and Hindu religious identity, see Dasgupta, Togawa, and Barkat (2011); Halder (2017). Bengali Muslims are around 25 percent of the population of Cooch Behar (2011 Census) while being the majority community in the neighboring districts of Bangladesh.

12. Thiranagama (2011, 7).

13. Heyman (1999), Jusionyte (2013), van Schendel and Abraham (2005).

14. Donnan and Wilson (1999, 2010), Wilson and Donnan (1998).

15. As suggested in the title of Willem van Schendel's magisterial book, *The Bengal Borderlands: Beyond State and Nation in South Asia* (2005), an influential work for spurring culturalist approaches to the study of this and other Asian borderlands. See also Scott (2010).

16. N. Ali (2019), R. Gupta (2019), Ibrahim (2019).

17. Coronil (1997), Taussig (1997). I am thinking with scholarship that engages the political affect of borderland communities and how they relate to the nation-state in a number of postcolonial and postsocialist contexts. See Aggarwal (2004), N. Ali (2019), Ibrahim (2009), Pelkmans (2006), Reeves (2011).

18. D. Chowdhury (2018), Cons (2016), D. Hussain (2013), Kikon (2019), Sur (2013).

19. "Ain o Salish Kendra (ASK)" (n.d.)

20. For ethnographic discussions of injury at and by border structures and architectures, see Jusionyte (2018) on the US-Mexico border and Vogt (2018) on the Mexico-Guatemala border.

21. Massey (2005).

22. Eaton (1993, xxiii).

23. Tracing the diffusion of Mughal culture in Bengal and the varying responses it received, Richard Eaton states that "Kuch Bihar was more than a political frontier" (1993, 187). He recounts the process of "the adoption of fictive genealogies appropriate for an upwardly mobile tribal dynasty" (187) by which tribes aspiring to economic power and political domination deployed Puranic mythology to establish their own links to the high gods of Hinduism, inserting themselves and their lineages into ritually pure Brahmin castes. These origin stories are in wide circulation even today. For a detailed study of sovereignty and political theology in Cooch Behar in the early twentieth century, see M. Banerjee (2018).

24. Samaddar (1999).

25. This was not least because several key India-Pakistan bilateral agreements, such as the evacuation of refugees and exchange of properties, were not applicable to the eastern border. See J. Chatterji (2009), van Schendel (2005, 2009).

26. Tripathi (2016), Murshid (2013).

27. D. Hussain (2013), Schendel (2005).

28. J. Chatterji (2007, 165). Partition caused not only displacement and migration across the international border but within provinces, as religious communities found themselves to be minority citizens and sought to resettle in areas where they would be numerically stronger.

29. Datta (2012).

30. The search for illegal Muslim immigrants occupies not only the state police but private employers, middle-class citizens, and right-wing party workers across the country, targeting the working-class poor in urban slums, trains, construction sites, and even upper-middle-class homes in gendered and sexualized figures of threat. See Ghosh and Mehta (2017), Bhatia and Mehta (2021).

31. For discussions of the Assam agitation, see Baruah (1999, 2009). The Nellie massacre of Bengali Muslims in rural Assam in 1983 (Kimura 2013) was probably one of the most devastating communal incidents in independent India. Its scars on the social fabric (Krishnan 2015) and in the figurations of the citizen and the illegal migrant run deep not only in Assam but across the regional political economy of India-Bangladesh.

32. Over the decades, this hostility has hardened and the nationalist anxiety is expressed at discrete sites, each referencing and shoring up the other—from recurrent questions that are tabled in parliamentary sessions to the Supreme Court panels that monitor the fencing of the India-Bangladesh border, ministerial campaign speeches, and middle-class anxieties in media narratives.

33. With the Ram Janmabhoomi movement and the demolition of the Babri Masjid in 1992, the early 1990s was a particularly important period for the consolidation of Hindutva ideology in India (Jaffrelot 1998).

34. While the shared Bengali identity encompasses both Hindu and Muslim affiliations and contains the possibility of a secular Bengali identity, many have pointed out the tensions that historically arose from the hegemony of a dominant-caste Hindu Bengali cultural identity (Sen 2014). In other South Asian border communities, the question of national loyalty becomes a flashpoint when there is a shared religious or linguistic past and identity (N. Ali 2019; Bal and Chambugong 2014; Gohain 2020; R. Gupta 2019). Minority borderland residents in both India and Bangladesh—whether Muslim in India or Hindu in Bangladesh—have faced social attacks without adequate state protections, which makes their properties, livelihoods, political identities, and cultural histories especially vulnerable.

35. I am building on the work of Subramanian (2009), Shneiderman (2010), Tahir (2017).

36. https://www.telegraphindia.com/india/bsf-enters-deeper-into-bengal-punjab-and-assam/cid/1834528.

37. Massey (2005).

38. Cons (2016), Reeves (2014, 5). For anthropologists and geographers, territory has been the mold, and the nation-state the scale in much of borderland studies.

39. Azoulay (2019, 370). I refer here to the potentiality of photography that she outlines as "an event and an archive," each image bearing the marks of its taking.

40. Haraway (1988, 585).

41. Massey (1994).

42. Aretxaga (2003, 403).

43. The constitutional right to the freedom to move as an Indian citizen that I could assert in the face of the BSF's surveillance and attempts to constrain my movements, I could not resort to in Bangladesh; I carried that knowledge every day, viscerally, and it shaped my fieldwork. Nationality, visa constraints, and gendered vulnerabilities intersect with caste and class privileges to produce a particular racialized experience of doing fieldwork on issues of national security in one's "home" context.

44. Kapur and Cossman (1996).

45. Readers expecting an account of borderland mobilities as resisting the militarization of the border and longing for the abolishment of borders altogether will be disappointed. Similar to James Ferguson's (2013) analysis of the pervasive "declarations of dependence" in southern Africa, my approach in this book is to grapple with the reality that residents' relationships with bordering confound liberal expectations of resistance, violence, and political action. I am attentive to how people may be willfully complicit in the making and reproduction of structures of injustice that demand different explanations beyond the victim/collaborator/perpetrator grid.

46. Ibrahim (2009, 66).

47. Sheller (2018, 10–11).

48. Smith (2020).

49. Bhasin and Menon (2000), Ramaswamy (2010), Anupama Roy (2005).

50. Yeh (2017, 11).

51. Stoler (2013). See also Kotef (2015), Mongia (2018), N. Sharma (2020). I am informed by Sunil Amrith's (2013) sweeping account of the connections of mobility within the hinterlands of subcontinental South Asia to the fortunes of those migrants that crossed the Bay of Bengal through the nineteenth and twentieth centuries.

52. See Bishara (2016) on the politics of fracture in solidarities.

53. Grewal and Kaplan (1994).

54. Lowe (2015).

55. Lowe (2015, 21).

56. By the twenty-first century, the term *transnational* has "become so ubiquitous in cultural literary and critical studies," that Inderpal Grewal and Caren Kaplan argued "much of its political valence seems to have become evacuated" (2001, 664). Heeding this caution, I follow Richa Nagar and Amanda Lock Swarr (2010) who deploy "transnational" as a critical tool of knowledge production that combines an ethical engagement of positionality with enacting accountability at every stage and scale of research and writing. A degree of narrative playfulness (cf. Visweswaran 2013) allows me to stage an analytical and methodological transnational feminist praxis.

57. Cox (2015), Nagar and Swarr (2010), Smith, Swanson, and Gökarıksel (2016).

58. Ahmed (2006).

59. Ibrahim (2011), Xiang (2013).

60. Haraway (1988, 584). See also Abu-Lughod (2008), John (1996).

61. I. Feldman (2019, 491), Ibrahim (2019).

62. Ibrahim (2019, 432).

63. Ali (2019), Robinson (2013).

CHAPTER 1

1. The burden of this history is complicated, for the British colonial state believed that the Rajbangsi and Muslim residents of the Rangpur and Cooch Behar region had a "low standard of intelligence" and that is because the "district had little contact with civilization . . . until railways were introduced 30 years ago" (*Rangpur District Gazetteer* 1913, 47).

2. Bayly (2000).

3. For resource extraction histories see Besky (2014), Cederlöf (2019b), Jayeeta Sharma (2011). For the agrarian settlement of the adjacent territories of Jalpaiguri and Goalpara, see S. Ray (2003) and Misra (2011), respectively.

4. J. Chatterji (2013), Munsī (1980).

5. R. Karim (2015).

6. I refer here to the rich tradition of the phenomenology of space and place that philosophers, historians, and geographers have contributed to such as Casey (2001), Ramaswamy (2004), Soja (1989), Tuan (1977).

7. Basso (1996), Besky (2014), Estes (2019), Ibrahim (2009), Kikon (2019), Subramanian (2009).

8. Cons (2016, 29). For the considerable scholarship on state territoriality and sovereignty in borderlands, see Paasi (1998), Rajaram and Grundy-Warr (2007), Reeves (2014), Wilson and Donnan (1998).

9. Cons (2016, 157).

10. Stoler (2013, 7), Ludden (2012).

11. Stoler (2013, 8).

12. Lefebvre (1992).

13. A. Gupta and Ferguson (1997), Gohain (2019), Harms et al. (2014), Ludden (2012).

14. Taking a sweeping historical view of *Uttarbanga*, or north Bengal, Samir Das (2018) observes that centuries of monarchical and colonial attempts to govern and settle the moving populations of the region into clearly demarcated homelands finally culminated with the postcolonial nation-state formations of 1947. While he focuses singularly on the subnational movements and demands for ethnic homelands within India—omitting a relational and transnational understanding of the development of political identities, whether across the border with Nepal or with Bangladesh—he offers vital historical analysis about the demographic upheavals and settlement across north Bengal in the early twentieth century, which rooted multiple homeland imaginaries instead of a singular, majoritarian Rajbangsi one.

15. Samir Das (2018), Debnath (2007), Ghosh (2006).

16. A. Ahmed (2012, 118). In his study of the politics of belonging and territory in the enclaves of the Cooch Behar–Rangpur region, Jason Cons (2016) has also written about the persistence of interethnic and linguistic boundaries between Rajbangsis and non-Rajbangsi Bengalis.

17. Charu Chandra Sanyal, *Janamat*, January 12, 1948.

18. Jiban Dey, *Octoberer Aloke Alokita*, p. 133–34, quoted by Ananda Gopal Ghosh (2006).

19. For example, Amanatullah Khan Chaudhury, the pro-Muslim League President of the Hitasadhani Sabha, was also the Revenue Minister of the Cooch Behar state in 1946. The British Resident at the Cooch Behar State allegedly nurtured the establishment of the Sabha because it was strongly against the Tebhaga movement that was organizing peasants across the region of northern Bengal at that time, including Cooch Behar, Jalpaiguri, Dinajpur, and Rangpur districts.

20. Reported and discussed widely in issues of the weekly Jalpaiguri-based journal, *Janamat;* quoted in Ghosh (2006).

21. Ghosh (2006). The activities of "pro-Pakistani elements" in Cooch Behar State were also fearfully noted by Nari Rustomji, then posted in the region as advisor to the governor of Assam.

22. Letter from Rajakanta Sarkar, State Prajamandal Cooch Behar to Sardar Patel, July 26, 1948 (D. Das 1971–72, 7:551–52).

23. The West Bengal chief minister wanted to take the political credit for Cooch Behar's accession to India to extend the influence of the Bengal Provincial Congress over the region, while bureaucrats loyal to the Central Congress cautioned national leaders that West Bengali, caste Hindu dominance in the region was greatly resented in Rajbangsi-dominated Cooch Behar, a resentment that simmers still today. Proposals were considered to accommodate the princely state as a centrally governed territory or even affiliate it to Assam instead of West Bengal (letter from AK Hydari, Governor of Assam, to Vallabhbhai Patel, Das 1971–72, 7:549–50).

24. Zamindar (2007, 229).

25. Chakrabarti (1990), H. Roy (2013), Samaddar (1999).

26. Ansari (2011), J. Chatterji (2013), Datta (2012), Sen (2014), Zamindar (2007), Murshid (2013).

27. In this section, I reproduce the spellings from the historical archives from which these stories are drawn.

28. Bangladesh National Archives (BNA) (CR) 20–1/50.

29. There is a much more sinister history of bodily violence on men in relation to Partition and Hindu-Muslim antagonisms. Urdu writer Sadat Hasan Manto portrays circumcision in one of his chilling short stories. See also Deepak Mehta (2000) on circumcision, masculinity, and the relation between ritual wounds and collective violence.

30. Zamindar (2007).

31. BNA, (CR) DO No 105718.

32. BNA, (CR) DO No 105718.

33. Butalia (2000), Menon (1998).

34. Goswami (2010, 114–25).

35. J. Chatterji (2013), Raghavan (2020).

36. Zamindar (2007).

37. See Raghavan (2020) for a historical account of diplomatic cooperation between India and Pakistan in this period.

38. Alexander, Chatterji, and Jalais (2014), Rahman and van Schendel (2003), van Schendel (2005).

39. Ramaswamy (2004, 6).

40. Sur (2021).

41. van Schendel (2005, 94).

42. T. Ali (2018).

43. The deployment of armed forces and repressive penal instruments in the borderlands was not exceptional in Pakistan at that time. As Saadia Toor (2009) notes in her essay on the repression of the Language Movement in East Pakistan, the new Pakistani state was particularly quick to use colonial instruments of power.

44. van Schendel (2005, 157).

45. Galemba (2008), Roitman (2008), Walker (1999).

46. A form of coinage in use until 1957 in India and 1961 in Pakistan, one *anna* in those days was a princely sum to land in the hands of a young peasant boy.

47. Reeves (2014, 104).

48. Glazier (1873), *Cooch Bihar State Gazetteer* (1905), *Rangpur District Gazetteer* (1913).

49. Vas (1911).

50. Boyle and Shneiderman (2020), Gohain (2019), Murton (2017), Rahman (2020).

51. MHA, *Home Ministry Annual Report 1964–65.*

52. Aggarwal (2004), Gagné (2017)

53. Bhan (2013, 16).

54. MHA, *Border Area Development Programme* (2007, 6).

55. Baruah (1999).

56. MHA, *Border Area Development Programme* (2007, 7).

57. MHA, Notice from the MHA to the Department of Border Management for 2015–16.

58. MHA, *Home Ministry Annual Report 1998–99.*

59. Bhan (2013, 129).

60. Bhan (2013).

61. In October 2021 the Indian government announced that the new jurisdiction for the BSF along the India-Pakistan and India-Bangladesh borders would be fifty kilometers.

CHAPTER 2

1. I write about the return journey with Aminul and Najma in Ghosh (2019c).

2. The Indian Home Ministry that oversees border security lists unfenced parts of the border as "sensitive." "Thinking with and through sensitive space," Jason Cons (2016, 7) writes in his ethnography of Dahagram, a Bangladeshi enclave in Indian Cooch Behar, links projects of border security with the creating and assertion of jurisdiction and "nationalist imaginations of territory as "blood and soil."

3. S. Ahmed (2006, 56).

4. "Phenomenology," Sara Ahmed (2006, 5) writes, "helps us explore how bodies are shaped by histories which they perform in their comportment, their posture, and their gesture." She builds here on the interventions made social theorists of embodiment such as Pierre Bourdieu (habitus) and Judith Butler (sedimentation as repetition).

5. *Saheb* refers to the BSF and police officers, while *babu* is reserved for bureaucrats; both are racialized terms of colonial origin and practice.

6. A. Feldman (1991, 155). Drawing on Irving Goffman's theory of performances through which inductions into closed institutions unfold, Feldman analyzes the rites of passage that mediate imprisonment in the "troubles" in Northern Ireland. I extend this analysis of disciplinary institutions by pointing to the social staging of these categories as events in everyday life.

7. The history of informers in South Asia is a vexed topic and pointed in the context of Bengal, where the Bengalis who aided the Pakistani army during the genocide of 1971 continue to be a hated target of Bangladeshi nationalism. See N. Chowdhury (2018) and Mookherjee (2006, 2015).

8. Here too, as Kamala Visweswaran notes, an attention to "language politics and semiotics" in contexts of militarized occupation from Kashmir to Kurdistan reveals that security introduces new lexicons in colloquial use (2013, 15).

9. Young (2003, 2).

10. See Basu (2015), Baxi (2013), I. Feldman (2007), Sriraman (2013), Peteet 2018.

11. Samaddar (1999, 131). See also Bishara (2016).

12. Shovon (2020).

13. McDuie-Ra (2009), Mohaiemen (2011).

14. The parts of the India-Bangladesh border that run through the densely populated agrarian regions of West Bengal and Assam are differentiated from the parts that run through the heavily militarized northeastern state of Mizoram and the hilly terrain of Tripura and Meghalaya, whose tribal communities are violently racialized by the Indian security state in manifold ways. See Kikon (2019), McDuie-Ra (2009), and Sur (2012).

15. Abu-Lughod (1990).

16. van Schendel (2005).

17. See Ibrahim (2021) and Rashid (2019) for similar arguments about the co-constitution of kinship and policing in forming affective regimes of rule in postcolonial South Asia.

18. Willen (2014). I am thinking with Nosheen Ali's passionate and important argument that the "feelings are not only central to the state-citizen relation but also active in the process of research and publication" (2019, 23).

19. Al-Bulushi, Ghosh, and Grewal (2022), Mushtaq (2018), Mushtaq et al. (2016), Zia (2019).

20. Ilana Feldman's (2015b) concept of "security society" for Gaza under Egyptian rule is resonant here.

21. See Ranabir Samaddar's discussion of bureaucratic efforts to fix—and thereby distinguish between—"migrants," "refugees," and "citizens" in the 1990s (1999, 64–69); see also Sriraman (2018). Central to these efforts was the work of T. N. Seshan, the Chief of the Election Commission (1990–96), who spearheaded electoral reforms including introducing mandatory photo identity cards. This is the "voter identity card" referred to here.

22. Lutz (2020).

23. I paraphrase Tobias Kelly's (2006) description, in the context of Palestine, of checkpoints as the key sites where the "texture of occupation is produced and felt."

24. I am drawing on Ajantha Subramanian's argument that state and subaltern actors must be viewed as intertwined and dialectically engaged in their efforts to scale politics "between locality and the nation, and nation and world" (2009, 28–31).

25. Scholars interested in resistance against occupation from Palestine to Kashmir have been especially attentive to how embodied knowledge allows people to navigate state's enclosures. See Bishara (2015), Junaid (2019), Peteet 2017.

26. I. Feldman (2015b, 52).

27. I resist the anthropological move to gloss *du-nombori* solely in terms of local moral economy, whereby that which is illegal in statist terms can be socially rationalized and flourish as licit. While I do not disagree with this argument—indeed, it is relevant here, too—the ambiguities and contestations through which residents and security forces understand the relational value of *du-nombori* are greater than the binary of the (il)licit and the (il)legal or the homogenizing framework of a moral economy.

28. N. Ali (2019, 9), al-Bulushi (2021).

29. Mona Bhan (2013) writes about these forms of subservience that are enforced by the armed forces in India-administered Kashmir.

30. Young (2003).

31. Reeves (2014, 179).

32. Ghosh (2022b).

33. Baud and van Schendel (1997, 216)

34. Das and Poole (2004), J. Heyman (1999, 2013), Jusionyte (2015).

35. Donnan and Wilson (1999, 2010), Wilson and Donnan (1998).

36. A. Feldman (1991, 63).

37. Peteet (2018, 54). Here I am thinking especially of her description of Palestinians' experience of waiting as "stealing time" by the Israeli occupation.

38. I explore this regulatory regime of documentation and identification in relation to cattle in Ghosh (2019b).

39. See also Cons (2016) as he describes a similar economy revolving around cattle slips in Dahagram, an Indian enclave in Bangladesh.

40. As scholars of protracted wars, conflicts, and counterinsurgencies have argued, democratic institutions and the norms of democracy are eroded when armed forces become superior in authority to civil administrations and democratically elected governments in time-spaces of national security. See Bhan (2013), Kikon (2019), Sundar (2016).

41. Berda (2017, 109).

42. Ruben Andersson has argued that accounting for the temporalities of migration controls is a way to overcome the limits of a singularly biopolitical understanding of contemporary border regimes: when they don't incarcerate or subjugate bodies, they "extract vitality" (2014, 806).

43. Junaid (2019, 7).

44. I make this connection between the routine imposition of Section 144 in the borderlands and the seemingly exceptional instances curfews and sieges in Kashmir as part of a collective feminist statement. See N. Ali et al. (2019).

45. Elsewhere I argue that militarization and the gendered logics of security rule at this "friendly" border can only be grasped within a heterogenous national security geography into which this is incorporated by contrast and distinction (Ghosh 2022b).

46. Bhuj is the western Indian state of Gujarat. See Ibrahim (2019) for descriptions of policing in the Bhuj borderlands.

47. Grewal (2006), Kotef and Amir (2007), Visweswaran (2012), Zia (2019).

48. Gold (1997).

49. See Govindrajan (2018a), Lamb (2001), Raheja and Gold (1994), Ramanujan (1991b).

50. For searing accounts of the Indian central paramilitary forces' use of sexual violence in counterinsurgency operations in the civil war against Maoists, see Sundar (2016); in Kashmir, see Mushtaq et al. (2016).

51. "Who are you?" in Hindi. Part of the joking and laughter shared between the Bengali women revolved around conversing in their broken Hindi in these exchanges.

52. Jeganathan (2018, 409).

53. Baxi (2013).

54. Bhan (2013).

55. Human Rights Watch 2010; Ghosh and Duschinski (2020).

CHAPTER 3

1. Constable (2010), Lindquist (2008).

2. Smith (2020, 81).

3. Ahmad (2017), Basch, Glick Schiller, and Blanc (1994), Gamburd (2000), Levitt (1998, 2007).

4. An important exception to this is Alexander, Chatterji, and Jalais's work (2014) on the Bengali Muslim Diaspora.

5. Remarkable oral history archives such as the 1947 Project gather stories of divided families, including for the eastern region. Extraordinary literary works in Bengali, such as the award-winning novel *Dayamoyir Kotha*, have attested to national schisms and losses between childhood and adulthood.

6. Bouquet (1996).

7. For a dynamic feminist reimagining of "generation" that pushes beyond static and successive conceptions of space and time, see Ghosh and Sehdev (2022).

8. This was not only a confusion regarding relations but shock from Rajbangsi and other Hindus in Bangladesh at my residence and commensality with Muslims as a Hindu woman. Deliberating on what kind of caste I belonged to based on my last name, Ghosh, and concluding that commensality could not be permissible in any case often led to tense conversations about minoritarian-majoritarian religious sentiments and rights in the subcontinent.

9. Carsten (2000), Collier, Yanagisako, and Bloch (1987), Yuval-Davis, Anthias, and Campling (1989). Farhana Ibrahim (2021) writes especially about policing practices within the borderland family and argues that the anthropology of kinship must be considered a primary site for the understanding of sovereignty and policing to maintain a contested social and moral order.

10. Rash Mela in Cooch Behar is a significant annual feature on the cultural calendar of north Bengal, an event dating back to the days of the Cooch Behar princely state. As a religious minority in Bangladesh, the scale and number of various fairs organized by Hindus are drastically smaller.

11. Harvey (2002).

12. S. Hussain (2015, 45).

13. Harms et al. (2014).

14. Di Leonardo (1987).

15. S. Ahmed (2006), Khatun (2018).

16. *Times of India* (2013).

17. Data collected from the District Collectorate, Cooch Behar. As they pulled out the records from their steel almirahs, the officers in the section that had previously administered it spoke about it fondly; they didn't understand why it had been discontinued.

18. This is especially true in a recent series of excellent work on Partition's legacies. See, for example, Butalia (2015) and. S. Kaul (2002).

19. Carsten (1995), Peletz (1995).

20. See Aramugam (2020) for a discussion about the pleasures of kinship for women, and Carsten (2000) for an expansive iteration of the idea of relatedness.

For discussions of debt and duty in Bengal, see Fruzzetti (1990). In north India, see Raheja and Gold (1994).

21. Lamb (2001, 537); see also Lamb (2000, 46–50), Gardner (2009).

22. I use quotation marks here to indicate that these proper names were used as such by Shahida Bibi in our conversation.

23. Charsley (2005), Charsley and Shaw (2006), Gardner (2009, 2002).

24. Rihan Yeh examines this fantasy of equivalence in the conversations between Mexican and American interlocutors in the Mexican border town of Tijuana (2017, 81).

25. Kapur and Cossman (1996).

26. Kapur (2005).

27. As the historiography and sociology of South Asia attests, caste and religious difference and hierarchy have profoundly shaped the horizons of community and conviviality, spatially and socially speaking. See Abraham (2018), Thiranagama (2019), Waghmore (2013), Singh (2011).

28. Thiranagama (2019, 295).

29. Massey (1994).

30. Mahler and Pessar (2001, 6).

31. See I. Feldman (2015b), Thiranagama (2018), and Ibrahim (2021).

32. Visiting Bangladeshi kin are not only stopped but also arrested by the BSF under the Foreigners Act. According to the officer-in-charge at the Dinhata Correctional Home, several of the Bangladeshi undertrials (people in jail awaiting trial) belonged to that unfortunate category: visiting kin.

33. Thiranagama (2019, 271).

34. See Sidharthan Maunaguru (2019) for an account of transnational marriages and intimacy across multiple hierarchies of nationality and class.

35. Alexander, Chatterji and Jalais (2014, 19),

36. Maunaguru (2019, 17). I echo Maunaguru's argument that viewing marriage as a process, extended over time and space, takes "in-between spaces" seriously to reveal "how communities affected by violence strive to reinhabit the world" (20). My analysis focuses on the fraught nature of transnational intimacy—an intergenerational reckoning with differences across which social reproduction must be consolidated.

37. Salih (2017, 757).

38. Carsten (1995, 21).

39. In oral accounts of political and regional history, the 1965 India-Pakistan War was referred to as *"chhoy Septemberer juddho,"* referring to the date on which hostilities formally broke out between the two countries.

40. Borneman (1992). In his account of marriages and relative intimacies in the two Berlins, Borneman stresses the importance of the state's ability "to make people into nations" (284).

41. This must be read in the context of ongoing political violence in neighboring Assam over the indiscriminate branding and violent intimidation of Bengali Muslims as "Bangladeshi infiltrators." For insights into the increasing religious polarization between previously co-existing Hindu and Muslim communities in the Bengal borderlands, see Jalais (2013).

42. J. Chatterji (2009), van Schendel (2005).

43. Trouillot (1995, 113).

44. Trouillot (1995, 48).

45. Ghosh and Sehdev (2022).

CHAPTER 4

1. Present district administrators in both India and Bangladesh boasted about the intensified and diversified agriculture of these areas of northern Bengal, as much as their colonial predecessors had dismissed the agrarian potential of these historically frontier spaces in favor of the agrarian settlement of the Bengal plains.

2. Guyer (2004).

3. Galemba (2012), Roitman (2005), Walker (1999).

4. Appadurai (1986).

5. Kopytoff (1986).

6. Ramamurthy (2014).

7. This paragraph is an homage to the brilliant exposition on tobacco and sugar by Fernando Ortiz (1947).

8. Appel (2019).

9. Galemba (2012), Garcia (2014), Roitman (2008), van Schendel and Abraham (2005).

10. I agree with Hannah Appel's discussion of *the* economy as a modular form (2019). Unlike her, I am more interested in the form of the national than the singularity of the economy.

11. Tsing (2005, 58).

12. Appel (2019, 213).

13. Scholar of agrarian markets Mekhala Krishnamurthy (2018) advocates this expansive and versatile method for a rejuvenated study of agrarian economies and markets in South Asia and beyond.

14. As if to confirm how this calculation fluctuated, more recent discussions with Amal-da revealed that the increased vigilance and associated risks and costs of Indian border security has meant that he chose to cultivate *motihari* in the 2019 and 2020 seasons so that he could safely sell to traders in Dinhata instead of relying on the Bangladeshi market. *"Bajar bhalo, kintu eto risk ke*

nebe, amar eto lobh nei [the market is good, but who will take such risks, I am not that greedy]," he told me over the phone. Greed, not legality, was his ethical compass.

15. Mitchell (1998, 89).

16. Cattle are smuggled from India to Bangladesh in large numbers; it is the most voluminous illegal trade across this border. On the Indian side, where the BSF is tasked with preventing cattle smuggling, one modus operandi for smugglers is to have the cattle wait in twos and threes in homes near the border, before they are collectively transported on the planned night in highly organized and elaborate operations. Smugglers will arrange for ten to twenty farmers to keep such cattle for a few nights for a modest fee. See Sur (2021) and Ghosh (2019b).

17. Historical references to the *haat* as a *bondor* reveal the riverine system of transportation that would have carried this commodity in the first half of the twentieth century. See Yang (1999), T. Ali (2018).

18. See Besky (2020), Krishnamurthy (2018).

19. Van Schendel (2002).

20. Saraf (2020).

21. T. Ali (2018), Besky (2014), Cederlöf (2019a), Misra (2011), R. Ray (1995).

22. See Ghosh and Sehdev (2022).

23. Appel (2019, 215).

24. As feminist analyses of the economic have observed, such coexistences are important to note in order to break down the hegemonic dualities of economic thought, such as that between market and non-market, precapitalist and postcapitalist, and as in this case, colonial and postcolonial. See Tsing (2009), Yanagisako (2012), Gibson-Graham (2006a).

25. Bose (1896, 196–98). Tirhut is in what became the state of Bihar in postcolonial India (Sinha-Kerkhoff 2014).

26. Tariq Omar Ali (2018) makes a persuasive argument in this vein by tracing the regulation of jute as a form of nationalism in the years after Partition in East Pakistan.

27. See T. Ali (2018) with respect to jute smuggling, and see chapter 1 for a discussion of conscripting the border as a tool of and for economic nationalism.

28. Goswami (2010).

29. For example, in 2015–16 the total acreage for tobacco in Lalmonirhat district was 11,074 hectares, making it the fourth most cultivated crop after rice (50,135 hectares), maize, and wheat.

30. Here I combine real place-names with the fictitious ones I have been using throughout the book to gesture to the broad region, including some particularly famed areas.

31. Besky (2020), Boyer (2005).

32. As Hannah Appel (2019) notes, the modularity of the economy is closely tied to the modularity of the nation-state form, as analyzed in Benedict Anderson's (2006) seminal work.

33. Appel (2019), Cooper and Stoler (1997), Escobar (2008).

34. Mitchell (1998).

35. Tsing (2009).

36. There are other agrarian crops that have become locally transnational commodities in these agrarian borderlands, such as maize, that I am unable to go into the details of here. All examples other than ganja, however, can be traced back to some form of official agrarian developmental intervention in one of the national economies.

37. According to Chattopadhyay (2018), with Bangladesh's zealous policing of narcotics, descendants in what would have been ganja farming families in the early 1900s do not admit to this past today.

38. This is similar to the domestic consumption of opium grown in this same region by farmers during the British colonial bid to monopolize the opium market; see Cederlöf (2019b).

39. The BSF forbade the cultivation of tall crops such as jute or maize, which interfere with their visibility as they keep watch over the land adjacent to the "zero line," as the borderline is called.

40. Hall (2011).

41. Jusionyte and Goldstein (2016, 4).

42. Guyer (2016, 206).

43. Gibson-Graham (2006b), Ramamurthy (2008, 2014), Yanagisako (2012).

44. Priti Ramamurthy (2014) theorizes the feminist commodity chain analysis as a particularly effective method for tracking how value is created in relation to patriarchy. See also Freeman (2001), Parreñas (2011).

45. Goswami (1998).

46. Goswami (1998, 624–25).

47. Ferguson and Gupta (2002); Reeves (2014) in showing how the state is spatialized in borderlands, and extending that to respond to a call (Schulz and Kuttig 2020) to think with the Bangladeshi state as an object of ethnographic study in South Asia.

48. Seized bundles of ganja often figure with their more dreaded and frequent companion, bottles of Phensedyl cough syrup.

49. Appel (2019).

CHAPTER 5

1. Ethnographers find that residents, especially men, of borderlands from Kargil and Kutchh on the western border to different regions of this eastern bor-

der face criminalization and struggle to establish their trustworthiness to the state. See Aggarwal (2004), R. Gupta (2019), D. Hussain (2013), Ibrahim (2011).

2. I draw on Pandian's (2009) exposition of the ethical horizon of "honest toil" as a means to cultivate virtue for the Piramalai Kallars, a community classified by the colonial state in India as a "Criminal Tribe."

3. Pandian (2008), Singha (2007), Yang (1987).

4. I follow Leela Fernandes (1997) in thinking about gender, class, and racialized religious and caste identities in an intersecting way.

5. While the links between internal migration within a country and international migration from that country have been widely established by scholars of migration (Alexander, Chatterji, and Jalais 2014, Paul 2017, Xiang and Lindquist 2014), methodological nationalism continues to occlude productive analyses of such connections.

6. Amrute (2015), Dattatreyan (2020).

7. Lowe (2015), 35.

8. Douglas and Wildavsky (1983).

9. For anthropological studies of risk's productive aspects in association with speculation and finance capitalism, see Appel (2019), Sawyer (2012), Zaloom (2004).

10. Human Rights Watch (2010).

11. According to the BGB, the number of Bangladeshis killed was 34 in 2012, 28 in 2013, 40 in 2014, 45 in 2015, 31 in 2016 and 21 until December 21, 2017 (*Dhaka Tribune* 2017). For a searing report on the use of nonlethal weapons in Kashmir by the BSF, among other forces, see Inzamam and Qadri (2016).

12. Bhonsle (2016), Kikon (2019), Misri (2019), Thiranagama (2011).

13. Human Rights Watch (2010).

14. Duschinski et al. (2018), Junaid (2016), N. Kaul (2018).

15. S. Ahmed (2013). For details on the violence by the army and the BGB, see HRW (2012).

16. C. Osella and F. Osella (2006, 118, my emphasis).

17. Anthropological scholarship on migration in the 1990s made the important intervention that migration was not solely an economic decision, isolated from other ongoing social and cultural processes in an individual and community's life. See Gamburd (2000), de Neve (2003, 2005), Shah (2006).

18. See Jeevan Sharma (2018) for a rich exploration of the meanings of migration and border-crossing for the formation and consolidation of Nepali masculinity.

19. Radhika Chopra, reflecting on her experience of being a woman conducting research on masculinity in rural Punjab, writes that the village street is not a site where a legitimate form of masculinity is produced and so there is no way that an outsider-anthropologist, despite the privileges and mobility that that outsider-ness affords, can justify being there as part of her work. It is not the

street as a public space per se that makes it "inaccessible" but the combination of gender, time, and space that "veils" this performance of masculinity (Chopra 2004, 48–50).

20. L. Karim (2008), Kar (2018).

21. In the context of widespread male migration to the Gulf in the southern Indian state of Kerala, hegemonic ideals of masculinity—and pushbacks to those ideals in terms of caste or class identity—shift considerably over distinct life courses (C. Osella and F. Osella 2000; C. Osella and F. Osella 2006). Cash earnings and distinct patterns of consumptions are vital avenues for individuals to fulfill and move across these life courses. See also Gidwani and Sivaramakrishnan (2003), J. R. Sharma (2018).

22. Those who worked in the garment industry in Dhaka expressed similar narratives. For scholarly and activist research on this topic, see Bangladesh Garment Sromik Samhoti (2014), L. Karim (2014).

23. Graeber (2001), Nakassis and Searle (2013).

24. Kaplan and Grewal (1994).

25. Bryan, G et al. (2014)

26. Kikon and Karlsson (2019, 39).

27. See Moodie (2010), Ghosh and Mehta (2017), Donthi (2018).

28. "Migration for Development" is a policy framework that unites the work of numerous organizations—such as the World Bank, the International Organization for Migration, the UNDP, and the EU. See Bryan et al. (2014) for a study by economists reflecting this framework of migration remittances as a developmental good. The assumptions of developmental gains is highly gendered: the ideal migrant is male.

29. Liberalization in South Asia, especially in India, and its attendant socioeconomic transformations, has been richly studied through the intersection of youth, caste, and education. See Jeffrey and Dyson (2008), Jeffrey, Jeffery, and Jeffery (2007), de Neve (2005).

30. Urban youth or migrant youth in cities have been the focus of much scholarship on youth in South Asia. For example, Dattatreyan (2020), Lukose (2009), Verkaaik (2003).

31. For instance, Hann and Parry (2018). I follow the approach of Breman (1985), de Neve (2005), and Shah (2006), who have consistently sought to place the agrarian question in conversation with those of gender and class identity while exploring precarities of labor and livelihood.

32. C. Osella and F. Osella (2006). Like Gabriel Dattatreyan (2020), who cautions against presuming a "South Asian" masculinity, I am less interested in a regional distinction. However, I am interested in the significance of *national* identity as one of the factors or forms of distinction that shape masculinity and worth as a man for Muslim and Rajbangsi Bengali men coming of age in these borderlands.

33. The Madhupur High School is the only one for that *union parishad;* there is another one in the neighboring *union parishad.*

34. BRAC and RDRS are large Bangladeshi NGOs; while the former is the largest Bangladeshi NGO, the latter was founded originally as a missionary organization in postwar relief and reconstruction, solely to work in this northern Cooch Behar-Rangpur region.

35. Ministry of Primary and Mass Education (2014). In India, recent studies show a disturbing trend of Muslim rural youth dropping out of education at higher rates than even their scheduled caste and other-backward caste peers (Jaffrelot and Kalaiyarasan 2019).

36. Jeffrey, Jeffery, and Jeffery (2007).

37. *Prothom Alo* (2015).

38. *Daily Star* (2015c, 2015d).

39. *Daily Star* (2015b).

40. See, for example, *Daily Star* (2015a).

41. World Bank (2006). In Bangladesh this national panic over youth drug addiction has recently coincided with the fear of misdirection by another powerful opiate: radical Islam (Hasan 2017).

42. *Daily Star* (2013).

43. This was part of a larger agenda to educate schoolgoers about prominent social issues relating to law and order—such as drug addictions, smuggling, child marriages, and gendered violence.

44. Foucault (2009). The colonial and casteist history of this kind of punitive policing and exercise of pastoral power in South Asia is significant and undoubtedly bears on the present, not least because India and Bangladesh have inherited colonial penal codes and policing institutions.

45. Camp and Heatherton (2016).

46. See, for instance, Govindrajan (2018a), Kikon and Karlsson (2019), Rinck (2020), J. R. Sharma (2018).

47. For a moving account of the Bengal famine of 1943 and its enduring legacy, see J. Mukherjee (2015).

48. In a searing analysis of the withholding of US food aid to Bangladesh during the "man-made famine of 1974," Rehman Sobhan (1979) analyses the broader political economy and geopolitics of food and famines in the 1970s.

49. Gidwani and Sivaramakrishnan (2003).

50. Pandian (2009, 146).

51. Roitman (2005, 21).

52. *Huffington Post* (2015).

53. Attacks on the BSF with stones and bamboo sticks by cattle smuggling groups (*The Hindu* 2015).

54. Take, for instance, the press coverage of the Modi-Hasina meeting in December 2020, and India's efforts to repair its strained friendship through

COVID vaccine diplomacy. Bangladeshi economist and public intellectual Anu Muhamad (19 December 2020) sardonically observed this was the "new heights" of "*soman-soman bondhutto*" (Chaudhary and Devnath 2020). The BSF and the BGB routinely exchange sweets for annual religious festivals such as Eid and Diwali, using these moments to visually propagate the narrative of friendliness.

55. Agamben (1998). For analyses of borders that derive from the space of exception framework, see Díaz-Barriga and Dorsey (2020), Jones (2011).

56. I am inspired by feminist historian Samia Khatun's (2018) call "to hear" histories and social realities of mobility that are not readily available in textual or visual archives.

57. In a pointed critique, Ranabir Samaddar reflects on the lack of connection between agrarian studies and the development of migration studies at the turn of the twenty-first century: "Migration studies has disciplined itself by depeasantizing its own corpus" (1999, 81).

CHAPTER 6

1. *Om* is a syllable that comes at the beginning and end of all Sanskrit prayers and the swastika is the Sanskrit word naming this symbol of auspiciousness.

2. According to art historian Dipti Khera (personal communication), small niches on the wall, usually on both sides of doorways, emphasize the axis of the threshold. They are also meant to hold small idols or talismanic objects. See also Hardgrove (2002).

3. This translates to "Victory to Bengalis," which was the battle cry of the freedom fighters during the War of 1971. Colloquially, the Liberation War is still referred to as "Joy Bangla" across Bangladesh.

4. For an overview of this voluminous literature, see Vertovec (2011). For an important critique, see Malkki (1992).

5. 72 percent of the world's refugees are hosted by neighboring countries within developing regions (UNHCR 2022).

6. J. Chatterji (2007), Dasgupta, Togawa, and Barkat (2011), Ispahani (2017), H. Roy (2013), Talbot and Singh (2009), Zamindar (2010).

7. J. Chatterji (2007, 166).

8. Luthra (1972, 15–17), quoted in J. Chatterji (2007, 105). These numbers are notoriously controversial—historians peg the number of Hindu migrants from East Pakistan to India from five to eight million.

9. J. Chatterji (2007, 166).

10. Kabir (2013, 9).

11. Stoler (2016).

12. See for instance, J. Chatterji (2013), Datta (2008), H. Roy (2013), Sen (2011, 201).

13. Hannah Arendt (1973) has explored the connections between home-lessness and statelessness. She writes that while the absence of legal protections and rights creates the abjection of the individual in statelessness, the experience of displacement in homelessness is not simply a material condition of losing a physical dwelling and legal status, but a deeply existential uprootedness.

14. Fouron and Schiller (2001), Kanaaneh and Nusair (2010), Yuval-Davis (2006).

15. Constable (1999).

16. Thiranagama (2011).

17. I. Feldman (2007).

18. Malkki (1995). There is a voluminous literature exploring the juridical and political exceptionality of camps as well as the intensity of regulation and government therein. For an overview, see I. Feldman (2015a).

19. J. Chatterji (2007), Robinson (2012).

20. Robinson (2012).

21. Sen (2011, 20). J. Chatterji (2007), Datta (2012), H. Roy (2013, 2), Zamindar (2007). Historians of South Asia studying documentary regimes that regulated mobility between India and Pakistan and through that define who was—and could be—an Indian or Pakistani citizen note the inconsistent ways in which domicile and religious identity came to define nationality. While Haimanti Roy (2013, 127) has argued that in the 1950s, "minorities were proxy citizens of the other nation," Vazira Zamindar (2007) reads between bureaucratic lines of sorting refugees from migrants, migrants from citizens.

22. Zamindar (2007, 119).

23. Steedly (2013, 9); also Abu-Lughod (2008, 15–18).

24. Ramanujan (1991a). See also Stuart Blackburn and A. K. Ramanujan (1986) for a discussion of South Asian traditions of storytelling, and Radhika Govindrajan (2018b) for an innovative feminist ethnography.

25. Ghosh and Sehdev (2022).

26. Rahman and van Schendel (2003). See also Joya Chatterji's (2007) discussion of the demographic reconstitution of borderlands in the years after partition.

27. Rahman and van Schendel (2003, 559).

28. See Friese (2015); *The Daily Observer* (2015).

29. For historical and ethnographic studies of the enclaves, see Cons (2016), van Schendel (2001); for experience of enclave-dwellers and incorporation into the Bangladeshi state, see Ferdoush (2021).

30. Jansen and Löfving (2009, 6).

31. Cleary (2002), Greenberg (2005).

32. Maunaguru (2019, 57).

33. See also Rahman and van Schendel (2003).

34. Both became districts only in 1984; until then, they were subdivisions of Rangpur district.

35. Datta (2012), Ferdous (2021).

36. Robinson (2012, 352).

37. Talbot (2011).

38. Chakrabarti (1990), J. Chatterji (2007), Datta (2012), Samaddar (1999).

39. Important work focuses on reconfigured gender roles and relations as Hindu refugee women begin to work outside the home (Sen 2011), but the discussion remains confined to privileged caste and class groups. For discussions of the exclusion of Dalit experiences of migration in eastern India, see Bandyopadhyay (1997); Sinharay (2019).

40. S. Feldman (1999, 168).

41. Dipesh Chakraborty (1996) discusses the term *bhitebari,* ancestral home, to argue that homelessness means the loss of a patrilineal foundation more broadly in this nostalgia for a lost rural idyll. The language and vision of a sacred, beautiful geography is central to Bengali Hindu partition literature, memoir, and cinema.

42. Stoler (2016, 7–8).

43. J. Chatterji (2009).

44. Gardner (2009).

45. The colony people's ostensible assimilation and lives as Bangladeshis today is mirrored in their erasure from national records of migration or recognition as refugees. My search in the state archives yielded no information at all about these colonies in East Pakistan. This disappearance from the historical record of the state contrasts sharply with the continued reference to the colony history in place names (e.g., Itepotha colony) and in local parlance (e.g., *colonir lok*).

46. See also van Schendel (2001).

47. Butalia (2000), Suranjan Das (1993), Pandey (2002).

48. V. Das (1995).

49. These incidents are not to be found in the national archives of either India or East Pakistan/Bangladesh. Nor were they reported in the national or regional dailies of the time. Historian of Assam Arupjyoti Saikia and Jishnu Baruah, a top-ranked bureaucrat in Assam, confirm that they were recorded in local police reports as "troubles" (personal communication).

50. The question of facticity and interpretation has long been central to debates in memory studies and oral history. See D. Chowdhury (2018), Nair (2011), A. G. Roy (2019). I follow anthropologist Michael Lambek (1996) in taking remembering to be a form of claims-making in the present.

51. This colony originally comprised seventy families, and each family received two acres of land. This was widely known and something all interviewees mentioned.

52. Bergman (2016).

53. Mohaiemen (2014).

54. McGranahan (2005, 571).

55. *Jotedari* was a particular kind of land tenure prevalent in northern Bengal.

56. Robinson (2013).

57. McConnell (2013), McGranahan (2005).

58. Siddiqi (2013).

59. Allan (2013, 39); see also I. Feldman (2019).

60. For discussions of the convergence of collective memory and commemoration, see Allan (2013). See also Alexander, Chatterji, and Jalais (2014). Dina Siddiqi (2013) terms these attachments, "estrangements," and forms of political identity "cracks in the national story"; extending her argument, we see the *transnational* grounds of the formation and instability of categories of belonging from the vantage point of borderlands.

61. Sen (2011).

62. See Sen (2011) for a similar account of lower caste Hindu refugees' narratives of resettlement in the harsh ecology of the Andaman Islands.

63. Rosaldo (2014, 167).

64. I. Feldman (2019).

65. Nguyen (2012, 13).

66. Siddiqi (2013, 155).

67. For instance, in September 2019 an engineering student at a premier institution in Bangladesh was beaten to death by members of the Chhatra League, the student wing of the Awami League, for his criticisms of the government's recently concluded bilateral agreements with India. This recent set of agreements—which allow India to withdraw water from the Feni River and install a coastal radar system along Bangladesh's marine borders, among other things—have been widely discussed in Bangladesh as reflections of the unequal and exploitative relationship between the neighboring countries.

68. For all practical purposes they live as citizens with the necessary identity documents. I say *tentatively* because as I show in detail elsewhere (Ghosh 2019a), they are vulnerable to the forms of policing and surveillance that saturate the borderlands in the search for the "illegal migrant."

69. Baruah (2009), Datta (2012).

70. For a comprehensive account of citizenship in India in relation to the categories of "migrants," "foreigners," and "refugees," see A. Roy (2011). For portraits and discussions of India's recently amended citizenship laws (the CAA), see the online collection at https://polarjournal.org/2020/09/07/indias-citizenship-amendment-act-caa.

71. Aretxaga (2003, 496).

72. *BBC News* (2015), *The Guardian* (2015).

73. There is considerable debate in Bangladesh about the rate of the "missing Hindu": the relative share of Hindu population has declined from 12.1 percent in 1981 to 9.2 percent in 2001, with arguably 2.8 million Hindus missing between 1991 and 2001 (Barkat et al. 2008; Dasgupta, Togawa, and Barkat 2011). It is a public secret that these Hindus have migrated clandestinely to India.

74. See Barkat et al. (2008), Feldman and Geisler (2012), and Yasmin (2015), for discussion of the legislative history and political economy of the Enemy Property Act and subsequently the Vested Property Act in Pakistan and Bangladesh, respectively.

75. For a discussion of this cinematic imagination and the Hindu refugee iconography, see A. J. Kabir (2013) and Sarkar (2009).

76. Chakrabarti (1990).

77. The BJP in northern West Bengal has been attempting to rouse this group of pious Hindus with its promise of centering the interests of Bengali Hindus, allegedly neglected by the ruling party, led by Mamata Banerjee's appeasement of the Muslim vote bank in West Bengal.

78. Levitt and Schiller (2004).

79. This proposed constitutional amendment was not approved in parliament in 2015. The bill was reintroduced and finally passed in 2019, amid massive countrywide and diasporic protests. Across the country, peaceful protests were met with brutal police violence, and dissenters and critics continue to be targeted and jailed by the Indian government.

80. I. Feldman (2015a, 2).

EPILOGUE

1. Besky (2017).

2. Mongia (2018), N. Sharma (2020). As Harsha Walia writes, such individual cases ought not to be understood as "domestic issues," but it is imperative that we diagnose their transnational relations by placing them "within globalized asymmetries of power—inscribed by race, caste, class, gender, sexuality, ability, and nationality—creating migration and constricting mobility" (2021, 4).

3. Ahmad (2017), Constable (2016), Murphy (2012), Osella and Gardner (2004), Parreñas (2017), Yanagisako (2020), Besky (2017).

4. Mongia (2018, 139); see also Walia (2021), N. Sharma (2020), Vijayan (2020).

5. Ayub (2019), The Hindu (2019).

6. Frayer (2019); for a record of lynchings since 2015, see *The Quint* (2015).

7. Daily Star (2015e).

8. Ghosh and Moral (2020), Saha (2021).

9. For analyses of the India-wide rise and hegemony of the Hindutva agenda,

see Chatterji, Hansen, and Jaffrelot (2019), Jaffrelot (2021); in the northeast, see Longkumer (2020); in West Bengal, see Bhattacharya (2020), M. Gupta (2021).

10. Riaz (2018), Siddiqi (2019).

11. Human Rights Watch (2021).

12. Smith (2020), Thiranagama (2021), Mountz (2011).

13. Malkki (1995).

14. Ferdoush (2021).

15. While Nina Glick Schiller has critiqued this tendency in migration studies as the orientation to take "state borders as societal boundaries" (2010, 111), historian Radhika Mongia (2018) lays this charge at the door of scholars of transnationalism as well.

16. Van Schendel (2005). Notable exceptions are Zamindar (2007), A. J. Kabir (2013), and Alexander, Chatterji, and Jalais (2016).

17. Fanon (2004, 179); see also Grewal and Kaplan (2001), McClintock, Mufti, and Shohat (1997).

References

UNPUBLISHED RECORDS

BNA   Bangladesh National Archives

Border   Area Development Programme. 2007. *Report of the Task Force.* July 2007, New Delhi.

CR   Government of East Bengal. Home (Political) Department, Branch Confidential Records.

MHA   Government of India. Ministry of Home Affairs Records.

Pol.   Government of East Bengal. Home (Political) Department, Branch Political Records.

PUBLISHED BOOKS AND ARTICLES

Abraham, Janaki. 2018. "'What Will the Neighbours Say?': Legitimacy, Social Control and the Sociocultural Influence of Neighbourhoods in India." *Diogenes*, February, 0392192117740042.

Abu-Lughod, Lila. 1990. "The Romance of Resistance: Tracing Transformations of Power Through Bedouin Women." *American Ethnologist* 17 (1): 41–55.

———. 2008. *Writing Women's Worlds: Bedouin Stories*. Berkeley: University of California Press.

Agamben, Giorgio. 1998. *Homo Sacer: Sovereign Power and Bare Life*. Translated by Daniel Heller-Roazen. Stanford, CA: Stanford University Press.

Aggarwal, Ravina. 2004. *Beyond Lines of Control: Performance and Politics on the Disputed Borders of Ladakh, India*. Durham, NC: Duke University Press.

Ahmad, Attiya. 2017. *Everyday Conversions: Islam, Domestic Work, and South Asian Migrant Women in Kuwait*. Durham, NC: Duke University Press.

Ahmed, Abbas-uddin. 2012. *Amar Silpi Jiboner Kotha*. Dhaka: Prothoma.

Ahmed, Sara. 2006. *Queer Phenomenology: Orientations, Objects, Others*. Durham, NC: Duke University Press.

———. 2013. *The Cultural Politics of Emotion*. London: Routledge.

"Ain o Salish Kendra (ASK) n.d. Accessed November 15, 2020. https://www.askbd.org/ask/category/publications-and-resources/human-rights-reports/.

Al-Bulushi, Samar. 2021. "Citizen-Suspect: Navigating Surveillance and Policing in Urban Kenya." *American Anthropologist 123 (4): 819–32.

Al-Bulushi, Samar, Sahana Ghosh, and Inderpal Grewal. 2022. "Security from the South: Postcolonial and Imperial Entanglements." *Social Text* 40 (3): 1–15.

Alexander, Claire, Joya Chatterji, and Annu Jalais. 2014. *The Bengal Diaspora: Muslim Migrants in Britain, India and Bangladesh*. London: Routledge.

Ali, Nosheen. 2019. *Delusional States: Feeling Rule and Development in Pakistan's Northern Frontier*. Cambridge: Cambridge University Press.

Ali, Nosheen, Mona Bhan, Sahana Ghosh, Hafsa Kanjwal, Zunaira Komal, Deepti Misri, Shruti Mukherjee, Nishant Upadhyay, Saiba Varma, and Ather Zia. 2019. "Geographies of Occupation in South Asia." *Feminist Studies* 45 (2–3): 574–80.

Ali, Tariq Omar. 2018. *A Local History of Global Capital: Jute and Peasant Life in the Bengal Delta*. Princeton, NJ: Princeton University Press.

Allan, Diana K. 2013. "Commemorative Economies and the Politics of Solidarity in Shatila Camp." *Humanity: An International Journal of Human Rights, Humanitarianism, and Development* 4 (1): 133–48.

Amrith, Sunil S. 2013. *Crossing the Bay of Bengal: The Furies of Nature and the Fortunes of Migrants*. Cambridge, MA: Harvard University Press.

Amrute, Sareeta. 2015. "Moving Rape: Trafficking in the Violence of Postliberalization." *Public Culture* 27 (2 [76]): 331–59.

Anderson, Benedict. 2006. *Imagined Communities: Reflections on the Origin and Spread of Nationalism*. London: Verso.

Andersson, Ruben. 2014. "Time and the Migrant Other: European Border Controls and the Temporal Economics of Illegality." *American Anthropologist* 116 (4): 795–809.

Ansari, Sarah. 2011. "Everyday Expectations of the State during Pakistan's Early Years: Letters to the Editor, Dawn (Karachi), 1950–1953." *Modern Asian Studies* 45 (Special Issue 01): 159–78.

Anwar, Anarjo. 2013. *Simantey Par-Abar*. Rangpur: Promiti.

Anzaldua, Gloria. 1987. *Borderlands/La Frontera: The New Mestiza*. San Francisco: Aunt Lute Books.

Appadurai, Arjun, ed. 1986. *The Social Life of Things: Commodities in Cultural Perspective*. Cambridge: Cambridge University Press.

Appel, Hannah. 2019. *The Licit Life of Capitalism: U.S. Oil in Equatorial Guinea*. Durham, NC: Duke University Press.

Aramugam, Indira. 2020. "Delighting in Kinship: Women's Relatedness and Casual Pleasures in Village Tamil Nadu." *Social Anthropology* 28 (2): 512–26.

Arendt, Hannah. 1973. *The Origins of Totalitarianism*. 1st ed. New York: Harcourt, Brace, Jovanovich.

Aretxaga, Begoña. 2003. "Maddening States." *Annual Review of Anthropology* 32 (1): 393–410.

Ayyub, Rana. 2019. "What a Rising Tide of Violence Against Muslims in India Says About Modi's Second Term." *Time*, June 28.

Azoulay, A. 2019. *Potential History: Unlearning Imperialism*, New York: Verso Books.

Bal, Ellen, and Timour Claquin Chambugong. 2014. "The Borders That Divide, the Borders That Unite: (Re)Interpreting Garo Processes of Identification in India and Bangladesh." *Journal of Borderlands Studies* 29 (1): 95–109.

Bandyopadhyay, Sekhar. 1997. *Caste, Protest and Identity in Colonial India: The Namasudras of Bengal, 1872–1947*. Richmond, Surrey: Curzon.

Banerjee, Milinda. 2018. *The Mortal God: Imagining the Sovereign in Colonial India*. Cambridge: Cambridge University Press.

Bangladesh Garment Sromik Samhoti. 2014. *Chobbishe April: Hazar Praner Chitkar (24th April: Outcries of a Thousand Souls)*. Dhaka: Bangladesh Garment Sromik Samhoti.

Barkat, Abul, Shafique Uz Zaman, Md. Shahnewaz Khan, Avijit Poddar, Saiful Hoque, and M. Taher Uddin. 2008. *Deprivation of Hindu Minority in Bangladesh: Living with Vested Property*. Dhaka: Pathak Shamabesh.

Baruah, Sanjib. 1986. "Immigration, Ethnic Conflict and Political Turmoil: Assam, 1979–1985." *Asian Survey* 26 (11): 1184–1206.

———. 1999. *India against Itself: Assam and the Politics of Nationality*. Philadelphia: University of Pennsylvania Press.

———. 2009. "The Partition's Long Shadow: The Ambiguities of Citizenship in Assam, India." *Citizenship Studies* 13 (6): 593–606.

Basch, Linda, Nina Glick Schiller, and Christina Szanton Blanc. 1994. *Nations Unbound: Transnational Projects, Postcolonial Predicaments, and Deterritorialized Nation-States*. London: Taylor & Francis.

Basso, Keith H. 1996. *Wisdom Sits in Places: Landscape and Language among the Western Apache*. Albuquerque: University of New Mexico Press.

Basu, Srimati. 2015. *The Trouble with Marriage: Feminists Confront Law and Violence in India*. Oakland: University of California Press.

Baud, Michiel, and Willem van Schendel. 1997. "Toward a Comparative History of Borderlands." *Journal of World History* 8 (2): 211–42.

Baxi, Pratiksha. 2013. *Public Secrets of Law: Rape Trials in India*. Delhi: Oxford University Press.

Bayly, C. A. 2000. *Empire and Information: Intelligence Gathering and Social Communication in India, 1780–1870*. Cambridge: Cambridge University Press.

BBC News. 2015. "Bangladesh Arrests 7,000 Opposition Activists." January 21, 2015, sec. Asia. https://www.bbc.com/news/world-asia-30917345.

Berda, Yael. 2017. *Living Emergency: Israel's Permit Regime in the Occupied West Bank*. Stanford, CA: Stanford Briefs.

Bergman, David. 2016. "The Politics of Bangladesh's Genocide Debate." *New York Times*, April 5, 2016. https://www.nytimes.com/2016/04/06/opinion /the-politics-of-bangladeshs-genocide-debate.html.

Besky, Sarah. 2014. *The Darjeeling Distinction: Labor and Justice on Fair-Trade Tea Plantations in India*. Berkeley: University of California Press.

———. 2017. "Fixity: On the Inheritance and Maintenance of Tea Plantation Houses in Darjeeling, India." *American Ethnologist* 44 (4): 617–31.

———. 2020. *Tasting Qualities: The Past and Future of Tea*. Berkeley: University of California Press.

Bhan, Mona. 2013. *Counterinsurgency, Democracy, and the Politics of Identity in India: From Warfare to Welfare?* New York: Routledge.

Bhasin, Ritu, and Kamala Menon. 2000. *Borders and Boundaries: Women in India's Partition*. 2nd ed. New Delhi: Kali for Women.

Bhatia, Monish, and Rimple Mehta. 2021. "Representations of Bangladeshis and Internal 'Others' in the Indian Press: The Cases of Felani Khatun, Zohra Bibi and the 'Woman in Red Sari.'" *From the European South* 9: 31–46.

Bhattacharya, Snigdhendu. 2020. *Mission Bengal: A Saffron Experiment*. New Delhi: HarperCollins.

Bhonsle, Anubha. 2016. *Mother, Where's My Country? Looking for Light in the Darkness of Manipur*. New Delhi: Speaking Tiger Books.

Bishara, Amahl. 2015. "Driving While Palestinian in Israel and the West Bank: The Politics of Disorientation and the Routes of a Subaltern Knowledge." *American Ethnologist* 42 (1): 33–54.

———. 2016. "Palestinian Acts of Speaking Together, Apart: Subalternities and the Politics of Fracture." *Hau: Journal of Ethnographic Theory* 6 (3): 305–30.

Blackburn, Stuart H., A. K. Ramanujan, and Joint Committee on South Asia. 1986. *Another Harmony: New Essays on the Folklore of India*. Berkeley: University of California Press.

Borneman, John. 1992. *Belonging in the Two Berlins: Kin, State, Nation*. Cambridge: Cambridge University Press.

Bose, Pramatha Nath. 1896. *A History of Hindu Civilisation during British Rule*. 4 vols. Calcutta: W. Newman. 1894–96.

Bouquet, Mary. 1996. "Family Trees and Their Affinities: The Visual Imperative of the Genealogical Diagram." *Journal of the Royal Anthropological Institute* 2 (1): 43–66.

Boyer, Dominic. 2005. "The Corporeality of Expertise." *Ethnos* 70 (2): 243–66.

Boyle, Edward, and Sara Shneiderman. 2020. "Redundancy, Resilience, Repair: Infrastructural Effects in Borderland Spaces." *Verge* 6 (2): 112–38.

Breman, Jan. 1985. *Of Peasants, Migrants, and Paupers: Rural Labour Circulation and Capitalist Production in West India.* Delhi: Oxford University Press.

Bryan, G., S. Chowdhury, and A. M. Mobarak. 2014. "Underinvestment in a profitable technology: The case of seasonal migration in Bangladesh." *Econometrica, 82*(5): 1671-1748.

Butalia, Urvashi. 2000. *The Other Side of Silence: Voices from the Partition of India.* Durham, NC: Duke University Press.

———, ed. 2015. *Partition: The Long Shadow.* New Delhi: Zubaan/Penguin.

Camp, Jordan T., and Christina Heatherton, eds. 2016. *Policing the Planet: Why the Policing Crisis Led to Black Lives Matter.* London:Verso.

Carsten, Janet. 1995. "The Politics of Forgetting: Migration, Kinship and Memory on the Periphery of the Southeast Asian State." *Journal of the Royal Anthropological Institute* 1 (2): 317–35.

———. 2000. *Cultures of Relatedness: New Approaches to the Study of Kinship.* Cambridge: Cambridge University Press.

Casey, Edward S. 2001. "Between Geography and Philosophy: What Does It Mean to Be in the Place-World?" *Annals of the Association of American Geographers* 91 (4): 683–93.

Cederlöf, Gunnel. 2019a. *Landscapes and the Law: Environmental Politics, Regional Histories, and Contests over Nature.* Delhi: Oxford University Press.

———. 2019b. "Poor Man's Crop: Evading Opium Monopoly." *Modern Asian Studies* 53 (2): 633–59.

Chattopadhyaya, Utathya. 2018. *Naogaon and the World: Intoxication, Commoditisation, and Imperialism in South Asia and the Indian Ocean, 1840-1940.* PhD Dissertation. University of Illinois.

Chakrabarti, Prafulla K. 1990. *The Marginal Men: The Refugees and the Left Political Syndrome in West Bengal.* Toronto: Lumière.

Chakrabarty, D. 1996. "Remembered Villages: Representation of Hindu-Bengali Memories in the Aftermath of the Partition." *Economic and Political Weekly* 31 (32): 2143–51.

Charsley, Katharine. 2005. "Vulnerable Brides and Transnational Ghar Damads: Gender, Risk and 'Adjustment' among Pakistani Marriage Migrants to Britain." *Indian Journal of Gender Studies* 12 (2-3): 381-406.

Charsley, Katharine, and Alison Shaw. 2006. "South Asian Transnational Marriages in Comparative Perspective." *Global Networks* 6 (4): 331–44.

Chatterji, Angana P., Thomas Blom Hansen, and Christophe Jaffrelot, eds. 2019. *Majoritarian State: How Hindu Nationalism Is Changing India*. Oxford: Oxford University Press.

Chatterji, Joya. 2007. *The Spoils of Partition: Bengal and India, 1947–1967*. Cambridge: Cambridge University Press.

———. 2009. "New Directions in Partition Studies." *History Workshop Journal* 67 (April): 213–20.

———. 2013. "Secularisation and Partition Emergencies." *Economic and Political Weekly* 48 (50): 42–50.

Chaudhary, Archana, and Arun Devnath. 2020. "India Seeks to Mend Bangladesh Ties with Coronavirus Vaccine Diplomacy." *Business Standard*, December 17, 2020. https://www.business-standard.com/article/current-affairs/india-seeks-to-mend-bangladesh-ties-with-coronavirus-vaccine-diplomacy-120121700533_1.html.

Chopra, Radhika. 2004. "Encountering Masculinity: An Ethnographer's Dilemma." In *South Asian Masculinities: Context of Change, Sites of Continuity*, edited by Radhika Chopra, C. Osella, and F. Osella. New Delhi: Kali for Women.

Chowdhury, Debdatta. 2018. *Identity and Experience at the India-Bangladesh Border: The Crisis of Belonging*. London: Routledge.

Chowdhury, Nusrat Sabina. 2018. *Paradoxes of the Popular: Crowd Politics in Bangladesh*. Stanford, CA: Stanford University Press.

Cleary, Joe. 2002. *Literature, Partition and the Nation-State: Culture and Conflict in Ireland, Israel and Palestine*. Cambridge: Cambridge University Press.

Collier, Jane Fishburne, Sylvia Junko Yanagisako, and Maurice Bloch. 1987. *Gender and Kinship: Essays toward a Unified Analysis*. Stanford, CA: Stanford University Press.

Cons, Jason. 2016. *Sensitive Space: Fragmented Territory at the India-Bangladesh Border*. Seattle: University of Washington Press.

Constable, Nicole. 1999. "At Home but Not at Home: Filipina Narratives of Ambivalent Returns." *Cultural Anthropology* 14 (2): 203–28.

———. 2010. *Cross-Border Marriages: Gender and Mobility in Transnational Asia*. Philadelphia: University of Pennsylvania Press.

———. 2016. "Reproductive Labor at the Intersection of Three Intimate Industries: Domestic Work, Sex Tourism, and Adoption." *Positions: Asia Critique* 24 (1): 45–69.

Cooch Bihar State Gazetteer, Statistics 1901–02. 1905. Calcutta: Bengal Secretariat Book Depot.

Cooper, Frederick, and Ann Laura Stoler. 1997. *Tensions of Empire: Colonial Cultures in a Bourgeois World*. Berkeley: University of California Press.

Coronil, Fernando. 1997. *The Magical State: Nature, Money, and Modernity in Venezuela*. Chicago: University of Chicago Press.

Cox, Aimee Meredith. 2015. *Shapeshifters: Black Girls and the Choreography of Citizenship*. Durham, NC: Duke University Press.

Cross, Jamie. 2010. "Neoliberalism as Unexceptional: Economic Zones and the Everyday Precariousness of Working Life in South India." *Critique of Anthropology* 30 (4): 355–73.

Daily Observer. 2015. "Bangladesh, India Start Joint Survey in the Enclaves." July 7. https://www.observerbd.com/2015/07/07/98516.php.

Daily Star. 2013. "Drug Addiction Alarming." November 24, 2013. https://www.thedailystar.net/drug-addiction-alarming-567.

———. 2015a. "Addictive Codeine-Based Cough Syrup." October 15, 2015. https://www.thedailystar.net/tags/addictive-codeine-based-cough-syrup.

———. 2015b. "Drug Smuggling on Rise under Aegis of AL Men." January 7, 2015. https://www.thedailystar.net/drug-smuggling-on-rise-under-aegis-of-al-men-58730.

———. 2015c. "Phensedyl Found in Vehicle Used by Cops." July 3, 2015. https://www.thedailystar.net/city/phensedyl-found-vehicle-used-cops-106666.

———. 2015d. "Sylhet DC's Car Chauffeur Arrested with Phensedyl." April 16, 2015. https://www.thedailystar.net/city/sylhet-dcs-car-driver-arrested-phensedyl-77491.

———. 2015e. "14 Hindu Idols Desecrated in Satkhira." October 7. https://www.thedailystar.net/country/14-hindu-idols-desecrated-satkhira-153181

Das, Durga, ed. 1971–72. *Sardar Patel's Correspondence, 1945–50*. Ahmedabad: Navajivan Press.

Das, Samir. 2018. *Migrations, Identities, and Democratic Practices in India*. Delhi: Routledge.

Das, Suranjan. 1993. *Communal Riots in Bengal, 1905–1947*. Delhi: Oxford University Press.

Das, Veena. 1995. *Critical Events: An Anthropological Perspective on Contemporary India*. Delhi: Oxford University Press.

Das, Veena, and Deborah Poole. 2004. *Anthropology in the Margins of the State*. Santa Fe, NM: School of American Research Press.

Dasgupta, Abhijit, Masahiko Togawa, and Abul Barkat, eds. 2011. *Minorities and the State: Changing Social and Political Landscape of Bengal*. New Delhi: Sage.

Datta, Antara. 2008. "Trouble on the Friendship Express?" *Economic and Political Weekly* 43 (21): 13–15.

———. 2012. *Refugees and Borders in South Asia: The Great Exodus of 1971*. London: Routledge.

Dattatreyan, Ethiraj Gabriel. 2020. *The Globally Familiar: Digital Hip Hop, Masculinity, and Urban Space in Delhi*. Durham, NC: Duke University Press.

Debnath, Sailen, ed. 2007. *Social and Political Tensions in North Bengal (Since 1947)*. Siliguri: N. L. Publishers.

Dhaka Tribune. 2017. "Why Border Killing Has Not Stopped." December 27, 2017. https://www.dhakatribune.com/bangladesh/2017/12/27/border-killing-not-stopped.

Díaz-Barriga, Miguel, and Margaret E. Dorsey. 2020. *Fencing in Democracy: Border Walls, Necrocitizenship, and the Security State*. Durham, NC: Duke University Press.

Donnan, Hastings, and Thomas M. Wilson. 1999. *Borders: Frontiers of Identity, Nation and State*. Oxford: Berg.

———, eds. 2010. *Borderlands: Ethnographic Approaches to Security, Power, and Identity*. Lanham, MD: University Press of America.

Donthi, Praveen. 2018. "How Assam's NRC Is Targeting and Detaining Bengali Muslims, Breaking Families." *Caravan*. July 1, 2018. https://caravanmagazine.in/politics/assam-supreme-court-nrc-muslim-families-breaking-detention.

Douglas, Mary, and Aaron Wildavsky. 1983. *Risk and Culture: An Essay on the Selection of Technological and Environmental Dangers*. Berkeley: University of California Press.

Duschinski, Haley, Mona Bhan, Ather Zia, and Cynthia Mahmood, eds. 2018. *Resisting Occupation in Kashmir*. Philadelphia: University of Pennsylvania Press.

Eaton, Richard M. 1993. *The Rise of Islam and the Bengal Frontier, 1204–1760*. Berkeley: University of California Press.

Escobar, Arturo. 2008. *Territories of Difference: Place, Movements, Life, Redes*. Durham, NC: Duke University Press.

Estes, Nick. 2019. *Our History Is the Future: Standing Rock versus the Dakota Access Pipeline, and the Long Tradition of Indigenous Resistance*. London: Verso.

Fanon, Frantz. 2004. *The Wretched of the Earth*. New York: Grove.

Feldman, Allen. 1991. *Formations of Violence: The Narrative of the Body and Political Terror in Northern Ireland*. Chicago: University of Chicago Press.

Feldman, Ilana. 2007. "Difficult Distinctions: Refugee Law, Humanitarian Practice, and Political Identification in Gaza." *Cultural Anthropology* 22 (1): 129–69.

———. 2015a. "What Is a Camp? Legitimate Refugee Lives in Spaces of Long-Term Displacement." *Geoforum* 66: 244–52. https://doi.org/10.1016/j.geoforum.2014.11.014.

———. 2015b. *Police Encounters: Security and Surveillance in Gaza under Egyptian Rule*. Stanford, CA: Stanford University Press.

———. 2019. "Afterword: Staying with the Ambiguity: Anthropological Encounters with Security and Surveillance." *Comparative Studies of South Asia, Africa, and the Middle East* 39 (3): 490–93.

Feldman, Shelley. 1999. "Feminist Interruptions." *Interventions* 1 (2): 167–82.

Feldman, Shelley, and Charles Geisler. 2012. "Land Expropriation and Displacement in Bangladesh." *Journal of Peasant Studies* 39 (3–4): 971–93.

Ferdoush, Md Azmeary. 2021. "Sovereign Atonement: (Non)Citizenship, Territory, and State-Making in Post-Colonial South Asia." *Antipode* 53 (2): 546–66.

Ferdous, S. 2021. *Partition as Border-Making: East Bengal, East Pakistan and Bangladesh*. London: Routledge India.

Ferguson, James. 2013. "How to Do Things with Land: A Distributive Perspective on Rural Livelihoods in Southern Africa." *Journal of Agrarian Change* 13 (1): 166–74.

Ferguson, James, and Akhil Gupta. 2002. "Spatializing States: Toward an Ethnography of Neoliberal Governmentality." *American Ethnologist* 29 (4): 981–1002.

Fernandes, Leela. 1997. *Producing Workers: The Politics of Gender, Class, and Culture in the Calcutta Jute Mills*. Philadelphia: University of Pennsylvania Press.

Ferry, Elizabeth Emma. 2013. *Minerals, Collecting, and Value across the U.S.-Mexican Border*. Bloomington: University of Indiana Press.

Foucault, Michel. 2009. *Security, Territory, Population: Lectures at the Collège de France 1977–1978*. New York: Picador.

Fouron, Georges, and Nina Glick Schiller. 2001. "All in the Family: Gender, Transnational Migration, and the Nation-State." *Identities* 7 (4): 539–82.

Frayer, Lauren. 2019. "'I Am Going to Die': India's Minorities Are Targeted in Lynchings." *National Public Radio*, August 21.

Freeman, Carla. 2001. "Is Local: Global as Feminine: Masculine? Rethinking the Gender of Globalization." *Signs* 26 (4): 1007–37.

Friese, Kai. 2015. "Marooned by History in India and Bangladesh." *New York Times*, July 3, 2015. https://www.nytimes.com/2015/07/04/opinion/marooned-by-history-in-india-and-bangladesh.html.

Fruzzetti, Lina M. 1990. *The Gift of a Virgin: Women, Marriage, and Ritual in a Bengali Society*. Oxford: Oxford University Press.

Gagné, Karine. 2017. "Building a Mountain Fortress for India: Sympathy, Imagination and the Reconfiguration of Ladakh into a Border Area." *South Asia: Journal of South Asian Studies* 40 (2): 222–38. https://doi.org/10.1080/00856401.2017.1292599.

Galemba, Rebecca. 2008. "Informal and Illicit Entrepreneurs: Fighting for a Place in the Neoliberal Economic Order." *Anthropology of Work Review* 29 (2): 19–25.

———. 2012. "Taking Contraband Seriously: Practicing 'Legitimate Work' at the Mexico-Guatemala Border." *Anthropology of Work Review* 33 (1): 3–14.

Gamburd, Michele Ruth. 2000. *The Kitchen Spoon's Handle: Transnationalism and Sri Lanka's Migrant Housemaids.* Ithaca, NY: Cornell University Press.

Garcia, Angela. 2014. "The Promise: On the Morality of the Marginal and the Illicit." *Ethos* 42 (1): 51–64.

Gardner, Katy. 2002. *Age, Narrative, and Migration: The Life Course and Life Histories of Bengali Elders in London.* London: Routledge.

———. 2009. "Lives in Motion: The Life Course, Movement, and Migration in Bangladesh." *Journal of South Asian Development* 4 (2): 229-51.

Ghosh, Ananda Gopal. 2006. *Uttarbanger Namer Sandhane.* Siliguri: N. L. Publishers.

Ghosh, Sahana. 2017. "Relative Intimacies: Belonging and Difference in Transnational Families." *Economic and Political Weekly* 52 (15). https://www.epw.in/journal/2017/15/exploring-borderlands-south-asia/relative-intimacies.html.

———. 2019a. "'Everything Must Match': Detection, Deception, and Migrant Illegality in the India-Bangladesh Borderlands. *American Anthropologist* 121 (4): 870–83.

———. 2019b. "Chor, Police and Cattle: The Political Economies of Bovine Value in the India–Bangladesh Borderlands." *South Asia: Journal of South Asian Studies* 42 (6): 1108–24.

———. 2019c. "Security Socialities: Gender, Surveillance, and Civil-Military Relations in India's Eastern Borderlands." *Comparative Studies of South Asia, Africa and the Middle East* 39 (3): 439–50.

———. 2022a. "Barbed Wire in an Agrarian Borderland." *Current Anthropology* 63 (3): 360–66.

———. 2022b. "Domestic Affairs: National Security and the Politics of Protest in India's 'Friendly' Borderlands." *Social Text* 40 (3): 61–82.

Ghosh, Sahana, and Rimple Mehta. 2017. "Under the Sign of Security—Why the Bogey of 'the Illegal Bangladeshi Immigrant' Is so Powerful across Urban Indian Homes: Sahana Ghosh & Rimple Mehta." *Kafila—Collective Explorations Since 2006* (blog), July 26, 2017.

Ghosh, Sahana, and Radhika Moral. 2020. "The Slipperiness of Documents: Notes from India's Eastern Borderlands." *Oxford Law Faculty* (blog), February 15, 2020. https://www.law.ox.ac.uk/research-subject-groups/centre-criminology/centreborder-criminologies/blog/2020/02/slipperiness.

Ghosh, Sahana, and Megha Sharma Sehdev. 2022. "Generations." *Feminist Anthropology* 3: 246–53.

Ghosh, Shrimoyee Nandini, and Haley Duschinski. 2020. "The Grid of Indefinite Incarceration: Everyday Legality and Paperwork Warfare in Indian-Controlled Kashmir." *Critique of Anthropology* 40 (3): 364–84.

Gibson-Graham, J. K. 2006a. "Imagining and Enacting a Postcapitalist Feminist Economic Politics." *Women's Studies Quarterly* 34 (1/2): 72–78.

———. 2006b. *The End of Capitalism (as We Knew It): A Feminist Critique of Political Economy.* Minneapolis: University of Minnesota Press.

Gidwani, Vinay, and K. Sivaramakrishnan. 2003. "Circular Migration and Rural Cosmpolitanism in India." *Contributions to Indian Sociology* 37: 339.

Glazier, E. G. 1873. *Report on the Rangpur District.* Calcutta: Calcutta Central Press.

Gohain, Swargajyoti. 2019. "Selective Access; or, How States Make Remoteness." *Social Anthropology* 27 (2): 204–20.

———. 2020. *Imagined Geographies in the Indo-Tibetan Borderlands: Culture, Politics, Place.* Amsterdam: Amsterdam University Press.

Gold, Ann. 1997. "Outspoken Women: Representations of Female Voices in a Rajasthani Folklore Community." *Oral Traditions* 12 (1): 103–33.

Goswami, Manu. 1998. "From Swadeshi to Swaraj: Nation, Economy, Territory in Colonial South Asia, 1870 to 1907." *Comparative Studies in Society and History* 40 (4): 609–36.

———. 2010. *Producing India: From Colonial Economy to National Space.* Chicago: University of Chicago Press.

Govindrajan, Radhika. 2018a. *Animal Intimacies: Interspecies Relatedness in India's Central Himalayas.* Chicago: University of Chicago Press.

———. 2018b. "Electoral Ripples: The Social Life of Lies and Mistrust in an Indian Village Election." *Hau: Journal of Ethnographic Theory* 8 (1–2): 129–43.

Graeber, David. 2001. *Toward an Anthropological Theory of Value: The False Coin of Our Own Dreams.* New York: Palgrave.

———. 2004. *Fragments of an Anarchist Anthropology.* Chicago: Prickly Paradigm.

Greenberg, Jonathan D. 2005. "Generations of Memory: Remembering Partition in India/Pakistan and Israel/Palestine." *Comparative Studies of South Asia, Africa and the Middle East* 25 (1): 89–110.

Grewal, Inderpal. 2006. "'Security Moms' in the Early Twentieth-Century United States: The Gender of Security in Neoliberalism." *Women's Studies Quarterly* 34 (1–2): 25–39.

Grewal, Inderpal, and Caren Kaplan, eds. 1994. *Scattered Hegemonies: Postmodernity and Transnational Feminist Practices.* Minneapolis: University of Minnesota Press.

———. 2001. "Global Identities: Theorizing Transnational Studies of Sexuality." *GLQ: A Journal of Lesbian and Gay Studies* 7 (4): 663–79.

The Guardian. 2015. "Bangladesh Rocked by Violence on Election Anniversary." January 5, 2015. https://www.theguardian.com/world/2015/jan/05/bangladesh-violence-election-anniversary-khaleda-zia.

Guha, Kamal. 2002. *Amar Jibon, Amar Rajniti (My Life, My Politics)*. Kolkata: Deep Prakashan.

Gupta, Akhil, and James Ferguson. 1997. *Anthropological Locations: Boundaries and Grounds of a Field Science*. Berkeley: University of California Press.

Gupta, Monobina. 2021. "Historical Roots of the Rise of Hindutva in West Bengal." *India Forum*, April 22, 2021. https://www.theindiaforum.in/article /historical-roots-rise-hindutva-west-bengal.

Gupta, Radhika. 2019. "There Is Never a Peace Time, It Is Just No War Time: Ambivalent Affective Regimes on an Indian Borderland." *Comparative Studies of South Asia, Africa, and the Middle East* 39 (3): 475–89.

Guyer, Jane I. 2004. *Marginal Gains: Monetary Transactions in Atlantic Africa*. Chicago: University of Chicago Press.

———. 2016. *Legacies, Logics, Logistics: Essays in the Anthropology of the Platform Economy*. Chicago: University of Chicago Press.

Halder, Tarun Kr. 2017. "Koch Rajbanshi Identity Question: An Analysis from Historical Perspective." *International Journal of Applied Research* 3 (7): 593–97.

Hall, Derek. 2011. "Land Grabs, Land Control, and Southeast Asian Crop Booms." *Journal of Peasant Studies* 38 (4): 837–57.

Hann, Chris, and Jonathan Parry. 2018. *Industrial Labor: Precarity, Class, and the Neoliberal Subject*. New York: Berghahn.

Haraway, Donna. 1988. "Situated Knowledges: The Science Question in Feminism and the Privilege of Partial Perspective." *Feminist Studies* 14 (3): 575–99.

Hardgrove, Anne. 2002. "Merchant Houses as Spectacles of Modernity in Rajasthan and Tamil Nadu." *Contributions to Indian Sociology* 36 (1–2): 323–64.

Harms, Erik, Shafqat Hussain, Sasha Newell, Charles Piot, Louisa Schein, Sara Shneiderman, Terence Turner, and Juan Zhang. 2014. "Remote and Edgy: New Takes on Old Anthropological Themes." *Hau: Journal of Ethnographic Theory* 4 (1): 361–81.

Harvey, David. 2002. *Spaces of Capital: Towards a Critical Geography*. London: Routledge.

Hasan, Mubashar. 2017. "Threats of Violent Extremism in Bangladesh Are a Symptom of Deeper Social and Political Problems." *Conversation*, January 11, 2017. http://theconversation.com/threats-of-violent-extremism-in-bangladesh-are-a-symptom-of-deeper-social-and-political-problems-70420.

Hashmi, Taj ul-Islam. 1992. *Pakistan as a Peasant Utopia: The Communalization of Class Politics in East Bengal, 1920–1947*. London: Taylor & Francis.

Heyman, Josiah, ed. 1999. *States and Illegal Practices*. Oxford: Berg.

———. 2013. "The Study of Illegality and Legality: Which Way Forward?" *PoLAR: Political and Legal Anthropology Review* 36 (2): 304–7.

The Hindu. 2015. "BSF Constable Killed by Cattle Smugglers," January 9, 2015. https://www.thehindu.com/news/cities/kolkata/bsf-constable-killed-by-cattle-smugglers/article6769464.ece.

Hossain, Adnan. 2019. "Sexual Nationalism, Masculinity and the Cultural Politics of Cricket in Bangladesh." *South Asia: Journal of South Asian Studies* 42 (4): 638–53.

Huffington Post. 2015. "'Killing or Smuggling a Cow Is Equivalent to Raping a Hindu Girl': RSS Spokesman." July 14, 2015. https://www.huffingtonpost.in/2015/07/03/india-bangladesh-beef_n_7719068.html.

Human Rights Watch. 2010. *"Trigger Happy": Excessive Use of Force by Indian Troops at the Bangladesh Border.* December 9, 2010. https://www.hrw.org/report/2010/12/09/trigger-happy/excessive-use-force-indian-troops-bangladesh-border.

———. 2012. *Bangladesh: Assist, Protect Rohingya Refugees.* August 22. https://www.hrw.org/news/2012/08/22/bangladesh-assist-protect-rohingya-refugees.

———. 2021. *Where No Sun Can Enter: A Decade of Enforced Disappearances in Bangladesh.* August 16, 2021. https://reliefweb.int/report/bangladesh/where-no-sun-can-enter-decade-enforced-disappearances-bangladesh.

Hussain, Delwar. 2013. *Boundaries Undermined: The Ruins of Progress on the Bangladesh-India Border.* London: Hurst.

Hussain, Shafqat. 2015. *Remoteness and Modernity: Transformation and Continuity in Northern Pakistan.* New Haven, CT: Yale University Press.

Ibrahim, Farhana. 2009. *Settlers, Saints, and Sovereigns: An Ethnography of State Formation in Western India.* New Delhi: Routledge.

———. 2011. "Re-Making a Region: Ritual Inversions and Border Transgressions in Kutch." *South Asia* 34 (3): 439–59.

———. 2019. "Policing in Practice: Security, Surveillance, and Everyday Peacekeeping on a South Asian Border." *Comparative Studies of South Asia, Africa, and the Middle East* 39 (3): 425–38.

———. 2021. *From Family to Police Force: Security and Belonging on a South Asian Border.* Ithaca: Cornell University Press.

Inzamam, Q., and H. Qadri. 2016. "In Kashmir, 'Non-Lethal' Weapons Cause Lethal Damage." *The Caravan.* 12 July.

Ispahani, Farahnaz. 2017. *Purifying the Land of the Pure: A History of Pakistan's Religious Minorities.* Oxford: Oxford University Press.

Jaffrelot, Christophe. 1998. *The Hindu Nationalist Movement in India.* New York: Columbia University Press.

———. 2021. *Modi's India: Hindu Nationalism and the Rise of Ethnic Democracy*. Translated by Cynthia Schoch. Princeton, NJ: Princeton University Press.

Jaffrelot, Christophe, and A. Kalaiyarasan. 2019. "The Political Economy of the Jat Agitation for Other Backward Class Status." *Economic and Political Weekly* 54 (7): 29–37.

Jalais, Annu. 2013. "Geographies and Identities: Subaltern Partition Stories along Bengal's Southern Frontier." In *Borderland Lives in Northern South Asia*, edited by David Gellner. Durham, NC: Duke University Press.

Jansen, Stef, and Staffan Löfving. 2009. *Struggles for Home: Violence, Hope and the Movement of People*. New York: Berghahn.

Jeffrey, Craig, and Jane Dyson. 2008. *Telling Young Lives: Portraits of Global Youth*. Philadelphia, PA: Temple University Press.

Jeffrey, Craig, Patricia Jeffery, and Roger Jeffery. 2007. *Degrees Without Freedom?: Education, Masculinities, and Unemployment in North India*. Stanford, CA: Stanford University Press.

John, Mary. 1996. *Discrepant Dislocations: Feminism, Theory, and Postcolonial Histories*. Berkeley: University of California Press.

Jones, Reece. 2011. "Spaces of Refusal: Rethinking Sovereign Power and Resistance at the Border." *Annals of the Association of American Geographers* 102 (3): 685–99.

Junaid, Mohamad. 2016. "The Restored Humanitiy of Commander Burhan Wani." *Raoit*. July 14. https://raiot.in/the-restored-humanity-of-the-kashmiri-rebel.

———. 2019. "Counter-Maps of the Ordinary: Occupation, Subjectivity, and Walking under Curfew in Kashmir." *Identities* 27 (3): 302–20.

Jusionyte, Ieva. 2013. "On and Off the Record: The Production of Legitimacy in an Argentine Border Town." *PoLAR: Political and Legal Anthropology Review* 36 (2): 231–48.

———. 2015. "States of Camouflage." *Cultural Anthropology* 30 (1): 113–38.

———. 2018. *Threshold: Emergency Responders on the US-Mexico Border*. Berkeley: University of California Press.

Jusionyte, Ieva, and Daniel M. Goldstein. 2016. "In/Visible—In/Secure: Optics of Regulation and Control." *Focaal* 75: 3–13.

Kabir, Ananya Jahanara. 2013. *Partition's Post-Amnesias: 1947, 1971 and Modern South Asia*. New Delhi: Women Unlimited.

Kabir, Ariful Haq. 2013. "Neoliberalism, Policy Reforms and Higher Education in Bangladesh." *Policy Futures in Education*, 11 (2): 154–66.

Kanaaneh, Rhoda Ann, and Isis Nusair. 2010. *Displaced at Home: Ethnicity and Gender among Palestinians in Israel*. Albany: SUNY Press.

Kaplan, Caren, and Inderpal Grewal. 1994. "Transnational Feminist Cultural Studies: Beyond the Marxism/Poststructuralism/Feminism Divides." *Positions: East Asia Cultures Critique* 2 (2): 430–45.

Kapur, Ratna. 2005. *Erotic Justice: Law and The New Politics of Postcolonialism*. London: Glasshouse Press.

Kapur, Ratna, and Brenda Cossman. 1996. *Subversive Sites: Feminist Engagements with Law in India*. New Delhi: Sage.

Kar, Sohini. 2018. *Financializing Poverty: Labor and Risk in Indian Microfinance*. Stanford: Stanford University Press.

Karim, Lamia. 2008. "Demystifying Micro-Credit : The Grameen Bank, NGOs, and Neoliberalism in Bangladesh." *Cultural Dynamics* 20 (5): 5-29.

———. 2014. "Disposable Bodies." *Anthropology Now* 6 (1): 52–63.

Karim, Rezaul. 2015. "Bangladesh, Bhutan, India, Nepal to Sign Deal in June Allowing Seamless Movement of Vehicles through Borders by End of 2015." *Daily Star*, May 23, 2015. https://www.thedailystar.net/backpage/no-border-vehicles-end-2015-85909.

Kaul, Nitasha. 2018. "India's Obsession with Kashmir: Democracy, Gender, (Anti-) Nationalism." *Feminist Review* 119 (1): 126–43.

Kaul, Suvir, ed. 2002. *The Partitions of Memory: The Afterlife of the Division of India*. Bloomington: Indiana University Press.

Kelly, Tobias. 2006. "Documented Lives: Fear and the Uncertainties of Law during the Second Palestinian Intifada." *Journal of the Royal Anthropological Institute* 12 (1): 89–107.

Khatun, Samia. 2018. *Australianama: The South Asian Odyssey in Australia*. Oxford: Oxford University Press.

Kikon, Dolly. 2019. *Living with Oil and Coal: Resource Politics and Militarization in Northeast India*. Seattle: University of Washington Press.

Kikon, Dolly, and Bengt G. Karlsson. 2019. *Leaving the Land: Indigenous Migration and Affective Labour in India*. Cambridge: Cambridge University Press.

Kimura, Makiko. 2013. *The Nellie Massacre of 1983: Agency of Rioters*. New Delhi: Sage.

Kopytoff, Igor. 1986. "The Cultural Biography of Things: Commoditization as Process." In *The Social Life of Things: Commodities in Cultural Perspective*, edited by Arjun Appadurai, 64–92. Cambridge: Cambridge University Press.

Kotef, Hagar. 2015. *Movement and the Ordering of Freedom: On Liberal Governances of Mobility*. Durham, NC: Duke University Press Books.

Kotef, Hagar, and Merav Amir. 2007. "(En)Gendering Checkpoints: Checkpoint Watch and the Repercussions of Intervention." *Signs* 32 (4): 973–96.

Krishnamurthy, Mekhala. 2018. "Reconceiving the Grain Heap: Margins and Movements on the Market Floor." *Contributions to Indian Sociology* 52 (1): 28–52.

Krishnan, Subasri, dir. 2015. *What the Fields Remember*. India: Public Services Broadcasting Trust.

Lamb, Sarah. 2000. *White Saris and Sweet Mangoes: Aging, Gender, and Body in North India*. Berkeley: University of California Press.

———. 2001. "Being a Widow and Other Life Stories: The Interplay between Lives and Words." *Anthropology and Humanism* 26 (1): 16–34.

Lambek, Michael. 1996. "The Past Imperfect: Remembering as Moral Practice." In *Tense Past: Cultural Essays in Trauma and Memory*, edited by Michael Lambek and P. Antze. New York: Routledge.

Lefebvre, Henri. 1992. *The Production of Space*. Hoboken, NJ: Wiley.

di Leonardo, Micaela. 1987. "The Female World of Cards and Holidays: Women, Families, and the Work of Kinship." *Signs: Journal of Women in Culture and Society* 12 (3): 440–53.

Levitt, Peggy. 1998. "Social Remittances: Migration Driven Local-Level Forms of Cultural Diffusion." *International Migration Review* 32 (4): 926–48.

Levitt, Peggy, and Nina Glick Schiller. 2004. "Conceptualizing Simultaneity: A Transnational Social Field Perspective on Society." *International Migration Review* 38 (3): 1002–39.

Lindquist, Johan A. 2008. *The Anxieties of Mobility: Migration and Tourism in the Indonesian Borderlands*. Honolulu: University of Hawai'i Press.

Longkumer, Arkotong. 2020. *The Greater India Experiment: Hindutva and the Northeast*. Stanford, CA: Stanford University Press.

Lowe, Lisa. 2015. *The Intimacies of Four Continents*. Durham, NC: Duke University Press.

Ludden, David. 2012. "Spatial Inequity and National Territory: Remapping 1905 in Bengal and Assam." *Modern Asian Studies* 46 (3): 483–525.

Lukose, Ritty A. 2009. *Liberalization's Children: Gender, Youth, and Consumer Citizenship in Globalizing India*. Durham, NC: Duke University Press.

Luthra, Pran Nath. 1972. *Rehabilitation*. New Delhi: Government of India, Ministry of Information and Broadcasting, Publications Division.

Lutz, Catherine. 2020. "The Military Normal: Feeling at Home with Counterinsurgency in the United States." Durham, NC: Duke University Press.

Mahler, Sarah J., and Patricia R. Pessar. 2001. "Gendered Geographies of Power: Analyzing Gender Across Transnational Spaces." *Identities* 7 (4): 441–59.

Malkki, Liisa. 1992. "National Geographic: The Rooting of Peoples and the Territorialization of National Identity Among Scholars and Refugees." *Cultural Anthropology* 7 (1): 24–44.

———. 1995. "Refugees and Exile: From 'Refugee Studies' to the National Order of Things." *Annual Review of Anthropology* 24 (1): 495–523.

Massey, Doreen B. 1994. *Space, Place, and Gender*. Minneapolis: University of Minnesota Press.

———. 2005. *For Space*. London: Sage.

Maunaguru, Sidharthan. 2019. *Marrying for a Future: Transnational Sri Lankan Tamil Marriages in the Shadow of War*. Seattle: University of Washington Press.

McClintock, Anne, Aamir Mufti, and Ella Shohat. 1997. *Dangerous Liaisons: Gender, Nation, and Postcolonial Perspectives*. Minneapolis: University of Minnesota Press.

McConnell, Fiona. 2013. "Citizens and Refugees: Constructing and Negotiating Tibetan Identities in Exile." *Annals of the Association of American Geographers* 103 (4): 967–83.

McDuie-Ra, Duncan. 2009. "Fifty-Year Disturbance: The Armed Forces Special Powers Act and Exceptionalism in a South Asian Periphery." *Contemporary South Asia* 17 (3): 255–70.

McGranahan, Carole. 2005. "Truth, Fear, and Lies: Exile Politics and Arrested Histories of the Tibetan Resistance." *Cultural Anthropology* 20 (4): 570–600.

Mehta, Deepak. 2000. "Circumcision, Body, Masculinity: The Ritual Wound and Collective Violence." In *Violence and Subjectivity*, edited by Veena Das et al, 79–101. Berkeley: University of California Press.

Menon, Vapal Pangunni. 1998. *Integration of the Indian States*. Calcutta: Orient Longman.

Ministry of Primary and Mass Education. 2014. *EFA 2015 National Review: Bangladesh*. UNESCO Digital Library.

Mintz, Sidney. 1985. *Sweetness and Power: The Place of Sugar in Modern History*. New York: Penguin Books.

Misra, Sanghamitra. 2011. *Becoming a Borderland: The Politics of Space and Identity in Colonial Northeastern India*. London: Routledge.

Misri, Deepti. 2019. "Showing Humanity: Violence and Visuality in Kashmir." *Cultural Studies* 33 (3): 527-49.

Mitchell, Timothy. 1998. "Fixing the Economy." *Cultural Studies* 12 (1): 82–101.

Mohaiemen, Naeem. 2011. "Flying Blind: Waiting for a Real Reckoning on 1971." *Economic and Political Weekly*, September 3, 2011, 40–52.

———. 2014. *Prisoners of Shothik Itihash*. ArtMap. Basel: Kunsthalle Basel. https://artmap.com/kunsthallebasel/exhibition/naeem-mohaiemen-2014.

Mongia, Radhika. 2018. *Indian Migration and Empire: A Colonial Genealogy of the Modern State*. Durham, NC: Duke University Press.

Moodie, Megan. 2010. "Why Can't You Say You Are from Bangladesh?: Demographic Anxiety and Hindu Nationalist Common Sense in the Aftermath of the 2008 Jaipur Bombings." *Identities: Global Studies in Power and Culture* 17 (5): 531–59.

Mookherjee, Nayanika. 2006. "'Remembering to Forget': Public Secrecy and Memory of Sexual Violence in the Bangladesh War of 1971." *Journal of the Royal Anthropological Institute* 12 (2): 433–50.

————. 2015. *The Spectral Wound: Sexual Violence, Public Memories, and the Bangladesh War of 1971*. Durham, NC: Duke University Press.

Mountz, Alison. 2011. "Where Asylum-Seekers Wait: Feminist Counter-Topographies of Sites between States." *Gender, Place & Culture* 18 (3): 381–99.

Mukherjee, Janam. 2015. *Hungry Bengal: War, Famine and the End of Empire*. Oxford: Oxford University Press.

Munsī, Sunīl Kumar. 1980. *Geography of Transportation in Eastern India under the British Raj*. Calcutta: K. P. Bagchi.

Murphy, Michelle. 2012. *Seizing the Means of Reproduction: Entanglements of Feminism, Health, and Technoscience*. Durham, NC: Duke University Press Books.

Murshid, Navine. 2013. *The Politics of Refugees in South Asia: Identity, Resistance, Manipulation*. London: Routledge.

Murton, Galen. 2017. "Making Mountain Places into State Spaces: Infrastructure, Consumption, and Territorial Practice in a Himalayan Borderland." *Annals of the American Association of Geographers* 107 (2): 536–45.

Mushtaq, Samreen. 2018. "Home as the Frontier." *Economic and Political Weekly* 53 (47): 7–8.

Mushtaq, Samreen, Essar Batool, Natasha Rather, Ifrah Butt, and Munaza Rashid. 2016. *Do You Remember Kunan Poshpora? The Story of a Mass Rape*. New Delhi: Zubaan Books.

Nagar, Richa, and Amanda Lock Swarr. 2010. "Introduction: Theorizing Transnational Feminist Praxis." In *Critical Transnational Feminist Praxis*, edited by Richa Nagar and Amanda Lock Swarr, 1–22. Albany: SUNY Press.

Nair, Neeti. 2011. *Changing Homelands: Hindu Politics and the Partition of India*. Cambridge, MA: Harvard University Press.

Nakassis, Constantine V., and Llerena Guiu Searle. 2013. "Introduction: Social Value Projects in Post-Liberalisation India." *Contributions to Indian Sociology* 47 (2): 169–83.

de Neve, Geert. 2003. "Expectations and Rewards of Modernity: Commitment and Mobility among Rural Migrants in Tirupur, Tamil Nadu." *Contributions to Indian Sociology* 37 (1–2): 251–80.

————. 2005. *The Everyday Politics of Labour: Working Lives in India's Informal Economy*. New York: Berghahn.

Nguyen, Mimi Thi. 2012. *The Gift of Freedom: War, Debt, and Other Refugee Passages*. Durham, NC: Duke University Press.

Ortiz, Fernando. 1947. *Cuban Counterpoint; Tobacco and Sugar*. New York: Knopf.

Osella, Caroline, and Filippo Osella, eds. 2006. *Men and Masculinities in South India*. New York: Anthem Press.

————. 2000. "Migration, Money and Masculinity in Kerala." *Journal of the Royal Anthropological Institute* 6 (1): 117–33.

Osella, Filippo, and Katy Gardner. 2004. *Migration, Modernity and Social Transformation in South Asia*. New Delhi: Sage.

Paasi, Anssi. 1998. "Boundaries as Social Processes: Territoriality in the World of Flows." *Geopolitics* 3 (1): 69–88.

Pandey, Gyanendra. 2002. *Remembering Partition: Violence, Nationalism and History in India*. Cambridge: Cambridge University Press.

Pandian, Anand. 2008. "Pastoral Power in the Postcolony: On the Biopolitics of the Criminal Animal in South India." *Cultural Anthropology* 23 (1): 85–117.

———. 2009. *Crooked Stalks: Cultivating Virtue in South India*. Durham, NC: Duke University Press.

Parreñas, Rhacel Salazar. 2011. *Illicit Flirtations: Labor, Migration, and Sex Trafficking in Tokyo*. Stanford, CA: Stanford University Press.

———. 2017. "Introduction: Special Issue on Technologies of Intimate Labour." *Sexualities* 20 (4): 407–11.

Paul, Anju Mary. 2017. *Multinational Maids: Stepwise Migration in a Global Labor Market*. Cambridge: Cambridge University Press.

Peletz, Michael G. 1995. "Kinship Studies in Late Twentieth-Century Anthropology." *Annual Review of Anthropology* 24 (1): 343–72.

Pelkmans, Mathijs. 2006. *Defending the Border: Identity, Religion, and Modernity in the Republic of Georgia*. Ithaca, NY: Cornell University Press.

Peteet, Julie. 2017. *Space and Mobility in Palestine*. Bloomington: Indiana University Press.

———. 2018. "Closure's Temporality: The Cultural Politics of Time and Waiting." *South Atlantic Quarterly* 117 (1): 43–64.

Pradeep, Jeganathan. 2018. "Border, Checkpoint, Bodies 1." In *Routledge Handbook of Asian Borderlands*, edited by Alexander Horstmann, 403–10. London: Taylor & Francis.

Prothom Alo. 2015. "Prokashhe madok sebon, bokhateder adda." November 28.

Raghavan, Pallavi. 2020. *Animosity at Bay: An Alternative History of the India-Pakistan Relationship, 1947–1952*. New York: Oxford University Press.

Raheja, Gloria Goodwin, and Ann Grodzins Gold. 1994. *Listen to the Heron's Words: Reimagining Gender and Kinship in North India*. Berkeley: University of California Press.

Rahman, Md. Mahbubar, and Willem van Schendel. 2003. "'I Am Not a Refugee': Rethinking Partition Migration." *Modern Asian Studies* 37 (3): 551–84.

Rahman, Mirza Z. 2020. "Infrastructuring Arunachal Pradesh Borderlands: A Case of Tawang Borderland." In *Tawang, Monpas, and Tibetan Buddhism in Transition*, edited by M. Mayilvaganan, et al., 103–13. Delhi: Springer.

Rajaram, Prem Kumar, and Carl Grundy-Warr. 2007. *Borderscapes: Hidden Geographies and Politics at Territory's Edge*. Minneapolis: University of Minnesota Press.

Ramamurthy, Priti. 2008. "Material Consumers, Fabricating Subjects: Perplexity, Global Connectivity Discourses, and Transnational Feminist Research." *Cultural Anthropology* 18 (4): 524–50.

———. 2014. "Feminist Commodity Chain Analysis: A Framework to Conceptualize Value and Interpret Perplexity." In *Gendered Commodity Chains: Seeing Women's Work and Households in Global Production*, edited by Wilma Dunaway, 38–54. Stanford, CA: Stanford University Press.

Ramanujan, A. K. 1991a. *Folktales from India: A Selection of Oral Tales from Twenty-Two Languages*. New York: Pantheon.

———. 1991b. "Toward a Counter-System: Women's Tales." In *Gender, Genre, and Power in South Asian Expressive Traditions*, edited by Arjun Appadurai, Frank Korom, and Margaret Mills, 429–47. Philadelphia: University of Pennsylvania Press.

Ramaswamy, Sumathi. 2004. *The Lost Land of Lemuria: Fabulous Geographies, Catastrophic Histories*. Berkeley: University of California Press.

———. 2010. *The Goddess and the Nation: Mapping Mother India*. Durham, NC: Duke University Press.

Rangpur District Gazetteer, Statistics, 1900–1901 to 1910–1911. 1913. Calcutta: Bengal Secretariat Book Depot.

Rashid, Maria. 2019. *Dying to Serve: Militarism, Affect, and the Politics of Sacrifice in the Pakistan Army*. Stanford, CA: Stanford University Press.

Ray, Rajat Kanta. 1995. "Asian Capital in the Age of European Domination: The Rise of the Bazaar, 1800–1914." *Modern Asian Studies* 29 (3): 449–554.

Ray, Subhajyoti. 2003. *Transformations on the Bengal Frontier: Jalpaiguri 1765–1948*. London: Routledge.

Reeves, Madeleine. 2011. "Fixing the Border: On the Affective Life of the State in Southern Kyrgyzstan." *Environment and Planning D: Society and Space* 29 (5): 905–23.

———. 2014. *Border Work: Spatial Lives of the State in Rural Central Asia*. Ithaca, NY: Cornell University Press.

Riaz, Ali. 2018. "More Than Meets the Eye: The Narratives of Secularism and Islam in Bangladesh." *Asian Affairs* 49 (2): 301–18.

Rinck, Jacob. 2020. *The Future of Political Economy: International Labor Migration, Agrarian Change, and Shifting Developmental Visions in Nepal*. PhD dissertation, Yale University.

Robinson, Cabeiri Debergh. 2012. "Too Much Nationality: Kashmiri Refugees, the South Asian Refugee Regime, and a Refugee State, 1947–1974." *Journal of Refugee Studies* 25 (3): 344–65.

———. 2013. *Body of Victim, Body of Warrior: Refugee Families and the Making of Kashmiri Jihadists*. Berkeley: University of California Press.

Roitman, Janet. 2005. *Fiscal Disobedience: An Anthropology of Economic Regulation in Central Africa*. Princeton, NJ: Princeton University Press.

————. 2008. "A Successful Life in the Illegal Realm: Smugglers and Road Bandits in the Chad Basin." In *Readings on Modernity in Africa*, edited by Peter Geschiere et. al, 214–20. Bloomington: Indiana University Press.

Rosaldo, Renato. 2014. "Grief and a Headhunter's Rage." In *The Day of Shelly's Death*, 167–77. Durham, NC: Duke University Press.

Roy, Anjali Gera. 2019. *Memories and Postmemories of the Partition of India*. London: Routledge.

Roy, Anupama. 2005. *Gendered Citizenship: Historical and Conceptual Explorations*. New Delhi: Orient Blackswan.

————. 2011. *Mapping Citizenship in India*. Oxford: Oxford University Press.

Roy, Haimanti. 2013. *Partitioned Lives: Migrants, Refugees, Citizens in India and Pakistan, 1947–65*. New Delhi: Oxford University Press.

Saha, Abhishek. 2021. *No Land's People: The Untold Story of Assam's NRC Crisis*. New Delhi: HarperCollins.

Salih, Ruba. 2017. "Bodies That Walk, Bodies That Talk, Bodies That Love: Palestinian Women Refugees, Affectivity, and the Politics of the Ordinary." *Antipode* 49 (3): 742–60.

Samaddar, Ranabir. 1999. *The Marginal Nation: Transborder Migration from Bangladesh to West Bengal*. New Delhi: Sage.

Saraf, Aditi. 2020. "Trust amid 'Trust Deficit': War, Credit, and Improvidence in Kashmir." *American Ethnologist* 47 (4): 387–401.

Sarkar, Tanika. 2009. *Rebels, Wives, Saints: Designing Selves and Nations in Colonial Times*. Ranikhet: Permanent Black.

Sawyer, Suzana. 2012. "Commentary: The Corporation, Oil, and the Financialization of Risk." *American Ethnologist* 39 (4): 710–15.

van Schendel, Willem. 2001. "Working Through Partition: Making a Living in the Bengal Borderlands." *International Review of Social History* 46 (3): 393–421. https://doi.org/10.1017/S0020859001000256.

————. 2002. "Geographies of Knowing, Geographies of Ignorance: Jumping Scale in Southeast Asia." *Environment and Planning D: Society and Space* 20 (6): 647–68. https://doi.org/10.1068/d16s.

————. 2005. *The Bengal Borderland: Beyond State and Nation in South Asia*. London: Anthem Press.

————. 2009. *A History of Bangladesh*. Cambridge: Cambridge University Press.

van Schendel, Willem, and Itty Abraham. 2005. *Illicit Flows and Criminal Things: States, Borders, and the Other Side of Globalization*. Bloomington: Indiana University Press.

Schiller, Nina Glick. 2010. "A Global Perspective on Transnational Migration: Theorising Migration without Methodological Nationalism." In *Transnationalism and Diaspora*, ed. Thomas Faist and Rainer Bauboeck. Amsterdam: Amsterdam University Press.

Schulz, M., and J. Kuttig. 2020. "Introduction: Ethnographic Perspectives on the State in Bangladesh." *Contributions to Indian Sociology* 54 (2): 125–51.

Scott, James C. 2010. *The Art of Not Being Governed*. New Haven, CT: Yale University Press.

Sen, Uditi. 2011. "Dissident Memories: Exploring Bengali Refugee Narratives in the Andaman Islands." London: Palgrave Macmillan.

———. 2014. "The Myths Refugees Live By: Memory and History in the Making of Bengali Refugee Identity." *Modern Asian Studies* 48 (1): 37–76.

Shah, Alpa. 2006. "The Labour of Love: Seasonal Migration from Jharkhand to the Brick Kilns of Other States in India." *Contributions to Indian Sociology* 40 (1): 91–118.

Sharma, Jayeeta. 2011. *Empire's Garden: Assam and the Making of India*. Durham, NC: Duke University Press.

Sharma, Jeevan R. 2018. *Crossing the Border to India: Youth, Migration, and Masculinities in Nepal*. Philadelphia: Temple University Press.

Sharma, Nandita. 2020. *Home Rule: National Sovereignty and the Separation of Natives and Migrants*. Durham, NC: Duke University Press.

Sheller, Mimi. 2018. *Mobility Justice: The Politics of Movement in an Age of Extremes*. New York: Verso.

Shneiderman, Sara. 2010. "Are the Central Himalayas in Zomia? Some Scholarly and Political Considerations across Time and Space." *Journal of Global History* 5 (2): 289–312.

Shovon, Fahim Reza. 2020. "Protesters at DU Demand Justice over Border Killing." *Dhaka Tribune*, January 25, 2020. https://www.dhakatribune.com/bangladesh/dhaka/2020/01/25/protesters-at-du-demand-justice-over-border-killings.

Siddiqi, Dina M. 2013. "Left Behind By the Nation: 'Stranded Pakistanis' in Bangladesh." *Sites: A Journal of Social Anthropology and Cultural Studies* 10 (2): 150–83.

———. 2019. "Exceptional Sexuality in a Time of Terror: 'Muslim' Subjects and Dissenting/Unmournable Bodies." *South Asia Multidisciplinary Academic Journal* 20 (May).

Singh, Bhrigupati. 2011. "Agonistic Intimacy and Moral Aspiration in Popular Hinduism: A Study in the Political Theology of the Neighbor." *American Ethnologist* 38 (3): 430–50.

Singha, Radhika. 2007. "Finding Labor from India for the War in Iraq: The Jail Porter and Labor Corps, 1916–1920." *Comparative Studies in Society and History* 49 (2): 412–45.

Sinha-Kerkhoff, K. 2014. *Colonising Plants in Bihar: Tobacco Betwixt Indigo and Sugarcane*. Delhi: Partridge India.

Sinharay, Praskanva. 2019. "To Be a Hindu Citizen: Politics of Dalit Migrants in Contemporary West Bengal." *South Asia: Journal of South Asian Studies* 42 (2): 359–74.

Smith, Sara. 2020. *Intimate Geopolitics: Love, Territory, and the Future on India's Northern Threshold.* New Brunswick, NJ: Rutgers University Press.

Smith, Sara, Nathan W. Swanson, and Banu Gökarıksel. 2016. "Territory, Bodies and Borders." *Area* 48 (3): 258–61.

Sobhan, Rehman. 1979. "Politics of Food and Famine in Bangladesh." *Economic and Political Weekly* 14 (48): 1973–80.

Soja, Edward W. 1989. *Postmodern Geographies: The Reassertion of Space in Critical Social Theory.* New York: Verso.

Sriraman, Tarangini. 2013. "Enumeration as Pedagogic Process: Gendered Encounters with Identity Documents in Delhi's Urban Poor Spaces." *South Asia Multidisciplinary Academic Journal*, no. 8 (December). http://samaj .revues.org/3655.

———. 2018. *In Pursuit of Proof: A History of Identification Documents in India.* New Delhi: Oxford University Press.

Steedly, Mary Margaret. 2013. *Rifle Reports: A Story of Indonesian Independence.* Berkeley: University of California Press.

Stoler, Ann Laura, ed. 2013. *Imperial Debris: On Ruins and Ruination.* Durham, NC: Duke University Press.

———. 2016. *Duress: Imperial Durabilities in Our Times.* Durham, NC: Duke University Press.

Strathern, Marilyn. 2020. *Relations: An Anthropological Account.* Durham, NC: Duke University Press.

Subramanian, Ajantha. 2009. *Shorelines: Space and Rights in South India.* Stanford, CA: Stanford University Press.

Sundar, Nandini. 2016. *The Burning Forest: India's War in Bastar.* New Delhi: Juggernaut.

Sur, Malini. 2012. "Bamboo Baskets and Barricades: Gendered Landscapes at the India-Bangladesh Border." In *Transnational Flows and Permissive Polities: Ethnographies of Human Mobilities in Asia,* edited by Barak Kalir and Malini Sur, 127–50. Amsterdam: Amsterdam University Press.

———. 2013. "Divided Bodies." *Economic and Political Weekly* 49 (13): 31–35.

———. 2021. *Jungle Passports.* Philadelphia: University of Pennsylvania Press.

Tahir, Madiha. 2017. "The Ground Was Always in Play." *Public Culture* 29 (1 [81]): 5–16.

Talbot, Ian. 2011. "Punjabi Refugees' Rehabilitation and the Indian State: Discourses, Denials and Dissonances." *Modern Asian Studies* 45 (Special Issue 01): 109–30.

Talbot, Ian, and Gurharpal Singh. 2009. *The Partition of India.* Cambridge: Cambridge University Press.

Taussig, Michael. 1997. *The Magic of the State*. New York: Routledge.

The Hindu. 2019. "65% of hate crimes against Dalits: Amnesty." March 5. https://www.thehindu.com/news/national/65-of-hate-crimes-against-dalits-amnesty/article26440412.ece.

The Quint. 2015. *Hunted: India's Lynch Files*. https://www.thequint.com/quintlab/lynching-in-india.

Thiranagama, Sharika. 2011. *In My Mother's House: Civil War in Sri Lanka*. Philadelphia: University of Pennsylvania Press.

———. 2018. "The Civility of Strangers? Caste, Ethnicity and Living Together in Postwar Jaffna, Sri Lanka." In *Civility: Global Perspectives*, edited by T. Kelly, C. Forment, and S. Thiranagama. *Anthropological Theory* 18 (2-3).

———. 2019. "Respect Your Neighbor as Yourself: Neighborliness, Caste, and Community in South India." *Comparative Studies in Society and History* 61 (2): 269–300.

———. 2021. "In Memoriam: Stories of Dissent in Sri Lanka." Talk given at the Centre for South Asian Studies, University of California, Santa Cruz.

Times of India. 2013. "41-Year-Old India-Bangladesh Passport Regime Ends." December 2, 2013. https://timesofindia.indiatimes.com/india/41-year-old-India-Bangladesh-passport-regime-ends/articleshow/26714666.cms.

Toor, Saadia. 2009. "Containing East Bengal: Language, Nation, and State Formation in Pakistan, 1947–1952." *Cultural Dynamics* 21 (2): 185–210.

Tripathi, Salil. 2016. *The Colonel Who Would Not Repent: The Bangladesh War and Its Unquiet Legacy*. New Haven, CT: Yale University Press.

Trouillot, Michel-Rolph. 1995. *Silencing the Past: Power and the Production of History*. Boston: Beacon.

Tsing, Anna Lowenhaupt. 2005. *Friction: An Ethnography of Global Connection*. Princeton, NJ: Princeton University Press.

———. 2009. "Supply Chains and the Human Condition." *Rethinking Marxism* 21 (2): 148–76.

Tuan, Yi-Fu. 1977. *Space and Place: The Perspective of Experience*. Minneapolis: University of Minnesota Press.

UNHCR. 2022. "Figures at a Glance." Accessed March 16, 2023. https://www.unhcr.org/figures-at-a-glance.html.

Vas, J. A. 1911. *Rangpur District Gazette*. Allahabad: Pioneer.

Verkaaik, Oskar. 2003. "Fun and Violence. Ethnocide and the Effervescence of Collective Aggression." *Social Anthropology* 11 (1): 3–22.

Vertovec, Steven. 2011. "The Cultural Politics of Nation and Migration." *Annual Review of Anthropology* 40 (1): 241–56.

Vijayan, Suchitra. 2021. *Midnight's Borders: A People's History of India*. New York: Melville House.

Visweswaran, Kamala. 2012. "Occupier/Occupied." *Identities* 19 (4): 440–51.

———. 2013. *Everyday Occupations: Experiencing Militarism in South Asia and the Middle East*. Philadelphia: University of Pennsylvania Press.

Vogt, Wendy A. 2018. *Lives in Transit: Violence and Intimacy on the Migrant Journey*. Oakland: University of California Press.

Waghmore, Suryakant. 2013. *Civility against Caste: Dalit Politics and Citizenship in Western India*. New Delhi: Sage Publications.

Walia, H. 2021. *Border and Rule: Global Migration, Capitalism, and the Rise of Racist Nationalism*. Chicago: Haymarket Books.

Walker, Andrew. 1999. *The Legend of the Golden Boat: Regulation, Trade and Traders in the Borderlands of Laos, Thailand, China, and Burma*. Honolulu: University of Hawai'i Press.

Willen, Sarah S. 2014. "Plotting a Moral Trajectory, Sans Papiers: Outlaw Motherhood as Inhabitable Space of Welcome." *Ethos* 42 (1): 84–100.

Wilson, Thomas M., and Hastings Donnan, eds. 1998. *Border Identities: Nation and State at International Frontiers*. Cambridge: Cambridge University Press.

World Bank. 2006. "India-Bangladesh Bilateral Trade and Potential Free Trade Agreement: Main Report." Working Paper no. 38932. http://documents. worldbank.org/curated/en/2006/12/7444102/india-bangladesh-bilateral-trade-potential-free-trade-agreement-vol-1-2-main-report.

Xiang, Biao. 2013. "Multi-scalar Ethnography: An Approach for Critical Engagement with Migration and Social Change." *Ethnography* 14 (3): 282–99.

Xiang, B., and J. Lindquist. 2014. "Migration Infrastructure." *International Migration Review* 48 (1_suppl): 122–48.

Yanagisako, Sylvia. 2012. "Immaterial and Industrial Labor: On False Binaries in Hardt and Negri's Trilogy." *Focaal* (64): 16–23.

———. 2020. *Producing Culture and Capital: Family Firms in Italy*. Princeton, NJ: Princeton University Press.

Yang, Anand A. 1987. "Disciplining 'Natives': Prisons and Prisoners in Early Nineteenth Century India." *South Asia: Journal of South Asian Studies* 10 (2): 29–45.

———. 1999. *Bazaar India: Markets, Society, and the Colonial State in Bihar*. Berkeley: University of California Press.

Yasmin, Taslima. 2015. "The Enemy Property Laws in Bangladesh: Grabbing Lands under the Guise of Legislation." *Oxford University Commonwealth Law Journal* 15 (1): 121–47.

Yeh, Rihan. 2017. *Passing: Two Publics in a Mexican Border City*. Chicago: University of Chicago Press.

Young, Iris Marion. 2003. "The Logic of Masculinist Protection: Reflections on the Current Security State." *Signs: Journal of Women in Culture and Society* 29 (1): 1–25.

Yuval-Davis, Nira. 2006. "Belonging and the Politics of Belonging." *Patterns of Prejudice* 40 (3): 197–214.

Yuval-Davis, Nira, Floya Anthias, and Jo Campling. 1989. *Woman, Nation, State*. Basingstoke, UK: Macmillan.

Zaloom, Caitlin. 2004. "The Productive Life of Risk." *Cultural Anthropology* 19 (3): 365–91.

Zamindar, Vazira Fazila-Yacoobali. 2007. *The Long Partition and the Making of Modern South Asia: Refugees, Boundaries, Histories*. New York: Columbia University Press.

———. 2010. Review of *The Spoils of Partition: Bengal and India, 1947–1967*, by Joya Chatterji. *Journal of Asian Studies* 69 (3): 939–40.

Zia, Ather. 2019. *Resisting Disappearance: Military Occupation and Women's Activism in Kashmir*. Seattle: University of Washington Press.

Index

Note: Pages in *italics* refer to illustrative matter.

Founded in 1893,
UNIVERSITY OF CALIFORNIA PRESS
publishes bold, progressive books and journals
on topics in the arts, humanities, social sciences,
and natural sciences—with a focus on social
justice issues—that inspire thought and action
among readers worldwide.

The UC PRESS FOUNDATION
raises funds to uphold the press's vital role
as an independent, nonprofit publisher, and
receives philanthropic support from a wide
range of individuals and institutions—and from
committed readers like you. To learn more, visit
ucpress.edu/supportus.